JUST ANOTHER STAR?

☆☆★☆☆ JUST ANOTHER STAR?

ANGLO-AMERICAN RELATIONS SINCE 1945

CHRISTOPHER GRAYLING
& CHRISTOPHER LANGDON

HARRAP

London

First published in Great Britain 1988
by HARRAP Ltd
19-23 Ludgate Hill, London EC4M 7PD

© Christopher Grayling and
Christopher Langdon 1988

ISBN 0 245–54603–0

Designed by Jim Weaver Design
Phototypeset by Falcon Graphic Art Ltd
Wallington, Surrey
Printed and bound in Great Britain
by Mackays of Chatham Limited

CONTENTS

PREFACE

THIS book was born out of the Westland crisis and the furore surrounding Mrs Thatcher's support for the American attack on Libya in the spring of 1986. The two incidents raised a fierce debate about the relationship between Britain and the United States. It seemed remarkable that such minor incidents should provoke so much hostility towards the country that has been Britain's ally in the Second World War and in peace. But what was even more remarkable was the level of ignorance about the nature of the relationship. There are many reasons for this. One has been the traditional official secrecy employed by successive British Governments over Britain's strategic relations. So many aspects of the nuclear and intelligence relationship are shrouded in secrecy.

At the same time there is a growing apart; new generations who haven't experienced wartime co-operation. While America has become more Pacific-orientated, Britain has become more European-orientated.

Then as the outlines of this book were taking shape came an incident which proved even more conclusively that the transatlantic connection was worth examining. President Reagan offered to negotiate away all the United States nuclear missiles at the Reykjavik Summit in October 1986. Had the summit not collapsed, this would have totally changed the post-war relationship. This time it was Mrs Thatcher who was horror-struck.

Those incidents demanded a reappraisal of the relationship between Britain and the United States nearly half a century after the current alliance between the two countries began.

It also seemed important to put the Anglo-American relationship in the international context, since national boundaries have become far less distinct with the internationalization of industry and economic systems, and the advent of organizations like the European Community and NATO which have reduced some of the autonomy of individual governments. In other words the relationship between Britain and the

United States is now far more than simply a bilateral one – it is also part of relations between North American and Western Europe, between the partners in the NATO alliance and in other international organizations.

The book focuses principally on the strategic and economic relationship because these are the issues at the heart of the debate.

Much has already been written about the transatlantic strategic and economic relationship – but most of that has been aimed primarily at the academic and specialist world. What we have set out to try to produce is a book written by journalists, that could offer a broad overview of the relationship between the two countries, the immediate historical background, as well as the current pressures on it in the 1980s.

The research is based on published and unpublished sources, as well as on the recollections and opinions of the many people to whom we have gone for advice, some of whom offered background information without wishing to be named. To all of those who helped us we offer our grateful thanks.

Among official sources, we are indebted to the American Chamber of Commerce and the American Embassy in London, and the Foreign Press Centre and British Embassy in Washington. Of the independent sources in Washington, Bill Arkin, and Andrew Burrows opened up their extraordinary store of documents, while John Barry and Stanley Sloan have provided continuing advice and information. In Britain, Richard Guthrie, Don Kerr and Malcolm Spaven have provided vital material. Assistance from Ray Cline, Harry Dean, Michael Hughes, Nelson Mews, Cord Meyer, John Paulus, Lars Pederson, and Jeff Richelson is also gratefully acknowledged.

Help from colleagues John Simpson, Martin Adeney, James Long and David Shukman has been much appreciated, as is the support from our bosses Tony Hall and Robin Walsh, which has given us the opportunity to write the book.

Warren and Ursula Vosseler, and Blair and Bill Lake provided us with much appreciated hospitality and insights into Anglo-American relationships. Our thanks also to Nick Clack for much needed research work, to our agent Andrew Lownie, and lastly, to Sue and Jeanette for their remarkable patience.

But it goes without saying that the faults are ours alone.

Chris Grayling
Chris Langdon   London June 1988

INTRODUCTION

THE relationship with the United States is one of the most contentious issues today. The Thatcher Government was nearly brought down by the Westland crisis in early 1986, and a few months later, opinion polls revealed widespread public disapproval of the use of British bases in the American raid on Libya. That October there was outrage in government circles over President Reagan's apparent willingness to trade all the United States nuclear weapons at the Reykjavik summit, and a potentially cataclysmic row between America and its European allies was only narrowly averted by a hurried meeting at Camp David between President Reagan and Mrs Thatcher.[1]

In January 1988 there were authoritative newspaper accounts of deep differences between Mrs Thatcher, the Foreign Office and the Ministry of Defence over the issues at the heart of the Westland affair; whether co-operation with Europe rather than America is the best course. Mrs Thatcher is maintaining her staunchly pro-American stance.

The relationship has been debated continuously since Churchill first used the phrase 'special relationship' in his famous 'iron-curtain' speech of 1946. His vision of close co-operation with America, although shared by the Labour Government, was soon challenged by a group of Labour left-wing politicians – including Michael Foot and Richard Crossman – who warned that 'Britain has been driven into a dangerous dependency on the USA'.[2] The Labour Government, like its Conservative successors in the fifties, advocated closer links with the United States, and resisted American pressure for closer European co-operation. Anglo-American relations should be seen therefore as a triangle consisting of the United States, Britain and continental Europe. Britain has had to accept that she has lost her position as the undisputed leader of the Western world to the United States. As the American Ambassador in London Lew Douglas reported in August 1948: 'Britain has never before been in a position where her national security and economic fate are so completely dependent on and at mercy of another country's decisions.'[3]

All British Governments, with the exception of the Heath Government in the early 1970s, have attempted to maximize links with the United States and cultivate a close relationship with the American President. The practical results of this policy, such as the purchase of American nuclear missiles, have allowed Britain to play the role of a medium-sized power – something it would otherwise have had difficulty in doing. This also meant ensuring that the United States was tied into the defence of Europe by providing bases on loose terms, in the late forties, when there were signs that the United States might re-adopt its pre-war isolationism. Although this strategy is successful in terms of Anglo-American relations, Britain's determination to maximize its trans-atlantic connection was a significant factor in the failure to develop coherent European co-operation – or the European Pillar, as Kennedy dubbed it. During the late fifties and early sixties attempts by two successive American administrations to dragoon Europe into closer defence co-operation were thwarted. A key factor – according to one of the most enthusiastic American advocates of greater European unity, George Ball, the Under Secretary of State in the Kennedy administration – was Britain's attitude. He said that as long as Britain thought 'she could by her own efforts, so long as she maintained a specially favoured position with the United States, play an independent great power role . . . it deflected from coming to terms with her European destiny.'[4] At the time there was no consensus that Britain had such a destiny. The lack of a co-ordinated European approach did not seem to matter while the United States was prepared to continue indefinitely to underwrite thousands of troops as well as nuclear weapons in Europe.

But the background to the defence relationship has changed dramatically since the post-war years – particularly in terms of the Western allies' relative economic strength. That has led to increasing questioning of the role played by the United States in the defence of Britain and Western Europe – on both sides of the Atlantic. Since the NATO alliance was founded in 1949, United States economic power has declined relative to that of its European allies. The United States no longer has the nuclear superiority over the Soviet Union that it possessed in the 1950s and it has also tasted military defeats and setbacks in Vietnam, Iran and Lebanon.

The United States Ambassador in London, Charles Price, warned of the changing attitudes in the United States, in a speech in 1987: 'The

American people accepted with much reluctance a world role. Many Americans, however, continue to think that the assumption of these duties was a mistake. Many more have reconciled themselves to this role, but in the most begrudging fashion.' A growing lobby in Washington wants to see the United States contribution to Europe's defence substantially reduced and believes that Western Europe must pay more for its own defences. Europe has been accused of freeloading on the United States, ploughing the money saved on defence into industries that will compete with rival American firms. The former United States Assistant Defence Secretary, Richard Perle, has warned: 'European members must do more. They must spend more. But I'm afraid nothing short of a real shock will awaken them.'[5]

In the 1940s and 1950s the United States was the economic centre of the Western world. Its industries produced a substantial proportion of the world's needs, and it paid for the reconstruction of Europe. That economic strength enabled it to establish a dominant position in the non-Communist world. In 1956 when Britain and France attempted to retake the Suez Canal, which had been nationalized by the Egyptians, the United States used economic pressure to stop action of which it strongly disapproved. Britain's power had ebbed so far that it was no longer able to launch a major military venture unless the United States was prepared to back it.

The years since Suez have seen the rise of other industrial powers: Japan, West Germany and the developing countries of the Far East, such as Taiwan and South Korea. In the post-war world the dollar was the rock on which international currency stability was founded but it is now as vulnerable to market forces as any other currency. The United States used to be the financier of the world – today it is the world's biggest debtor, dependent on foreign finance to sustain its massive budget deficit.

The relative decline in America's economic power has coincided with the internationalization of finance and business. New York has moved from its position as the world's financial centre to being only one part of an international trading system, which crosses geographical boundaries and time zones using the latest communications systems. International markets can undermine an economy or a currency in seconds – as happened in October 1987 when stock markets around the world crashed, prompted by anxieties about the United States economy. This internationalization of finance has restricted the autonomy of democratic governments in the West – including that of the United States.

Politicians can no longer act unilaterally. If, for example, American investors dislike British Government policy, they can undermine sterling by selling it as fast as they can. Likewise, Europeans and Japanese can undermine the dollar if they feel – as they did in 1987 – that the American economy has major problems.

The relative decline in the economic strength of the United States has had several direct effects on her relationship with Britain and the rest of Western Europe. Firstly, it has increased pressure in Washington for the other NATO allies to spend more on their own defence, and for cuts to be made in the number of American conventional forces stationed in Europe. The 1987 stock market crash not only symbolized the weakness of the American economy – it also provided valuable ammunition to those who see the Western Europeans as freeloaders, living off Uncle Sam.

The pro-European lobby in Congress has tried to counter this anti-European sentiment by promoting the idea of greater collaboration – and hence cost-saving – in developing new defence systems in NATO. In the 1960s the United States achieved near domination of the world's defence markets through a combination of economies of scale and aggressive marketing – some of it highly dubious, as the Lockheed bribes scandal later showed. The success of the Pentagon's sales machine forced Western European industries to collaborate in many key projects, in an attempt to create economies of scale similar to those enjoyed by American industry. To date there has been considerable progress on European collaboration in military and in civil aviation spheres.

The transatlantic relationship is under increasing pressure. There are a myriad of explanations: including a greater Pacific orientation in the United States, or a new generation, which has no experience of wartime co-operation. Certainly, in both Europe and the United States there has been public disapproval of the other's politics and actions. Particularly during the Reagan presidency, Europeans have expressed concern at the White House's gung-ho approach to international affairs. The British, for example, were furious at the American invasion of Grenada in 1983. Politicians and pressure groups alike have voiced doubts about American policies on Central America. And most of the European allies refused to back the American decision to attack Libya for its involvement in international terrorism, a decision which provoked fury in the United States.

Concern about American policies has been reflected in public opinion surveys. After the Libyan raid in April 1986, an opinion poll revealed that most people in Britain regard the United States as posing as big a threat to world peace as the Soviet Union. Not since Kennedy has there been an American President really respected in Britain – and Ronald Reagan is viewed as particularly incompetent. The satirical television programme *Spitting Image* even ran a series of items called 'The President's brain is missing'. Suspicions about the intentions of the American leadership were intensified by NATO's decision in December 1979 to deploy land-based Cruise missiles in Britain. They were heightened by a sharp change in American foreign policy. Within a month of the Cruise decision the Soviet Union had invaded Afghanistan. President Carter introduced sanctions and in so doing began a new period of Cold War, embraced with enthusiasm by his successor, Ronald Reagan. This provoked a resurgence in the British anti-nuclear movement, which attracted a degree of support not seen since the 1950s. And the Labour Party adopted a non-nuclear defence policy at its conference in 1980 – something which has threatened to bring it into direct political confrontation with the United States in the event of it winning power.

The mounting suspicions about the American nuclear presence in Britain and Europe, and opposition to many of the Reagan administration's policies has prompted concern in Washington. It prompted the warning issued by the American Ambassador Charles Price that anti-Americanism poses a severe threat to the Atlantic alliance. 'Once entrenched', he said, 'it spreads to every segment of society and, over time, undermines the mutual respect our alliance requires.'

It is by no means clear that greater European co-operation – the solution advocated by pundits on all sides of the alliance – will necessarily lead to a smoother relationship with the United States. A closer, more integrated Europe is likely to be more forthright in tackling the United States on issues of international concern like Central America or the Siberian gas pipeline dispute in 1982. If the United States is to continue to fund much of Europe's defence, then the Americans are bound to carry on thinking of themselves as leaders of the free world, and to expect their allies to close ranks behind them at times of crisis. But if Europe is to contribute more to NATO, as the United States clearly wants, that situation cannot continue. NATO will have to become still more of a coalition, where Europe has a powerful voice, and where the United States sometimes has to accept the European line even if it doesn't want to. In short, what is required is a new transatlantic bargain, in which the United States would accept a loss of political influence in NATO in exchange for a reduction in its own NATO commitments. But, although Britain is certain to continue improving co-operation with its European allies, it is by no means clear that the scale of the shift in resources which the Americans will require has been accepted in Europe. And so far there is no evidence that the United States is prepared to address itself to the changes that would have to take place in the political balance.

1

☆☆★☆☆

THE ERA OF
UNITED STATES SUPREMACY

*It may be that we shall have to consider the British Isles as an
Eastern Extension of a strategic area, the centre of which is the
American continent.*

Clement Attlee, 1946

IN THE years immediately after 1945 the United States totally
dominated the Western world. Alone among the victorious allies its
territory and industries were unscathed, and its economy left stronger
than ever. By contrast mainland Europe had been devastated by five
years of bitter fighting against Hitler's Germany. Most countries had
seen their industrial base destroyed in the fighting; food production was
down to 50 per cent of pre-war levels, and transport facilities, trucks,
railway wagons, and passenger transport, were either destroyed or
unserviceable. Britain had fared better, but had nonetheless lost
400,000 dead and had suffered enormously from German bombing. Its
people would continue to live off rations for almost a decade.

Much of the strength of the United States economy stemmed from
the huge wartime demand. Share prices on Wall Street were at record
levels. Farmers, who had suffered terribly during the recession of the
thirties, were now more prosperous than ever. 'The American people',
said the director of the Office of War Mobilization and Reconversion,
'are in the pleasant position of having to learn to live 50 per cent better
than they have ever lived before.'[1] The strength of the American
economy in 1945 made the adjustment to a peacetime economy simple.
Demand for housing was so high that there were shortages. Companies
which had spent four years manufacturing tanks, aircraft and military
equipment adapted their production lines and started building cars, civil
airliners and refrigerators instead. They couldn't make them fast
enough. In the absence of industrial competition the United States built
up a dominant position as the largest supplier of goods to world

markets. In 1945 and 1946 American exports were worth some $10 billion, in 1947 the figure reached $14 billion – a third of the world's total exports – and in 1947 American industry produced half the world's total industrial output.

Not only was such economic supremacy inevitable because of the lack of alternative producers, but it was also actively encouraged by the Truman administration which saw the spread of international trade and economic interdependency as a way to ensure a long period of peace and prosperity. The Truman administration had a clear view of the lessons that had to be learned from the 1930s. The Great Depression had been caused because the international trading system had broken down as individual countries used protectionist policies to defend their economies. That had caused hardship and suffering, and had ultimately led to the rise of Nazism. If the past was not to be repeated, there had to be a new economic system immune from hurried shifts towards protectionism, where prosperity and security were guaranteed.

The financial mechanism for the creation of a new economic system was the 1944 Bretton Woods agreement, formulated when it became clear that the war was won and it was only a matter of time before reconstruction would have to begin. The agreement was the result of the work of two men: the world-famous British economist John Maynard Keynes, and Harry White, an adviser to the United States Treasury. Keynes wanted an ambitious plan – with a huge international fund centred on the United States aimed at helping countries that ran into economic difficulties. White agreed in principle, but was less ambitious, and ultimately it was the Americans who prevailed.

The aim of Bretton Woods was to provide a secure framework for international trade. That was to be achieved by instituting a system of fixed exchange rates, with all currencies set at a particular level against the dollar. The dollar itself was to have its value pegged to gold. If a country did run into difficulties with its balance of payments, and the markets lost confidence in its currency, rather than having its currency fall sharply making vital imports, perhaps food, much more expensive, or having to put restrictions on trading, it would be able to borrow money from the international community to tide it over the crisis. This money was to be provided through the establishment of the International Monetary Fund (IMF), which would be funded by subscriptions from the member countries – much of it from the United States. Britain and the United States between them provided more than half the initial funding for the IMF. The Bretton Woods conference also paved the way for the establishment of the World Bank, or International Bank for Reconstruction and Development as it is officially known. The World Bank was set up as a finance house for international investment in the post-war world. Both the IMF and the World Bank were dominated by the United States, as the major shareholder in both, and through them it wielded enormous economic power, able to dictate policy throughout the Western sphere of influence. That power was increased still further as the dollar replaced the pound as the world's foremost international currency.

The other institution to emerge as a cornerstone of the post-war economic order was the General Agreement on Tariffs and Trade (GATT), brought about as a result of a conference of twenty-three nations in Geneva in 1947. It again embodied the Truman administration's vision of a world able to trade without the restrictions and protectionism that had hampered economic recovery after the 1929 'crash'. The signing of the GATT coincided with a whole series of bilateral arrangements between the participating countries which reduced trading preferences, and numerous tariffs. The American determination to secure a world able to trade freely was one reason for the Truman administration's hostility to the British commitment to the Empire. For years the British had given preference to Empire products, a policy which ran directly contrary to the free-trade principles embodied in the GATT.

In sharp contrast to the United States, Britain was in a desperate economic state in 1945. Foreign investments worth £1,118 million had been sold off to pay for essential imports of wartime supplies; 15.9 million tons of shipping had been lost during the U-boat attacks, and the total bomb damage was estimated at around £1,500 million. Added to that was the effect of lack of investment in the economy during the war. Railways and coal-mines, for example, had been worked to the limit during the previous six years, but without the regular updating and replacement of machinery that should have taken place. At the same time Britain had built up huge foreign debts – including some £3,355 million borrowed from countries within the Empire.

In August 1945 the United States, which had been effectively financing the British economy through the system of lend-lease – under which the Americans leased British overseas assets in exchange for finance and war supplies – unilaterally halted the arrangements. It was a move which left Britain in a serious predicament. Their revenue simply wasn't great enough to meet current obligations, and the Attlee

Government which came to power in 1945 was forced to turn back to Washington in search of additional finance to stave off an economic crisis.

After lengthy negotiations the Americans agreed to lend Britain $1,100 million, intended to tide them over until export revenues could recover. The money was to be repaid from 1951 onwards, and the interest rate was to be 1.6 per cent. But included in the terms of the loan were a number of clauses which the British clearly did not want but which were forced upon them by the Americans. The most controversial was the convertibility clause which allowed any other country with sterling deposits to trade them in with Britain for dollars a year after the loan agreement came into force. The American intention was to undermine the role of sterling as the major trading currency in many parts of the world. If holders of sterling could convert their pounds into dollars it would increase the role of the dollar as a world trading currency. This provoked strong opposition in the British Parliament. Conservatives accused the Attlee Government of selling out the Empire, and 269 MPs – including Churchill – voted against or abstained when the matter was put to a vote. Many of their fears were justified. When the clause came into force in July 1947 the effect on the loan money was devastating – other countries rushed to convert their pounds into dollars, and within five weeks the clause had to be dropped, but not before causing Britain severe economic difficulties. It was a problem that had been foreseen, but as Prime Minister Clement Attlee put it later: 'We weren't in a position to bargain – we had to have the loan.'[2] Britain was no longer a truly independent world power.

Although the two countries had been close wartime allies, their political ties were not as strong as they might have been in the immediate aftermath of the fighting. The root of the differences lay in their attitudes to the Soviet Union. Whereas Churchill made public in 1946 his concern that the Soviet Union would try to expand its influence in Europe after the war, causing an 'iron curtain' to fall across the continent – concerns which were shared by Ernest Bevin, who was Foreign Secretary in the post-1945 Labour Government – the Americans took longer to realize the nature of the Soviet threat. Indeed Roosevelt, before his death in 1945, had been far more suspicious of British post-war intentions than of the Russians, convinced that Churchill's aim was to rebuild the British Empire and to expand Britain's influence in Western Europe. This suspicion did not disappear with Roosevelt's death. The Truman administration, in its early days at least, did not share British fears about the USSR.

It soon became clear, however, after the war that Stalin's Soviet Union was now bent on expansion, not just within the states right on its borders, but further afield as well. Britain tried to counter Stalin's ambitions, with Bevin taking a lead by promoting German reconstruction through investment and the restoration of economic stability; but they no longer had the financial resources to commit huge amounts of money abroad.

Bevin, realizing this, played a key role in drawing the United States into a position of political, as well as economic, leadership of the West. His first move was bold, but ultimately decisive. He told the Americans that Britain could no longer afford to provide military and other support to Greece and Turkey, and that all aid would be stopped at the end of March 1947. Inevitably, that decision would have created a political vacuum in the Eastern Mediterranean, and given the Soviet Union the opportunity to expand its influence in the region. Bevin was, without doubt, calling the Americans' bluff, and made his decision in the confident belief that the United States was by now sufficiently suspicious of Soviet motives to want to fill that vacuum itself. There were other concerns too. Western Europe's economy was taking far longer than expected to recover, and in some countries, particularly France and Italy, strong Communist movements had emerged. And there was the problem of Communist expansion in Eastern Europe. In 1945 the Russians had set up a Polish Government that would obviously be subservient to them, and the other Eastern European post-war governments, particularly that of Benes in Czechoslovakia, were threatened by increasingly strong, Soviet-backed Communist Parties.

Bevin had judged his moment and the mood of the American administration well. Truman's appointment of George Marshall as Secretary of State in early 1947, and Dean Acheson as Marshall's Under-Secretary, had brought a new realism and strength of purpose to the State Department. Under the influence of Marshall the Truman administration began to take a much firmer line in its foreign policy and to adopt the role of political as well as economic leader of the West. But the Americans were put out by the suddenness of the British action over Greece and Turkey. 'Such abrupt action', Marshall wrote to Bevin, 'makes co-operation unnecessarily difficult.'[3] In March 1947 the American President responded to Bevin's initiative on Greece and Turkey by announcing what has come to be known as the Truman Doctrine. He told a joint session of Congress that he was making available an immediate package of $400 million of aid for Greece and Turkey. And he launched a strong attack on the Soviet Union saying he believed it was the duty of the United States to 'support free peoples who are resisting attempts of subjugation by armed majorities or outside pressure'.[4]

Truman's announcement was only the first stage in the United States' move to bolster Europe against Soviet pressure. In a speech at Harvard on 5 June 1947, Marshall announced a programme of American economic aid to bolster European recovery, conditional on the Europeans themselves working out a co-ordinated recovery programme. He emphasized that it was for the Europeans to take the initiative. American money and other aid was there only if they could create a system to put it to good use.

In London, Bevin welcomed the Marshall proposals and indicated that he was willing to take up the gauntlet. 'I said to myself at once,' he said, 'and the Cabinet agreed: "it is up to us to tell them what we want; it is up to us to produce the plan." '[5] The offer was put to the whole of Europe, including the Soviet Union, although its terms – which would have given the United States a degree of influence in Soviet affairs – effectively made Soviet participation impossible. When the sixteen European countries met in Paris in September 1947 to discuss the proposals, the Soviet Union and its allies refused to attend. The following month the sixteen participants submitted a joint programme to the United States for consideration, and the Marshall Plan was launched.

Over the course of four years in which the plan – the European Recovery Programme as it also became known – was in operation, the United States provided loans and grants to Europe worth around $12 billion. It also afforded an interesting insight into the American attitude to post-war Britain. When the proposals were first announced, Bevin pressed the Truman administration not to bracket Britain with the rest of Europe, even though Britain certainly needed the aid. Instead he argued that Britain should be a partner in – rather than just a recipient of – the aid. Bevin's request was firmly resisted by the Americans.[6] The Marshall Plan marked both the birth of the Western Bloc and the era of United States' domination over Western Europe. Britain had already demonstrated its economic dependence on the United States and in the Marshall system it was no more than one among many recipients of aid.

The United States was drawn still further into Europe by the formation of the NATO (North Atlantic Treaty Organization) alliance in 1949. It was again Ernest Bevin who provided the initial impetus for some kind of formal Western political union to resist the advance of the Soviet Union. In early 1947 Britain and France had signed the rather vague Treaty of Dunkirk which provided for co-operation if either country came under attack, and in January 1948 Bevin told the House of Commons that talks had been arranged with the three Benelux countries aimed at broadening that agreement into a wider co-operative union. The result was the Brussels Treaty, signed two months later, which later established the Western European Union. It was to last for fifty years and provided for all the five signatories to come to the aid of the others if they were attacked.

Bevin believed that the United States should also be involved in the Brussels treaty, and the events of 1948 made his task of persuading them easier. In February the Communists overthrew Benes's short-lived democratic Government in Czechoslovakia. The news horrified many in the West, and destroyed many illusions about the Soviet Union's intentions in Eastern Europe. Then in early March the Norwegian Ambassador told Bevin that he thought his country might be pressed into signing a pact with the Russians. The two events led Bevin to approach Marshall and propose some kind of Atlantic security system. 'We can turn the whole world away from war', he told the Americans, 'if the rest of the nations outside the Soviet system become fully organized, and in turn save Russia herself.'[7]

Opinion in Washington had shifted dramatically following the events in Czechoslovakia – the legislation enacting the Marshall Plan, for example, had had little opposition when it passed through Congress. Marshall himself was enthusiastic about a treaty – he replied to Bevin on 12 March saying that the Truman administration was prepared to go ahead immediately with proposals for a pact.[8] Within a few weeks officials from Britain, the United States and Canada met in Washington to discuss the possibility of setting up an Atlantic defensive alliance. The delegates focused primarily not on the principle of an alliance but on whether the end product should be a formal alliance or a simple presidential declaration of support for the democracies of the West. Moves towards the formation of an Atlantic alliance were made possible two months later with the passage through Congress of the Vandenberg Resolution, which supported the concept of mutual security pacts with America's allies. And by the time negotiations about the possible creation of an international security pact could begin, international events had taken a sudden and unexpected turn.

On 24 June 1948 the Soviet Union cut off all the land and water routes into the western sector of the occupied German capital Berlin. On 15 July the National Security Council in Washington agreed to deploy B-29 bombers in Britain, from where they could be used against Moscow. For almost a year the British and American military operated an air lift to supply Berlin. The crisis removed most of the objections to the formation of NATO, and the treaty was signed in Washington in April 1949.

The formation of NATO showed as clearly as any of the economic developments in the post-war years just how dependent Europe had become on the United States, and how relatively powerless Britain now was. It was only nine years since the Battle of Britain, but now there was no question of Britain standing alone. Britain and the NATO allies needed the United States, for its might was their only real protection against Russia. And the United States was well aware of the position – during the early negotiations which led to the formation of the alliance, the British Embassy in Washington reported in a memorandum back to London: 'They still feel that they are in the position of a kind of fairy godmother handing over favours to the less fortunate Western European countries – provided always that the latter can justify their claims for such favours.'[9] When, during the early negotiations American delegates hinted at the possibility of Britain joining a united Europe, Bevin protested bitterly that Britain was not 'a small country of no account'. But the world had changed since Churchill's protestation during the war that he hadn't 'become the King's First Minister to preside over the dismantling of the British Empire'. In 1945 Britain was in no state to retain the Empire and the United States was in no mood to let it.

But it was the Suez crisis of 1956 which highlighted the extent to which Britain had become subordinate to, and dependent on, its transatlantic ally. President Nasser's decision to nationalize the Suez Canal was a drastic blow to Britain's national pride and status in the world, as well as a threat to the key oil routes to the Middle East. Prime Minister Anthony Eden, in particular, felt that the Egyptian leader could not be allowed to get away with such a challenge to the British presence in the region. Nasser's action effectively nullified Britain's lease of the Canal. The waterway had to be retaken, and Nasser overthrown to protect British interests and to secure the safe flow of oil from the Middle East, Eden believed.

The French were equally concerned by Nasser's action. Not only was the Suez Canal Company partly owned by the French; France also had good reason to believe that the Egyptians had provided support to a revolt against French rule in Algeria in 1954. They saw Nasser's continued presence and growing strength in the region as likely to carry on undermining their position there.

Immediately after the seizure of the Canal an international conference was held in London. It called for the Canal to be put under international control – a suggestion rejected by the Egyptians. The United States' compromise proposal for the formation of a Suez Canal Users Association, which would negotiate the level of tolls charged, was eventually accepted by the Egyptians. But by the time this proposal was accepted the British and French had decided to retake the Canal by force. Secret talks between the British and French Governments were held at Deauville to discuss tactics. The result was a plan to use an Israeli attack on Egypt by land as a pretext for reoccupying the Canal. On 29 October Israeli troops crossed into the Sinai and started driving the Egyptians back towards the Canal. The following day Britain and France issued an ultimatum to both sides: both armies to withdraw to positions ten miles from the Canal on either side, and to let British and French forces occupy the zone in between as a buffer. The Egyptians refused to comply, as it would have forced them to surrender the Canal and most of the Sinai Peninsula. The British and French responded by sending an expeditionary force to occupy the Canal.

But the British totally misjudged the mood in Washington. Perhaps believing that the close ties between the two countries would induce the United States to condone their actions, regardless of the consequences, they failed to realize that the move to reoccupy Suez would rekindle all the American hostility to British imperialism that had existed after the Second World War. America had originally backed Nasser's coup, and President Eisenhower was implacably hostile to the idea of using force to retake the Suez Canal.

However, it was the inherent weakness of Britain's economy and its dependence on the United States that enabled Washington to tilt the political balance and force Britain and France to withdraw. The British Treasury had already warned that the crisis might leave sterling in difficulties – whether or not Nasser survived any attempt to oust him. When it became clear that Britain was going to become involved in a war over the Canal, there was a sudden run on sterling which left the British economy in desperate difficulties. Furthermore, Britain's action not only forced tankers to be re-routed round South Africa at great expense, but also cut it off from its normal oil supplies, making it virtually impossible for the British to obtain Arab oil. The situation became so bad that petrol rationing was introduced for a time.

The problems facing sterling were compounded when the United States responded to the British and French move by ordering its Sixth Fleet into the Eastern Mediterranean to demonstrate that the action did not have its backing. As the Anglo-French fleet steamed towards Egypt, Britain asked the IMF for money to see it through the sterling crisis. But the money was not forthcoming: the Eisenhower administration, to the total surprise of the British Government, blocked Britain's right to withdraw the funds. The United States' domination of the IMF, and the fact that America was the only real alternative source of oil for Britain, gave it the weapon with which to force a ceasefire. In short, despite Eden's determination to go through with the reoccupation of the Canal, economic reality forced him to back down. Without the help of the United States to bolster the pound and provide extra oil, Britain had to do what it was told. On 6 November, the day after British and French paratroops were dropped on Egyptian soil, Eden's Government accepted the ceasefire. The French were left with little option but to do likewise.

The United States kept up the intense economic pressure on Britain until every soldier was removed from the Canal Zone, and the recently declassified Government papers from that period highlight the weakness of the position Britain found itself in. Even after the ceasefire, sterling remained under intense pressure, as investors continued to switch their money to other currencies. One cable from the Washington Embassy to London perfectly sums up Britain's situation:

'In a conversation yesterday with the Economic Minister, the Secretary to the Treasury expressed concern about the strain on our balance of payments caused by the re-routing of tankers and the necessity to purchase oil from sources other than the Middle East. But in his opinion the burden would have to be met by the United Kingdom and French Governments from their own resources. For the United States to offer financial aid to the United Kingdom and France in the light of our actions in the last ten days would be totally unacceptable politically in the United States for some considerable time.'[10]

Then on 12 November, after the Treasury had warned that the economic situation was worsening: 'It is clear that we shall not get any substantial help from the United States before the political situation is clearer.' A week later Harold Macmillan, the Chancellor of the Exchequer, made a direct appeal to the United States, warning the administration that the economic crisis in Britain was so serious there was a danger that he would be forced to cut back NATO and Comonwealth commitments if no American help was forthcoming. He went on:

'I know there has been a deep division between our two countries in the action which we and the French took in Egypt. We took that action not only to secure our interests, but also those of the entire free world. I can only hope that time will show that we were not wrong. In the meantime it would be tragic – and as I have said, a major victory for the Communists – if we were to allow what has happened to result in an economic disaster for the free world. We can prevent it, but only if we act together and act speedily. That is why I most earnestly ask your help.'[11]

The strain of the crisis was too much for Eden. His health failed, and he was forced to go away to Jamaica to rest. While he was away the Government, temporarily led by Rab Butler, yielded its position in Egypt to the United Nations, which sent an emergency force to keep the peace and reopen the Canal.

More than anything else Suez showed the changes that had taken place after the war. Britain, the once great imperial power, was now unable to mount a relatively minor offensive in the Third World if the United States wanted to stop it.

But if the Suez crisis marked a low point for Britain, it also marked the zenith of American post-war power. Ahead lay the start of self-doubts: the Soviet Union's sudden and unexpected success in launching the first space rocket, the Bay of Pigs fiasco, the assassination of Kennedy and the Vietnam War. With the hindsight of the 1980s it seems extraordinary that any country should have dominated in the way the United States did after the war, and that this was the era that should have provided the concept of a 'special relationship' between London and Washington – a time when the British needed American money and defence against the ambitions of Russia and when the United States was openly advocating the dismantling of the British Empire.

But the United States of the 1980s, enormously strong though it remains, is not the power it was in the heyday of the 'Pax Americana', as those years have become known. The relationship between Britain and the United States has also changed. It is barely thirty years since Suez – in the eighties it seems like a different era.

2

☆☆★☆☆

POLITICAL TIES

*It would be utter folly to expect sixteen democratic nations, embracing
some 630 million free people, to agree all of the time and in every
particular. It would be equally foolish, as well as dangerous, to expect
them to disguise their disagreements. It is not, however, foolish to
expect them to be temperate in their criticism of each other.*

Charles Price, United States Ambassador to London.

SURPRISINGLY, perhaps, neither the Suez crisis, nor any of the
less serious disputes between Britain and the United States in the
years since the Second World War have had a long-term effect on their
political relationship. American leaders have been periodically suspicious of the policies of their British counterparts, as Eisenhower was
over Eden's 'imperialism'. The British have sometimes harboured grave
doubts over American actions – never more so than during the invasion
of Grenada in 1983. But on the whole political and diplomatic ties
between the two Governments have been good despite policy differences. Ronald Reagan and Margaret Thatcher are only the latest in a
long series of British and American leaders to be friends as well as
allies. Macmillan, for example, enjoyed a close friendship with
Eisenhower, with whom he had worked during the war, and then went
on to develop a close personal relationship with Kennedy in the early
sixties.

But it is really not since the assassination of John Kennedy in 1963
that British public opinion has had true confidence in an American
President. There was hostility towards the Johnson administration
because of the burgeoning Vietnam War; Richard Nixon's image and
reputation were destroyed by the Watergate revelations; Gerald Ford
was only in the White House for two years, and was viewed as
simple-minded; and Jimmy Carter was seen as vacillating and weak.

Even the close ties between Reagan and Thatcher have come at a
time when the British as a whole have lost confidence in the American
leadership. Ronald Reagan is seen in Britain as a fool – and sometimes

as a dangerous fool – particularly in the early part of his presidency when his anti-Soviet rhetoric was at its strongest.

The close personal relations between successive British and American leaders since the war have probably done as much as anything to ensure that Britain has continued to have some influence over American foreign policy – even though that influence has not always been particularly effective.

For example the recovery of relations after Suez would surely have been slower if Eden and not Macmillan had been Prime Minister. Macmillan had been an adviser to Eisenhower during the war, and the American President was delighted when he took over the Premiership. He wrote:

'Dear Harold,

'This morning, upon learning of your designation by Her Majesty as the new Prime Minister, I sent you a formal message of congratulations, the kind that is approved even by State Departments. The purpose of this note is to welcome you to your new headaches. Of course you have had your share in the past, but I assure you that the new ones will be to the old like a broken leg is to a scratched finger . . . Knowing you so long and so well I predict that your journey will be a great one. But you must remember the old adage, "Now abideth faith, hope and charity – and greater than these is a sense of humour".

'With warm regard, As ever, D.E.'[1]

This from an American President to a British Prime Minister only weeks after what was, by far, the most serious rift between the two countries this century.

Ronald Reagan and Margaret Thatcher have been – at least from an outside perspective – as close as Macmillan and Eisenhower, and subsequently Macmillan and Kennedy (who developed almost an uncle–nephew relationship) have been. When the two leaders met in Washington a month after Reagan's inauguration the *Washington Post* remarked: 'It is hard to remember when a President of the United States and a British Prime Minister have been so remarkably of one mind, not just on their economic theories, but on their fundamental world view.' Mrs Thatcher has been one of Reagan's most fervent admirers in public. 'As you know,' she told *The Times* in 1985, 'I am his greatest fan.' And in 1981 she told the United Nations that 'The election of a man committed to the cause of freedom and the renewal of America's strength has given encouragement to all those who love liberty.'[2] Reagan repays her compliments. In January 1988, when Mrs Thatcher overtook Asquith to become Britain's longest serving Prime Minister, he praised her unreservedly in a BBC profile. 'I think we're very good friends,' he said, 'and it's a friendship that I treasure very much. At the same time, in the economic summits, where the seven Heads of States sit around the table and all, I've noticed that we usually and without any pre-planning, we usually seem to wind up on the same side of the subject.'[3] Even though Mrs Thatcher assumes the role of his greatest fan in public, behind the scenes she is said to treat him more like one of her ministers, hectoring him and browbeating him as they discuss various issues.

A former Cabinet Minister has described the relationship: 'I've seen her banging on and on in front of Reagan, and the poor man can't get a word in edgeways. The whole thing washed over him.' But he seemed not to mind, according to a former diplomat: 'The President acquiesces, when the Prime Minister hogs the floor. He's probably quite relieved. He can sit back and think of Hollywood.' Another British diplomat was less patronizing, saying Reagan finds Mrs Thatcher's approach of lavish praise in public and intense criticism in private somewhat duplicitous. For that reason perhaps, she has to temper her criticism, as one Minister recalled: 'I've seen her beside herself with frustration. But she's quite right not to let him see it.'[4]

But whereas the bonds between successive leaders have served to provide a degree of continuity in the political relationship between the two countries, they have tended to ease the impact of – rather than prevent – major disputes between London and Washington. Apart from Suez, which was something of a special case, disputes between the two leaders have tended to arise when there has been a lack of consultation between the Western allies at times of crisis. A classic example occurred during the 1973 Middle-East War between Israel and its Arab neighbours. Anglo-American relations were already at a low ebb over the then Prime Minister Edward Heath's determination that Britain's future was in Europe. Indeed the Secretary-General of NATO Dr Joseph Luns accused Heath of deliberately worsening his relations with the United States to improve relations with Europe. These tensions were brought into the limelight when Heath refused to allow the Americans to use the British airbase in Cyprus to transport supplies for any military intervention in the October 1973 Middle-East War. Henry Kissinger, President Nixon's National Security Adviser, complained that the British had made it clear the Americans should not ask because they would be refused. And the war also provided another incident which caused fury in London and other European capitals.

On 24 October 1973, at the height of the fighting between Israel and her Arab neighbours, the Americans put their forces on a full nuclear alert to warn the Soviet Union against intervening in the conflict to stop an Egyptian defeat. The British Ambassador was only consulted an hour *after* the alert had been raised, even though it included all the American nuclear forces in Europe. This incident highlighted the tenuous control that countries such as Britain have over the use of American nuclear bases in Europe, and provoked an angry reaction in the United Kingdom. James Callaghan, then shadow Foreign Secretary, accused the Americans of 'brusqueness and insensitivity' in declaring the alert without consultation.

James Schlesinger, the American Defence Secretary, conceded that the alert wasn't handled well. 'There was time for consultation,' he ackowledged,[5] although his Cabinet collegue Henry Kissinger remarked acidly in his memoirs that 'British officials fell in with the prevailing brouhaha over inadequate consultation'.[6]

Disputes over consultation have not been limited to times when relations between London and Washington have been at a low ebb. In 1983, with Margaret Thatcher in Downing Street and Ronald Reagan in the White House, there was a major rift between the two countries over the American decision to invade Grenada. The United States, and particularly the Reagan administration, had long been concerned about the threat of growing Soviet influence in Central America and the Caribbean. Well before the invasion on 25 October Washington had been keeping the tiny island of Grenada under scrutiny because of its avowedly left-wing Government. Grenada had originally been a British colony, and was now part of the Commonwealth. Washington officials were irritated that the British should have allowed their influence in the region to decline, and the Soviet Union to move in. Indeed there were long-established plans for Grenada to be invaded by the American marines and the marines had even staged a mock invasion of a similar island in 1981.

American anxieties were brought to a head when Grenada's left-wing Government was overthrown by an even more extreme administration. The coup caused alarm in the more moderate Caribbean states, and the United States felt obliged to intervene. It happened at the time of the abortive peace-keeping mission to Lebanon – which ended in massive loss of life when the United States Marines' base in the city was blown up by a suicide bomber – and the Reagan administration desperately needed a foreign policy success. After a week of complex negotiations and discussions, American forces were sent to Grenada. Consultation with Britain was minimal. Only hours before the invasion, the British Foreign Secretary Sir Geoffrey Howe told the House of Commons that he knew of no American intention to launch an invasion. 'Consultations', he later told MPs, 'fell far short of what was desirable.' Britain was only officially told of America's plans minutes before the invasion began.

Although there has been strong criticism of the British Foreign Office's failure to anticipate the invasion, there is evidence that the Americans held back intelligence information which would normally have been shared with the British. As one Pentagon official said afterwards: 'You don't collaborate with allies in spying on yourself.'[7] Margaret Thatcher is reported to have been furious when the White House contacted London to say that the President had issued the orders to invade. She telephoned Reagan to protest, but received a cold response. The conversation lasted five minutes. Later, she is said to have ordered an inquiry into why her intelligence services hadn't kept her better informed.[8]

After he retired, Tip O'Neill, the then Speaker of the United States House of Representatives, recalled the evening – when he met the President to be told of the invasion plans. ' "Grenada is part of the British Commonwealth," I said; "what does Mrs Thatcher think about all of this?" "She doesn't know about it," said the President. That didn't sound right to me. Mrs Thatcher was our closest ally so how could we go into Grenada without informing her? Clearly in the excitement about the invasion the White House had overlooked the British connection. Sure enough as we left the meeting Bob Michel, the House Republican Leader, told me that the President was on the phone to Mrs Thatcher. We could hear Reagan's side of the conversation, and from his fumbling and apologies it was obvious she was outraged.'[9]

In the days following the invasion Mrs Thatcher was – unusually for her – openly critical of the American action. She told a radio interviewer that the Reagan administration had gone too far: 'I have always said that the West has defensive forces in order to defend our own way of life. But when things happen in other countries that we do not like, we don't just march in. We try to do everything to persuade.'[10] But while Britain felt rebuffed because it had not been consulted before a Commonwealth country was invaded, the American administration found it hard to understand British objections, viewing the action in the same way Mrs Thatcher had regarded the Falklands War, as the use of force to restore democracy over lawlessness. Ultimately, however, even President Reagan acknowledged that consultation with Britain had been inadequate.

But though the United States claims it will give its allies full consultation in times of crisis, the White House will act unilaterally if it thinks it necessary. Henry Kissinger said after the 1973 crisis that 'imminent danger did not brook an exchange of views, and to be frank we could not have accepted a judgement different to our own . . . emergencies are sure to arise again and it will not be in anyone's interest if the chief protector of world security is hamstrung by bureaucratic procedures in the face of imminent Soviet intervention'.[11] And in 1983, before the Grenada crisis, after the European allies had complained about the lack of consultation about East-West issues, Vice-President George Bush said: 'I'm sorry. The United States is leader of the free world, and under this administration we are beginning once again to act like it.'[12]

Henry Kissinger attributes the fact that such rifts have failed to damage seriously the ties between the two countries to 'statesmanship on both sides'. He argues that, though there have been differences, the British have in fact adapted well to the changing circumstances of the post-war years. He acknowledges that whereas Britain is not strong enough to put pressure on Washington to change its policies, it has been able quietly to build up a position of counsellor to the United States. 'By discreet advice,' he says, 'the wisdom of experience, and the presupposition of common aims, she made herself indispensable, so that American leaders no longer thought of consultations with London as a special favour, but as an inherent component of their own decision-making. The wartime habit of intimate, informal collaboration thus became a permanent practice, obviously because it was valuable to both sides.'[13]

Kissinger has admitted that during his period of office, 'the British played a seminal part in certain American bilateral negotiations with the Soviet Union – indeed, they helped draft the key document. In my White House incarnation then, I kept the British Foreign Office better informed and more closely engaged than I did the American State Department – a practice which, with all affection for things British, I would not recommend be made permanent. But it was symptomatic.'[14]

Margaret Thatcher has also played an important role in the improving

climate between the Soviet Union and the West since Mikhail Gorbachev took office. She had liaised closely with the White House at the
time of meetings between her and the Soviet leader and, after she met
Mr Gorbachev at RAF Brize Norton before the Washington summit in
December 1987, she immediately telephoned the White House to brief
Ronald Reagan. Another hint of the close links between Downing Street
and the White House was revealed shortly before the start of the 1988
presidential primaries. The Senate majority leader Robert Dole, who
had emerged initially as one of the two front runners for the Republican
nomination, boasted that when his poll ratings began to match briefly
those of his main rival George Bush, Margaret Thatcher began to
accept his phone calls herself.

The Thatcher Government has been, in political terms, by far the
most loyal and supportive of America's European allies – despite
disputes that have arisen between London and Washington. In 1984
Britain readily agreed to an American request for British troops to join
the ill-fated international peace-keeping force in the Lebanon. Britain
was the only nation to back the United States when it attacked targets in
Libya in April 1986, in response to alleged Libyan support for terrorist
acts against Americans. That support was widely condemned by Mrs
Thatcher's opponents. Mrs Thatcher was also the first Western leader
to offer the Americans support in their efforts to keep the Persian Gulf
open to shipping in the summer of 1987, though not without some
hesitation. At the end of July the American Ambassador Charles Price
lodged a formal request for British minesweepers to go to the gulf to
help clear Iranian mines and keep the shipping lanes open. Initially the
Foreign Office refused, mindful of the aftermath of its support for the
Libyan raid and fearful of the consequences of British forces being
drawn into conflict with Iran. Other European governments took a
similar view. But two weeks after the initial American request, and after
intense wrangling between the Foreign Office and Downing Street, the
British and French broke ranks following the discovery of mines off
Oman, and agreed to back the Americans in the Gulf. Only then did
other NATO allies agree to follow suit.

But although the United States has shown that it can direct the
foreign policy of the Western world, it has not always been able to
compel Britain to fall into line. In 1964, for example, Britain refused to
support the Americans in Vietnam. President Johnson had made it clear
that he was looking for a symbol of British backing – even a token
presence, 'a platoon of bagpipers' would have been sufficient.[15] But

Wilson refused and the issue remained a running sore between the two administrations. Johnson's Secretary of State Dean Rusk angrily told a journalist: 'All we needed was a regiment. The Black Watch would have done. But you would not; well don't expect us to save you again. They can invade Sussex and we wouldn't do a damn thing about it.'[16]

But though Britain was not prepared to give any kind of public commitment to the war in Vietnam, it offered assistance where necessary behind-the-scenes. This included any Vietnamese radio traffic intercepted by the British signals intelligence outstation in Hong Kong and jungle training for American marines with the SAS in Borneo.[17]

The divisions between Britain and the United States over the Vietnam War were curiously mirrored in the early days of the dispute between Britain and Argentina in 1982 over the Falklands. In the 1960s the British were hostile to American military action, but nonetheless provided covert support where needed. In 1982 the British Government's decision to send a large naval force to the South Atlantic in an attempt to retake the Falkland Islands was greeted with a mixture of anger and disbelief by Washington. But even so the United States provided essential military assistance behind the scenes. Without that help it is arguable that Britain would have lost the Falklands War.

In public, however, the United States greeted the news of the Argentine invasion by taking up a position of strict neutrality. Although the American people as a whole and a sizeable lobby in the American capital were pro-British, there were those key officials, such as the then Ambassador to the United Nations Jeanne Kirkpatrick, who took an actively pro-Argentinian stance. 'The Argentinians have been claiming for 200 years that they own those islands. If they own those islands, then moving troops into them is not armed aggression.'[18]

President Reagan attempted to mediate in the dispute. His Secretary of State Alexander Haig was despatched to both capitals in an attempt to find an acceptable compromise. Privately both Haig and Reagan made it clear to the British that if pushed to an extreme they would have to back the attempt to recapture the Islands. But they made no attempt to hide their fury at what the British were doing. President Reagan said publicly that he couldn't understand the British fixation with what he called 'a little ice-cold bunch of land down there'. It was revealed later that Reagan had even asked Haig whether Margaret Thatcher's honour would be satisfied if one Argentine ship was sunk.[19] The British Prime Minister was incensed – as Johnson had been with Wilson eighteen years earlier – by the initial American refusal to provide immediate public support for what she saw as an entirely legitimate response to unwarrranted aggression. But when Alexander Haig's peace efforts failed in the face of Argentinian intransigence, the United States imposed sanctions against Argentina and publicly offered the British military aid.

The United States also had strategic reasons for disappproving of Britain's action. When Britain sent her naval task force to the South Atlantic without consulting Washington, it left serious gaps in NATO's defences. The despatch of submarines to the area left NATO sea patrols under capacity, and the departure of a sizeable part of the British Navy created a serious vacuum. However, in private, the British had been receiving tacit military assistance from the very first days of the crisis. That assistance came not from the administration, but from the Pentagon, anxious about the damage a British defeat would do to the credibility of NATO's defences.

In the early days of the Falklands War, at the same time as Alexander Haig was attempting to maintain the illusion of even-handedness in his negotiations between London, Washington and Buenos Aires, the Pentagon, under Caspar Weinberger, was shipping volumes of essential military supplies to the British military staging post on Ascension Island. And the flow of supplies increased after the Reagan administration had committed itself to Britain. The former United States Secretary of the Navy, John Lehman, says that the Falklands War would almost certainly not have been won without this support – and that was what Weinberger was told by his analysts at the time.[20]

The United States also provided Britain with other support: with important intelligence information, with 12.5 million gallons of fuel, and with essential weapons systems, including anti-ship missiles, and the latest generation of Sidewinder missiles for use by the British Harrier aircraft, as well as with ammunition and explosives. The Sidewinders forced the Argentinian pilots to fly low; as a result, many of their bombs failed to go off as their fuses were not set for low-level bombing. This saved a number of Royal Navy ships. In addition, the Pentagon provided Britain with communications satellites – the decision to sink the Argentine battleship the *General Belgrano* was probably conveyed to the submarine *HMS Conqueror* through an American communications network made available while the United States was still officially neutral. And the Pentagon made an unofficial offer that if one of the two British carriers, *HMS Invincible* or *HMS Hermes*, were sunk by the

Argentinians, they would replace it immediately with an American ship, the *USS Guam,* to be manned by British naval personnel.[21]

In early 1988 Weinberger was given an honorary knighthood by the British in recognition of his support. At a dinner to mark the occasion, Mrs Thatcher said there was no American she would rather welcome to London.

Yet although the Falklands conflict revealed a continuing commitment to the alliance in Washington, it also showed how the importance of that alliance has diminished over the years. The role played by Jeanne Kirkpatrick and others in pushing the Argentinian side of the Falklands argument – and particularly stressing United States' strategic interests in South America – provided an important lesson for Britain and Western Europe.

During the Cold War events in Europe had been of paramount consideration in American strategic planning. Today, the United States has important strategic interests throughout the world: in South America, in the Far East, and in the Pacific. That strategic change has been accentuated by a gradual shift in the political balance of the United States.

This is one of two factors contributing to an underlying pressure on the political relationship between Britain and the United States. The second lies in the political changes that have taken place in the United Kingdom. Although there has long been anti-American sentiment in Britain, most notably during the 1950s with the growth of the Campaign for Nuclear Disarmament and later with the anti-Vietnam movements, this has grown in the past decade. Since the 1970s anti-Americanism has been most closely associated with the resurgent anti-nuclear movement in Britain. The Campaign for Nuclear Disarmament had been semi-dormant since the early 1960s when NATO announced its decision, in 1979, to deploy Cruise and Pershing missiles in Western Europe. That decision coincided with the election of Ronald Reagan to the White House, a man seen widely in Europe at the time as an irresponsible anti-Communist whose rhetoric against the Soviet Union suggested that the United States had entered a new era of militarism. He was the man who called the Soviet Union an 'evil empire', and presided over the biggest arms build up in recent American history.

But anti-Americanism hasn't been limited to the left wing of British politics. There is also a tradition of anti-Americanism on the right of British politics among those hostile to what they see as the brash and vulgar approach of the United States in international affairs. But in the

1980s this view has little influence. And there have been concerns outside politics. Thousands of people, many without political backgrounds, joined the protest marches against the deployment of Cruise. After the Libyan Raid in 1986 an opinion poll found that more people thought the 'special relationship' with the United States was harmful rather than beneficial to Britain.

The decision to deploy Cruise missiles resulted in a sudden and dramatic burgeoning of the anti-nuclear movement in Britain and elsewhere in Western Europe, and there were calls from the left wing of British politics for the United Kingdom to become neutral. In 1980 the Labour Party adopted a policy of unilateral nuclear disarmament at its annual conference. That policy entails not only the dismantling of Britain's own nuclear deterrent, but also the closure of American nuclear bases in the United Kingdom – a prospect that has caused anguish and horror in Washington. The then Assistant Defence Secretary Richard Perle, a right-winger strongly critical of the British opposition, said on television in 1986 that he regarded the Labour Party's defence policy as 'so wildly irresponsible . . . that I think a Labour Government which stood by its present policies would, if it did not destroy the alliance, at least diminish its effective ability to do the task for which it was created'.[22]

Indeed the United States Government has worked hard to discredit Labour as a serious political force capable of international negotiation. The current Labour leader Neil Kinnock has met President Reagan twice in Washington since taking over from the veteran unilateralist Michael Foot after the 1983 election. On the second occasion, in March 1987, shortly before the General Election that saw Margaret Thatcher returned to power for the third time, Kinnock was diplomatically cold-shouldered by the White House. He was only given twenty minutes of the President's time (although afterwards there was some dispute over the actual duration of the meeting and Kinnock said it had lasted longer). The White House described the brief encounter as 'polite and businesslike' – the normal diplomatic euphemism for cool and frosty. It was made clear to Kinnock – and the world in general – that Reagan did not agree with Labour's nuclear policy. Caspar Weinberger has warned on several occasions that he views the Labour Party as likely to wreck NATO if it doesn't change course. Indeed, although the Reagan administration decided in the run-up to the election to avoid interfering in the British electoral process, Weinberger appeared on a platform in London with Norman Tebbit, then Conservative Chairman, a week before the 1987 general election. Although he made no direct references to the campaign, his remarks about the need to strengthen NATO and the threats it faced from within were clearly aimed at Kinnock and the Labour Party. 'It would', he said, 'be terribly naïve and worse, given the bloodshed we have suffered in this century, to believe that free peoples can disentangle themselves from the world arena.'[23]

Some of Labour's most prominent left-wingers have expressed the fear that the United States would force a left-wing Labour Government to give up its policies. And one left-wing MP Chris Mullin has written a novel based on the election of a radical 'left' government in Britain, in which American pressure and the tacit connivance of the British establishment forced a change of policy and leadership.[24]

The question of pro-American opinion in Britain acting to prevent a serious rift with Washington is an interesting one. The Editor of the *Sunday Telegraph* Peregrine Worsthorne has said that he could imagine a situation under a radical Labour Government when 'one were approached by a CIA official who sought to enlist one's help in a project designed to "destabilize" this far-left Government. Would it necessarily be right to refuse cooperation?'[25]

American disquiet over unilateralism in Britain, and particularly the way it has manifested itself politically, have remained of little direct importance while the Conservatives remain in office. But that disquiet, combined with widespread hostility towards the United States over issues like Central America, and the American raid on Libya, does have an impact in Washington. Because of the enormous American commitment to European defence, any visible anti-Americanism in Europe provokes hostility in Washington, particularly from those who feel that America's European interests are given too high a priority. That has become a matter for great concern to the pro-Europe lobby within the United States' political establishment. Charles Price warned recently that anti-Americanism in Europe could push the United States back into isolationism: 'When', he said, 'the accusations reach a fevered pitch, when Americans see their national interests scorned . . . then the call issues forth, from senators and from salesmen, from pundits and from plumbers: "bring our boys home".' The implications of such sentiments for the defence of Europe are discussed more fully in a later chapter. But there is no doubt that the political implications are serious, too.

In 1956 the United States Government used direct economic pressure to force the British to back down over Suez. In the 1980s the international economy is far more complex than it was thirty years ago,

and it is doubtful that the United States would have the same ability to
force a Labour Government to change its policies. If a Labour
Government was elected and it attempted to introduce a radical defence
policy of the kind espoused by the Party in the 1987 General Election,
there would probably be a major rift between London and Washington.
That would certainly be reflected in the financial markets, and the value
of the pound and of British shares would certainly fall sharply. But
although there would be damage to the British economy, most analysts
believe that the effects would be short lived. The markets would almost
certainly settle in a short space of time – as one London observer put it:
'The will to make money soon overrides political considerations.' The
United States can apply pressure through the IMF, but that action
would only be really effective at a time when the British economy was
weak, and dependent on foreign finance. According to Gavyn Davies of
the American bank Goldman Sachs, who has advised Labour on
economic matters, the United States could put pressure on Labour if, as
happened in 1976, Britain had a serious balance of payments crisis and
needed help from abroad. Then the British were forced to turn to the
International Monetary Fund for bridging finance to tide the economy
through a serious balance of payments crisis. The IMF attached
stringent conditions to the loan, including sharp cuts in public borrowing
which was running at a very high level. The IMF's firm approach was
certainly inspired by the view of the Ford Administration and the United
States Treasury that British public spending was too high and should be
cut. It was, though, also professional economic advice given at a time of
financial crisis – and not simply an American tool to influence the
domestic policies of a Socialist Government in Britain.

In other circumstances direct economic pressure might be limited to
restrictions, for example, on British takeovers of American firms. The
strongest weapon available to an American administration looking to halt
what it saw as an undesirable defence policy in Britain would be through
pressure from its other European allies. Threats of American troop cuts
in West Germany could put enormous strain on Britain's relations with
its partners in the European Community. Direct pressure within the
Community could force a change of policy in London.

Although the problems unilateralism poses to Anglo-American relations may prove to have been changed dramatically by the Intermediate
Nuclear Forces (INF) treaty between the United States and the Soviet
Union – to scrap land-based medium-range missiles – the implications of
the debate remain. By the time of the next General Election in Britain,

talks on arms reductions may well have reached a point where any new government can credibly disarm by offering the British deterrent as part of a new treaty. But the debate over Labour's nuclear policy has highlighted the fact that Britain, by becoming part of the Western alliance, has lost some of its own freedom of manoeuvre. The British Government cannot do what it wants regardless of the opinions of its allies. Although there is no firm evidence to indicate that the Americans would be able to block unilateralist policies, such a proposition has been given serious consideration on both sides of the policital spectrum. Though there is majority support in Britain for NATO and for the links with the United States, there has clearly been a price to pay for the security those links have provided.

But the balance of the relationship between London and Washington has changed since Suez. Over many issues Britain is now only one component of a European response, whether it be refusing to impose sanctions against Libya in 1986, or formulating European proposals for Middle East peace – as happened in 1984. European Community foreign ministers now meet regularly to formulate joint approaches to policy, and they can and do differ from the United States over major international issues such as Libya and Central America. But events such as the invasion of Grenada show that though the Western world is now increasingly politically interdependent, in the final analysis the United States will act alone and unsupported – regardless of the opinions of its closest allies.

3

☆☆★☆☆

ECONOMIC LINKS

*Economists seeking to explain America's policy options tend to use
Mexico or Brazil as analogies, not Japan or Germany. Some
quipsters have even taken to calling Reagan a 'banana Republican'.*

Fortune Magazine, 7 December 1987.

THE shift in the relative economic position of the two countries is at
the root of the changing relationship between Britain and the
United States in the 1980s. That change has profound implications not
only for the way the economic ties between them are likely to develop in
the future, but also for the future of the transatlantic political and
defence relationships. Today Britain and the United States are no
longer truly sovereign economic powers. Instead they are both part of
an increasingly international economy, where both business and financial markets are global rather than national.

This means that governments have increasingly seen their ability to
act freely as restricted by the mood of international markets, which are
able to switch money from one side of the globe to another in seconds.
Economies can be undermined in an instant – as happened in the 1987
stock market crash. This is well understood by the money men, but
perhaps less so by politicians. One of America's leading bankers, Walter
Wriston of Citibank, said recently: 'At the end of the day it's a new
world, and the concept of sovereignty is going to change. Politically, the
new world is an integrated market in which nobody can get away with
what they used to. You can't control what your people hear, you can't
control your capital flows. The idea of fifteenth-century international law
is gone. It hasn't laid down yet, but it's dead. It's like the three-mile
limit in a world of Inter-Continental Ballistic Missiles.'[1]

The relative economic strength of the United States has also
declined. In the 1940s and 1950s it was the economic centre of the
world. But from the early 1950s onwards that supremacy began to

wane, and by the end of the 1960s – burdened by the cost of the Vietnam War, the United States' overseas commitments, and social spending at home – it had been enormously eroded. Between 1950 and the early 1970s the economies of France, Germany and Italy all grew twice as fast as the United States's, while Japanese growth was four times higher. Today the United States is acknowledged as only one of three major international economic centres, along with Japan and Western Europe. It also faces an increasing challenge from the more successful of the developing countries, notably Taiwan, South Korea and Hong Kong.

International pressure from the financial markets has already put strain on the transatlantic defence relationship. It was the dramatic expansion of defence spending during the early years of the Reagan administration which caused the United States' current budget deficit problems. Those problems sparked the 1987 stock market crash, and will dominate American economic policies in the years ahead. The American commitment to NATO is certain to suffer, in terms of both money and manpower, as America cuts spending to ease its deficit difficulties.

The economic strength of the United States in the post-war years was founded on three main features. Firstly the size of its own domestic market and industry ensured that it was the focal point of Western economic activity. Its role in the post-war financial institutions, particuarly the IMF, gave it tremendous direct political influence over other economies. And the role of the dollar as the world's main reserve currency and trading medium again ensured that the United States was the focal point of economic activity in the industrialized world, although in the immediate post-war years sterling remained very much the world's number two currency, and Britain was second in the economic hierarchy. But Britain's partnership with the United States in building the Western economic system was more symbolic than real.

And by the 1960s even that degree of symbolism was disappearing. Britain's continuing overseas commitments, in both the old Empire and the Commonwealth, were a heavy burden. The economy grew slower than all her major competitors throughout most of the fifties and sixties. By 1958 British Gross Domestic Product per head was lower than that of the United States, Canada, Sweden, Australia and New Zealand. By 1963 it was lower than France and Germany as well. The economic weakness made it impossible to keep sterling at the levels it had been set at after the war. Throughout those years the strength of the pound had far more than the pure economic significance it has today. It was still widely used as a trading currency by Commonwealth countries; and in the remaining colonies, any devaluation of the pound to bring it to more realistic levels against the dollar meant that Commonwealth countries would find their finances depleted as the pound was set at lower levels. It could, at worst, destabilize the Commonwealth – and perhaps even break it up.

During the 1950s Churchill and Eden both tried to maintain British international interests, regarding devaluation as an evil to be avoided at all costs. In fact, keeping the pound at a high level against the dollar hampered Britain's economy, making imports cheap and British products expensive abroad. Pressure on the balance of payments forced one devaluation as early as 1949 – though other currencies were revalued against the dollar at the same time. However, by 1967 the economic situation had become so bad that Britain had unilaterally to devalue sterling and abandon most of her remaining overseas commitments. Today the British still consider the pound an important and influential world currency. That is not the case. In the United States the media don't generally even quote the exchange rate between the pound and the dollar, except on the specialist financial pages. Economists in other financial centres regard the pound as part of 'the Mark zone' – as tied to the fortunes of Europe's most prosperous economy, West Germany. The German mark is regarded in world financial circles as one of the three major trading currencies, along with the yen and the dollar.

The historic strength of London as an international financial centre was based on both the importance of sterling as a world trading currency and on the vast foreign investments built up by the British throughout the last century. By the end of the Second World War Britain had become a debtor nation and its currency played second fiddle to the American dollar. Furthermore, until 1979 exchange controls severely limited the flow of money in and out of Britain, making it impossible for British investors and institutions to participate directly in the international financial markets. Yet despite those limitations and the decline in Britain's relative economic strength, the City of London has managed to maintain its position as one of the three key international financial centres, alongside Wall Street and Tokyo.

The reason for this lies, quite simply, in the failure of the United States to allow its own institutions to compete freely in international financial markets. In the 1950s what was known as the Euromarket built up in London – primarily as a result of the Cold War. Countries from the Communist Bloc had sizeable stocks of dollars which they wanted to deposit, but not inside the United States. Several London bankers came up with a solution – dollars could be held by banks based in London, beyond the jurisdiction of the Americans. The British authorities had no reason to interfere with dealings in another country's currency, so long as such dealings had no effect on the British economy.

In 1963 the Kennedy administration imposed capital controls restricting the flow of dollars to other countries. That created enormous problems for New York's international bankers, who saw their business dramatically curtailed, and much of America's international banking business decamped to the Euromarkets as the big banks opened operations in London. Throughout the 1960s and 1970s the City was able to offer a relatively free environment for trading in foreign currencies, while at the same time the Bank of England and successive governments kept a tight rein on dealings in sterling.

A huge international wholesale market in dollars and other currencies developed. American banks flocked to London throughout the sixties and seventies – so much so that at one point there were more American banks operating in London than there were in New York. The freedom which they enjoyed in London was highlighted by the Iran hostage crisis in 1979. When President Carter froze Iranian assets held by American banks, the restriction could not be applied to Iranian money on deposit at branches of American banks in the City of London.

Even though capital controls in the United States were lifted in 1974, it was the Euromarket in London rather than Wall Street which became the principal repository for the deposits of the oil-rich nations of the Middle East throughout the mid-1970s. The Arabs had no wish to deposit their money in the coffers of a country that was the biggest backer of their greatest enemy. The Euromarkets became enormously popular internationally for the lack of regulation they afforded; whether for political or other reasons. As one prominent banker put it in 1970: 'They afforded a marvellous platform from which it is easy to rebound, in any direction, to any country, into any currency – and with anonymity.'[2]

Much of the money deposited in the London Euromarkets was redirected by the banks into long-term loans to Third-World countries via the IMF. Because of the large number of international banks represented in the City of London by that time, it became the ideal centre point for the syndication of these huge loans – even though many of them were put together and largely funded by American banks. Getting dozens of bankers together to sign agreements was much easier when they all had offices in such a small area. By 1980 there were more than 350 foreign banks operating in London. Indeed, as Denis Healey took the British begging bowl to the IMF in 1976 during the balance of payments and budget deficit crisis which followed the 1973 oil crisis, the City of London was booming – boosted by massive flows of international capital in and out of its institutions. British finance houses – particularly the four big clearing banks – did manage to establish themselves in these highly profitable markets, although only on a relatively small scale. Those syndicated loans financed by British banks amounted to some ten per cent of the total, but that figure represented only around the same as that of the biggest American bank operating in the field – Citicorp.

The United States banks' highly profitable business in large syndicated loans arranged in London was undermined by the monetary policies of the American Government in the early 1980s. The anti-inflationary policies pursued by the Reagan administration in the USA after 1981 and, with less international effect, by the Thatcher Government in Britain, used high real interest rates as a monetary tool to keep the money supply down and hence keep inflation under control. High interest rates in the United States had two chief effects on the international capital markets. Firstly, the majority of the loans to Third-World countries had been arranged with a floating, rather than a fixed, interest rate. That meant that when United States rates went up, the borrowers had to increase their own foreign currency revenues to service their debts. In addition, the attractive rates of return available in the United States forced up the value of the dollar which left the Third-World debtors needing even greater resources to buy enough dollars to meet their obligations.

In 1982 Mexico announced that it couldn't pay its debts. Brazil followed suit shortly afterwards, and by 1984 they had been joined by thirty-three other countries. Few could even pay the interest they owed, let alone begin making repayments. It was a crisis point for the international banking community, which found itself with vast amounts of bad debts on its books. A major collapse was avoided after emergency efforts by Western governments and the IMF to arrange rescheduling of loans and interim financing for the countries in difficulties. But the problems facing many of the Third-World debtors effectively spelt the end of the American-dominated syndicated loan market in

London. Many lenders and investors turned to safer arrangements, such as investing in the secure British mortgage market, and, in particular, lending money to the Reagan administration to fund its budget deficit.

At the same time changes within the American financial structure had begun to alter the relative strengths of Wall Street and the City. Arrangements introduced in 1981 allowed the creation of an offshore dollar market on Wall Street, through what are known as International Banking Facilites (IBFs). The end of the syndicated loan boom had already made London a far less attractive place for American banks to operate in, and the creation of IBFs led many of them to begin to run down – or even close – their operations there.

In the years after 1979 the City of London was also under pressure from American and Japanese institutions, both in its domestic activities and in the field of international finance. Soon after the Thatcher Government came to power it lifted exchange controls – for the first time in nearly half a century. Since then, particularly because of the revenue from North Sea oil, there has been a substantial outflow of capital from Britain to the rest of the world – so much so, indeed, that the United Kingdom is now the world's second largest foreign investor after Japan.

But very little of the financial service work that such a massive flow of capital created came to British companies, principally because of the way the domestic financial market in the United Kingdom operates. Although for two decades London had been at the centre of the international finance market, the biggest British financial institutions were all small by world standards, and the Stock Exchange, in particular, was old-fashioned and parochial. It continued to operate a scheme of fixed minimum commissions for its members, as well as a two-tier system of dealing, with investors buying their shares through a broker and a jobber. The broker acted as agent for the investor, while the jobber acted as market maker, buying shares on the market from brokers acting for investors, marking the price up a few pence and then selling them on to other investors through their brokers. The combination of the fixed commissions plus the jobbers' mark-ups – together with stamp duty imposed by the British Government on all share transactions – made London an extremely expensive place to buy and sell shares. (In Tokyo and New York the system was both simpler and cheaper.) That meant that many international share markets, such as mining, which had long-standing links with London, were increasingly based elsewhere, most of them in New York.

And from the early 1980s onwards the domestic share market began to emigrate as well, with companies like ICI, and Jaguar dealing in sizeable quantities in New York so as to be seen as part of the world's leading stock market. The pace of the emigration was so rapid that many prominent British shares ended up being traded in greater numbers on Wall Street than in London. Some British investment institutions went so far as to begin trading in British shares in the form of American depository receipts – essentially promissory notes which were held in place of shares that were lodged with American banks in London – so avoiding stamp duties and fixed commissions. In addition, in the late 1970s, the Labour Government under James Callaghan began to take a close interest in the way the City operated. This led to an investigation into the City's practices under the Restrictive Practices Act, which continued after the election of the Thatcher Government in 1979.

All these factors combined to induce the financial authorities in London to restructure the City and restore its position in what was becoming, with the advent of new technology, an increasingly international market in securities and equities. That restructuring culminated in the so-called 'Big Bang' in the autumn of 1986, when the fixed commissions were abolished and the divide between brokers and jobbers removed. In the run up to 'Big Bang' there was heavy foreign investment in the City of London as American and other financial institutions tried to buy their way into the new stock market. Most of London's leading stockbrokers and jobbing firms were bought by financial institutions who saw the future in terms of large-scale operations able to offer a wide range of financial services to clients – this at a time when businesses were turning away from conventional bank loans as a means of raising finance. The buyers included many of the biggest American banks, most notably Citicorp and Chase Manhattan, as well as Japanese and other foreign institutions. In addition, the successful companies would need to have long-term financial strength to enable them to compete in a world becoming increasingly dominated by the giant international finance houses.

London could also offer the Americans a geographical position, mid-way, in terms of time, between Tokyo and New York – the two largest markets. It is now possible for a dealer to operate in London with both the other two major trading centres on the same working day. At a time when stock trading is increasingly global, this is a vital advantage for the London market.

This has resulted in an international, harmonized trading system operating twenty-four hours a day – first in Japan, then in Britain and then in New York. And though the links between the City and Wall Street are close, both because of language and the number of American institutions in London, they are also components of a much broader world structure.

The integration of financial markets has resulted in increased co-operation between the British and the American Governments in policing the activities of companies and financial institutions. This development evolved out of a dispute between the two countries over attempts by the United States to apply its laws beyond its boundaries – in this case when the United States Department of Justice ordered a Canadian bank based in Florida to hand over records relevant to a narcotics investigation. Those records were held in the Cayman Islands – a British colony. The American action was directly in contradiction of British bank secrecy laws, and provoked an angry response. But the circumstances of the dispute convinced both sides that some kind of mechanism was needed to exchange information in such cases, and has led to a series of agreements to share financial information in criminal proceedings.

These agreements have been enormously successful. In more than a hundred cases the United States has asked for financial information to help in inquiries, and the arrangement has also led to the exposure of Britain's biggest financial scandal for many years – the Guinness affair. The revelation that one of Britain's most prominent companies had acted fraudulently to win an important takeover battle rocked the City of London at the end of 1986. The information that led to the arrest of several prominent businessmen and bankers came out of an insider trading investigation in Wall Street. Investigators from the Securities and Exchange Commission looking into the activities of the American financier Ivan Boesky discovered that he had been involved in what appeared to be illegal transactions linked to the Guinness takeover bid for the Scottish-based Distillers Group. That information was passed on to a representative of the Department of Trade and Industry who was in Washington on another matter. He took various documents back to London with him, and ten days later Guinness's headquarters were raided. At the time of writing there are rumours that the DTI is investigating other recent takeovers as a result of information provided by Boesky to the American authorities.

Since the 1960s the United States' relative economic position has undergone a dramatic transition. Within four years of Wilson's devaluation of sterling in 1967, the American currency was also undermined with the final collapse in the early seventies of the system of fixed exchange rates established at Bretton Woods. Several factors made the change inevitable. The United States was now running a massive deficit on its international account, paying the huge costs of its NATO commitments and the Vietnam War. The revival of Japan and Europe meant that the dollar became more and more overvalued, and hence American industry was less able to compete. And the independent offshore dollar markets made it increasingly difficult for the United States to manage a dollar-based international currency system. Towards the end of the sixties the United States' reserves came under pressure as investors sold dollars. The crunch came in 1971, with the rush out of the dollar reaching crisis proportions. Facing a desperate situation, the Nixon administration devalued the dollar, thus ending twenty-five years of stability, and put a temporary ten per cent surcharge on imports to stop the flow of money abroad.

The end of the Bretton Woods system of exchange rates fixed to the dollar was the first clear sign that the economic hegemony enjoyed by the United States in the post-war era was over. The dollar, for so long the mainstay of the international financial structure, was now vulnerable, and the United States' economy itself was clearly liable to the same periodic crises that had affected other countries. In late 1971 the industrialized countries attempted to create a new fixed-rate system, with a substantial realigning of the dollar against the other leading currencies. But by the beginning of 1973 it had become widely recognized that this alternative wasn't working properly either – the pound, for example, had been upgraded against the dollar in the 1971 arrangements to a level that the performance of the British economy did not justify. The other Western nations responded by abandoning the principle of fixed exchange rates, leaving their currencies to float freely rather than remain tied to the dollar.

The post-Bretton Woods era has seen the dollar continuing in its position as the world's most important trading currency. Oil and gold, for example, are still priced in dollars. But the dollar is now no longer any less vulnerable to economic fluctuations than the other leading currencies. In fact, it is currently more vulnerable because Reagan's policies have been domestically orientated, causing some anxiety to major overseas holders of dollars, whether banks, nations or corporations. Since the ending of the Bretton Woods system the dollar has twice run into serious difficulties, and fallen sharply. In 1977 the cumulative effects of the 1973 oil crisis left the United States with a large balance of payments deficit, and so undermined the value of the dollar. And in the 1980s the dollar has again been in trouble. The Reagan administration's expansion of defence spending, combined with the President's commitment to cut taxes, left the American Federal Government with a massive shortfall of funds to meet its commitments. The deficit was funded by American domestic investors who bought government bonds with their savings, but more significantly, by attracting large amounts of money from overseas investors – particularly from a Japanese economy awash with earnings from its huge trade surpluses with the rest of the world. Under Reagan the United States Government borrowed more money than under all the other thirty-nine presidents combined. The apparent strength of the American economy, particularly after Reagan's landslide victory in 1983 when he was at the height of his popularity, seemed to assure foreigners that the investment would be worthwhile. But it also ensured that the dollar remained strong, pushing it to levels where American exporters found their products unable to compete overseas.

In September 1985 the Finance Ministers of the major industrial countries met at the Plaza Hotel in New York to halt the rise of the dollar. The Plaza Agreement, as it became known, aimed to bring down the United States' currency by cutting American interest rates, and so making it more attractive to invest in other countries. In the event, it worked too well, and the dollar plummeted, so much so that the Finance Ministers had to meet again – at the Louvre in Paris in February 1987 – to try to halt the dollar's slide.

The Louvre agreement was a watershed in the history of the dollar, and in the post-war economic position of the United States. Like the Bretton Woods agreement it attempted to stabilize exchange rates, though this time within a small, set range. It set down that central banks, like the Bank of England, could intervene in the currency markets to keep exchange rates from fluctuating beyond the set limits. The United States was to start cutting its budget deficit, while Germany and Japan agreed to boost their economies to cushion any slowdown in world economic activity after the American action. In short, the agreement demonstrated quite clearly that the United States was no longer capable of solving its economic difficulties independent of the other Western industrial powers. Although there are still those in

America who believe their country ought to act unilaterally in matters of economic policy – Richard Gephardt made his early running in the 1988 Democratic Presidential Primaries campaign on just such a platform – but the fact that the build-up of the budget deficit has left the United States as the world's biggest debtor nation makes that view absurd. Indeed, analysts such as Michael Hughes of the merchant bank Barclays de Zoete Wedd now believe that it is only a matter of time before the Japanese yen replaces the dollar as the world's chief currency.

The contrast with Britain is revealing. Ronald Reagan and Margaret Thatcher openly share the same economic ideals: both were elected on a promise to cut taxes and public expenditure, and to reduce the burden of government on the people. After nine years of Thatcher Government the overall burden of taxation is only marginally lower and public spending has increased. But Nigel Lawson, Chancellor of the Exchequer since 1983, has also managed to keep public borrowing to its lowest level for two decades. By contrast the Reagan administration has successfully cut taxation, but has also allowed expenditure to rise, making it impossible to keep public borrowing under control. Two leaders, widely perceived to share economic ideas, have presided over contrasting economic developments. Britain, the pauper of the seventies, has evolved into a major overseas investor; the United States, the power that dominated the Western world for two decades, is now the world's biggest debtor.

The Louvre agreement did not halt the fundamental weakness of the dollar, but simply diverted the problem. Since 1985 investors have been increasingly concerned about America's economic difficulties, particularly the trade and budget deficits. As the United States' national debt builds up, the repayments of interest take up more and more public money, leading the Government into serious financial difficulties. Although the United States cut its budget deficit significantly after the Louvre agreement, investors continued to sell their dollars. Those dollars were bought by the central banks of the other major industrial powers – New York economists estimate that in the seven months before the October 1987 crash Britain, West Germany and Japan had spent well over $50 billion supporting the American currency. Much of that money was spent in their own currencies buying dollars from investors who wanted to sell, to try to stop the price falling too far. Those central banks now hold large reserves of dollars which, as the value of the United States' currency goes down, are also losing value. If the central banks decided to offload dollars to halt their losses, the amounts they would be selling would cause the once mighty currency to collapse completely. In short, in 1987 the stability of the United States' currency – the world currency of the past forty years – depends on the co-operation and support of the bankers and politicians of the other main industrial countries.

That reality was one of the factors behind the stock market crash in the autumn of 1987. The crash began on what has since been nicknamed 'Black Monday' – 19 October 1987. In less than a week all the major financial centres saw losses averaging around 20 per cent, and in many cases the figures were much worse. In purely numerical terms it made the 1929 Wall Street crash look small. The incident that triggered the crash perfectly symbolized the change in the structure of the world financial and economic system, and the relative decline of the United States as an economic power. In the week before the falls began, there was a public row between the American Treasury Secretary James Baker and the West Germans over the international currency co-operation that had followed the Louvre agreement. Baker claimed that a rise in German interest rates and plans for some tax increases were directly contradictory to the spirit of economic co-operation established by the agreement, and were slowing the expansion of the German economy. The Germans responded angrily, saying that they had no intention of letting their own economic policies be directed by the fact that American consumers were spending too much on imports.

This opened up highly undesirable possibilities to international investors in Wall Street. A breakdown in international currency management which prompted another fall in the value of the dollar would cost them money as the relative value of investments in dollars fell too. Those fears were heightened by a small rise in United States interest rates – again apparently a move away from the Louvre agreement which would make investment by American companies locally more expensive and would hit economic growth.

The result was a sharp, and sudden fall in share prices on Wall Street as investors rushed to pull out of the United States. On the first day of the crash the main New York index, the Dow Jones average, fell by some 500 points – around 20 per cent of its total value – to be followed by heavy losses in other markets around the world. In the days that followed the London market fell by around a third, and Tokyo a fifth, before they too recovered ground. And in what turned out to be a disastrous decision the Hong Kong market was suspended for a week, ostensibly to prevent panic selling, but in practice to give time to prepare a rescue package for local dealers vulnerable to a large market fall. When the market reopened a week later it was down around a third, and the credibility of Hong Kong as an international financial centre was severely damaged.

There is an old adage about America sneezing, and the rest of its allies catching cold. Although that is less evident today, the way in which the original 1987 stock market falls on Wall Street spread to other markets indicated that what happens in the United States still has a profound effect on confidence around the world.

It is symbolic of the international economic integration of recent years that the British market, perhaps somewhat overpriced and yet backed by a solid economy, should follow so closely the lead provided by Wall Street. While there was every reason for Wall Street to crash, there was little apparent need for more than a technical correction on a relatively small scale in London. The British Chancellor of the Exchequer Nigel Lawson blamed what he called the 'globalization of the herd instinct' – now electronic.

In the weeks after the crash there was a further indication of the way the economic balance has tilted over the past two decades. The crash coincided with an attempt by the Thatcher Government to sell off its remaining minority shareholding in the oil giant British Petroleum as part of its privatization programme. The plan was to raise £5¼ billion. The issue opened the day after 'Black Monday', and closed before any real recovery had begun. As a result the share price, which had been pitched at an attractive level for the small investor in the pre-crash market, became hopelessly expensive and the issue was massively undersubscribed.

The shares had been underwritten by most of the major British financial institutions, and by foreign banks looking to take a part in what had been – in previous issues – a highly profitable transaction. Four American banks – Goldman Sachs, Morgan Stanley, Shearson Lehman and Salomon Brothers – were among the biggest underwriters, along with Japanese and Canadian institutions. In the eighties the participation of foreign banks in such transactions has become a normal part of international financial practice, in a way that would never have happened in the past. In the sixties, for example, it would have been inconceivable for American institutions to lose heavily because of internal developments in the United Kingdom. The four American banks are estimated to have lost around $100 million each from the BP issue, even though the British Government fixed a floor price to limit the underwriters' losses. At one stage in the controversy, the United States Treasury Secretary James Baker tried to put pressure on the British Government to drop the issue because of the effect the losses suffered by the four American banks would have on the United States' market! That in itself is a remarkable event – a generation ago no part of the British Government's domestic economic plans could have prompted such attention from the Treasury Department in Washington.

In the aftermath of the crash, American economists like John Paulus of Morgan Stanley believe that Britain and Western Europe will suffer as the United States addresses the economic problems that have been building up since the mid-eighties. Transatlantic trade now amounts to some $120 billion a year, and though the United States trade deficit is primarily with Japan and the other industrial economies of the Far East – Taiwan, Hong Kong, South Korea and Singapore – if the deficit is reduced, European producers will be adversely affected. But unless increased action is taken to address the American trade and budget deficits, the dollar is likely to remain weak – a situation that will also hinder European producers looking to sell goods in the United States. British and European companies are also put at a disadvantage by the fact that the currencies of the smaller Far Eastern countries are, by and large, fixed against the dollar. Unless they agree to a revaluation, their producers will remain just as competitive if the dollar goes on falling.

Japan, which has by far the largest single trade surplus with the United States, has done much to shield itself against the effects of America's economic difficulties. It has stimulated consumer demand at home, and its corporations have invested heavily in property and factories overseas – particularly in the United States. Britain has nothing like the same dependence on the United States for its exports – most British trade is now within the European Community. A survey by the London Business School in the aftermath of the October 1987 crash suggested that even the worst possible scenario – a recession in the United States caused by massive cuts in the budget deficit or by pushing up interest rates to stop the dollar collapsing – would hit the British economy. But it suggested that that impact might well do no more than halve growth and halt the decline in unemployment – serious but not catastrophic developments.[3] The American cold need not give Britain pneumonia. Although if problems in the United States led to the collapse of a major bank, the effects would be more serious. However the readiness of the authorities to support troubled institutions in recent years makes this very much a worst-case scenario. Even so, a serious downturn in the American economy would affect Europe far more than any economic development in Britain and Europe could affect the United States.

It is, then, a paradox. The United States now operates as part of an international monetary and economic bloc, and has to rely, at least in part, on the support and co-operation of other major economies. Yet it remains the largest and potentially most influential member of that bloc – and decisions taken in Washington have implications for the prosperity of the whole of the Western world. In short, the United States is no longer able to give the clear economic lead it has given in the past – a fact acknowledged by Paul Volcker, who later became Chairman of the Federal Reserve, in 1982. 'Power is more fragmented,' he said. 'The United States can't play the same role that it did in the earlier post-war period.'[4] But at the same time it remains the largest and most influential Western economy. Despite the argument that the world is moving towards an era of Japanese economic supremacy, there is little evidence to indicate that the Japanese are willing to play a more active role in international economic management.

In terms of the financial relationship Britain remains a minor partner. It is only the importance of the City of London as a financial centre that gives Britain a place in the front line of international economic affairs. Indeed recently the Italians argued that they should replace Britain as one of the five members of the Group of Five (G-5) forum for meetings between the leading industrial nations, because, they said, they were now the economically stronger country. In 1988, the Chancellor Nigel Lawson started advertising the successes of the British economy since the mid-eighties – and the contrast this provides with the deficit in the United States – as a reason why he believes that Britain now plays a more influential role in the management of Western economics. Although the close relationship between Margaret Thatcher and Ronald Reagan, coupled with respect in Washington for Nigel Lawson's achievements, undoubtedly gave the British Government better access to American decision-making, it is hard to see that Britain could play a major role in the future. In the same way that Keynes gave Britain added influence at Bretton Woods, so Lawson and Thatcher may have a degree of personal influence over the Reagan administration and its successors. But to the United States what happens in West Germany is more important.

However, the fact that Britain and the other developed nations have deemed it necessary to spend enormous amounts of money supporting the dollar in recent months is a clear sign that the relative decline in the importance of United States' currency should not be overestimated. The globalization of world finance has inevitably diminished the United States economic muscle. As economies have become more intertwined, so nations have become more interdependent in financial terms. Britain no longer needs the United States – but a break in the economic links between the two countries would certainly hurt the British far more than it could ever hurt the Americans.

4

☆☆★☆☆

THE UNITED STATES
AND THE
BRITISH NUCLEAR DETERRENT

*Britain became conceptually and morally a satellite of the United
States . . . once it relied on the United States for its own nuclear
deterrent.*

Enoch Powell – former Conservative Minister.

THERE are two areas where there really is a special relationship
between Britain and the United States – in intelligence matters and
also in the field of nuclear technology. Indeed, the unofficial view at the
American Embassy is that intelligence apart, the special relationship *is*
the nuclear relationship.

British and American scientists worked together during the Second
World War to create the nuclear weapons that would destroy Hiroshima
and Nagasaki. And while the relationship broke down for a decade after
the war, there is now close co-operation between the nuclear establishments on both sides of the Atlantic.

The key to the nuclear relationship has been the United States
agreement to provide Britain with its own nuclear deterrent. In fact,
although Britain has made great play of having an independent nuclear
capability, since the early 1960s it has relied on the United States for
the technology needed for that 'independent' deterrent. Indeed, Britain
is the only country to have been allowed access to what is one of
America's most preciously guarded technologies.

Britain's Polaris missiles are American. And when those missiles are
phased out in the 1990s, their replacement – the Trident missile system
– will also be American.

The first steps towards nuclear co-operation between the two
countries were taken after the United States entered the war against
Germany at the end of 1941. Both countries had been working on their
own nuclear programmes, although, despite America's neutrality, there

had been some interchange of information from the autumn of 1940.[1] In 1941 the Americans twice proposed a joint nuclear programme at a time when Britain was well ahead technically. The British refused, reluctant to hand secrets to a neutral power. This was to prove a mistake – when the two countries did eventually link up, American research was far more advanced and British influence correspondingly smaller. A team of British scientists visited their American counterparts in early 1942 to see for themselves their research effort. They were surprised by the result. Britain had been at the forefront of early nuclear research, and the scientists had thought that their project, which had been concealed behind the innocuous sounding name of Tube Alloys, was well ahead of the American project. The visit to the United States convinced them that they were wrong. Back in London the scientists reported that the progress they had witnessed, together with the vastly greater resources of the United States, would enable the Americans to leave the British behind in developing nuclear weapons and reactors. A member of the British team reported: 'Their resources for working out schemes quickly are vastly greater than ours.'[2] They recommended an approach to the American Government proposing that the two projects should be merged.

The proposal initially provoked hostility in the United States. Some of the scientists involved in the American research, known as the Manhattan Project, suspected that Britain's real intention was to get access to American technology that could be used to develop a civil nuclear programme after the war. Now the boot was on the other foot, and to begin with the Americans rejected the British approaches. It came as a 'bombshell' and was 'quite intolerable', Sir John Anderson, project chairman, wrote to Churchill.[3]

But eventually the two sides reached an agreement following a diplomatic offensive by Britain. The agreement was signed by Churchill and Roosevelt at a meeting in Quebec in August 1943, and it pledged that the two countries would never use atomic weapons against each other, would always consult the other before any nuclear bomb was used against another country, and would consult fully before letting anyone else have access to nuclear technology. This was the only time an agreement between the two countries has given Britain a right of veto over the use of American nuclear weapons. American fears about Britain's commercial interest in the programme were assuaged by a stipulation that after the War the United States President would have the right to decide under what terms the jointly developed technology could be released for civil use. British scientists were sent to the United States and Canada to work on the Manhattan project, and they played an important part in developing the weapons used to defeat the Japanese.

Towards the end of the war the United States turned its attention to the way nuclear research would be handled when the war was over. In September 1944 Roosevelt and Churchill signed a memorandum known as the Hyde Park Aide-Mémoire, agreeing not to disclose any information about the Manhattan project to other countries. But it also proposed 'full collaboration between the United States and the British Government in developing Tube Alloys for military and commercial purposes'. Disastrously for the British, as it turned out, the American copy was mistakenly filed in a folder on naval matters, the code name having been taken literally.[4]

Scientists working on the project wanted to share the nuclear research with the Russians, and to set up an international forum for managing nuclear technology in the post-war years. They feared there would otherwise be a post-war arms race between the United States and the Soviet Union.

But after the war, and with Roosevelt dead, the situation changed catastrophically for the British. There was strong pressure from the United States' nuclear establishment and from influential people on Capitol Hill against a continuation of the joint Anglo-American programme, because of fears that Britain would use American research to its own commercial advantage. President Truman was forced to revise the American position. He told the Labour Prime Minister Clement Attlee that the United States was prepared to carry on with a full exchange of basic research information and co-operation in developing nuclear raw materials, but that it was under no obligation to provide details of the production systems of the American research into building a nuclear reactor. He felt it would be unwise to extend co-operation further while moves were underway to try to establish some kind of international control.

In July 1946 Congress passed the McMahon Act which made it illegal to pass over nuclear information overseas until an effective system of international control had been established. Senator McMahon later said he would never have pushed such a tough bill through the Senate if he had known about the Hyde Park Aide-Mémoire.

The McMahon Act effectively ended the co-operative programme between Britain and the United States. Britain felt a deep sense of betrayal, particularly in Whitehall and among the scientists who had worked alongside their American counterparts during the war. However, some parts of the joint programme remained intact – the two countries continued to control supplies of uranium together, and a handful of British scientists went on working in the United States on the development of nuclear weapons, many of them becoming American citizens. Nuclear research in Britain had been relatively limited during the later stages of the war, since most of the allied effort was concentrated in the United States and Canada on the weapons programme. But even before the MacMahon Act was passed the Attlee Government had already taken the decision in January 1946 to start work on a British nuclear reactor. Now with the cut off of American information the scientists assigned to the project were forced to pursue their own lines of development.

At the same time the RAF began lobbying for Britain to acquire its own atomic bomb able to be carried to targets in a new generation of high-speed and high-altitude bombers. The RAF first stated its requirement for an atomic bomber in August 1946 and the detailed specification stated it had to be capable of carrying a 'special bomb' to a range of 1,500 miles.[5] The decision to press ahead with the development of a British atomic weapon was taken on 8 January 1947 by a handful of ministers – the full Cabinet, Parliament and the Labour Party were not told.

As well as the immediate need to decide whether to continue work on the project, Britain had two other reasons for pressing on alone and developing an independent nuclear capability. The first was simply the question of her role as a great power. Although the war had dramatically changed Britain's role in the world – more than most British politicians appreciated at the time – Britain still saw itself as a significant world power. As Attlee himself put it later: 'The stupid McMahon Act prevented our acting fully with them. And they were inclined to think they were the big boys and we were the small boys; we just had to show them they didn't know everything.'[6] The decision was justified by Bevin, who arrived late at a Cabinet Committee set up in October 1946 to decide on building nuclear facilities; as Attlee summed up the case against, Bevin expostulated: 'No, Prime Minister that won't do at all . . . we've got to have this . . . I don't mind for myself, but I don't want any other Foreign Secretary of this country to be talked at, or to, by a Secretary of State in the United States as I have just had in my discussions with Mr Byrnes. We have got to have this thing over here whatever it costs . . . We've got to have the bloody Union Jack flying on top of it.'[7] In other words, not to press ahead with the development of what was clearly the weapon of a new age would be to consign Britain to the position of second division nation with no role as a great power in the post-war world – and able to be ordered around by the United States. The political considerations behind the nuclear programme were amply demonstrated in the 1950s when a relatively low priority was given to trying to build up Britain's nuclear stockpile, once the first British nuclear weapons were deployed. The West only had limited amounts of uranium. Strategically it was more important for the American deterrent to be built up for the security of the West. Britain wanted its bomb for more symbolic reasons. It was more important to be a nuclear power for diplomatic reasons than to have a huge nuclear arsenal for military purposes.

The second consideration was the future of Britain's defence. Enough doubts existed about the American commitment to the defence of Britain in the immediate post-war years to make it appear foolhardy for the British not to have the atom bomb. It was, after all, only six years since the United States had abandoned its pre-war period of isolationism to join the allied war effort. Attlee himself explained years later:

> 'At that time we had to bear in mind that there was always the possibility of their withdrawing and becoming isolationist once again. The manufacture of a British atomic bomb was, therefore, at that stage vital to our defence. You have to remember this was all prior to NATO. NATO has altered things. But at that time, although we were doing our best to make the Americans understand the realities of the European situation – the world situation – we couldn't be sure we'd succeed. In the end we did. But we couldn't take risks with British security in the meantime.'[8]

The anxieties behind the decision were increased enormously by the explosion of the Soviet Union's first nuclear device in 1949, years earlier than had been expected. Suddenly the security threat was all too real.

The American and British nuclear programmes functioned separately for some eleven years after the breach in 1946. During that time both countries expanded their nuclear arsenals considerably and made great headway in the development of nuclear reactor technology. But the British programme was dogged, as indeed it has been for much of the past forty years, by almost immediate obsolescence. Britain's first atom bomb was exploded in the Monte Bello Islands off Australia on 3 October 1952. A month later the United States programme moved into a different league with the explosion of the vastly more powerful H-bomb on Eniwetok atoll in the Pacific. Britain was then forced to begin developing an H-bomb itself to keep up with the United States, despite the enormous extra cost.

Discussions between the two sides resumed in 1947. The United Nations Atomic Energy Commission, which had spent fourteen months in negotiations, had failed to find a satisfactory formula for the international control of nuclear power, and Marshall and Truman felt the United States could justifiably begin working with the United Kingdom again. But the United States entered the talks largely out of self-interest, recognizing that the burgeoning American nuclear programme would be limited if it couldn't secure access to uranium stocks that fell partly under British control. 'What we need urgently in the near future is more of what you have,' Secretary of State Marshall wrote to Bevin in December 1947. There was also growing anxiety in the United States about the stipulations of the 1943 Quebec agreement which gave Britain the right of veto over America's use of atomic weapons. Members of Congress were outraged to learn that the United States had apparently accepted unconstitutional limitations over its ability to use its own weapons.

Britain made a number of concessions to the United States in the talks, particularly in allowing the United States to have a larger share of the uranium controlled by the two countries, and allowing the Quebec agreement to lapse in 1948 – in an agreement called the *modus vivendi*. In return, the United States agreed to increase the free exchange of scientific information between the two countries' nuclear programmes. The readiness to accept these one-sided agreements showed the strength of Britain's desire to resume co-operation. But although Britain accepted that it could not dictate the use of nuclear weapons by the United States in situations in which it was not involved, the question of the control of American nuclear weapons stored in Britain has been contentious ever since.

Negotiations with the new American Secretary of State Dean Acheson, about loosening the provisions of the McMahon Act, collapsed after the arrest of the atom spies Fuchs and Nunn May in 1950. 'The talks with the British and Canadians returned to square one,' wrote Acheson.[9] Attempts to co-ordinate the separate nuclear development programmes only began in the early fifties, when the two countries had a change of leaders. Churchill, back as Prime Minister in 1951, was prepared to accept a reduction in the independence of the British atomic development programme in order to restore some of the old ties, so long as the principle of the independent nuclear deterrent and British research facilities remained intact. As long as Britain had the bomb – and the status it accorded – he was happy. Otherwise, building up the military strength of NATO was more strategically important than a large British stockpile of weapons. Eisenhower, who succeeded Truman in 1953, believed the divorce of the two programmes in 1946 had been excessively harsh on Britain. But the political will for restoring collaboration was, at first, hampered by the strength of the restrictions imposed by the laws passed in 1946. Churchill met Eisenhower at Bermuda in December 1953 armed with a photocopy of the original Hyde Park Aide-Mémoire, and Eisenhower promised to ask Congress to relax the laws. After a long and complex series of political negotiations, Congress passed a new Atomic Energy Act in 1954. The Act gave the President the authority – unless Congress disagreed – to share a much wider range of nuclear information with an ally.

Although there were diplomatic motives for opening the doors to co-operation with the United Kingdom, there were military considerations as well. During the 1950s nuclear weapons were beginning to play a key role in NATO strategy. In December 1954 the NATO Council of Ministers declared that it was ready to use nuclear weapons against a conventional Soviet attack. The new Atomic Energy Act made it possible for the United States to give Britain details about the size and weight of its nuclear weapons. More important, it allowed Britain access to information that would allow it to adapt its own fleet of V-bombers – the planes planned to carry the British deterrent – so that they could hold American designs of bombs as well. Those provisions provided the basis for the Anglo-American negotiations that followed the Suez crisis two years later.

Although Suez severely jolted Anglo-American political relations, it had little impact on the growing co-operation in nuclear matters. In the aftermath of the crisis, members of the Conservative Government argued that Britain had either to become an independent power capable of acting without the sanction of the United States, or should rebuild bridges and accept the realities of the status of a junior partner. Harold Macmillan, who succeeded Sir Anthony Eden as Prime Minister after Suez, moved in both directions for a time. In his first broadcast to the nation a week after taking office he emphasized the commitment to the

United States, but also the determination to remain independent. 'We don't intend to part from the Americans, and we don't intend to be satellites. I am sure they don't want us to be. The stronger we are, the better partners we shall be.' Cabinet papers recently released show that in a secret briefing paper it was accepted that: 'we should become dependent on the United States for some of the most important of our future weapons'. But that was, the paper said: 'no more than a recognition that our national security is already dependent on the United States'.[10]

Macmillan pressed ahead with the independent British programme, developing Blue Streak, a missile system capable of carrying warheads. He also continued negotiations aimed at increasing still further the ties between the two nuclear programmes. He was helped both by his close relationship with Eisenhower, and by the explosion in May 1957 of the first British H-bomb on Christmas Island, which brought Britain's technology back into the top flight.

By the end of 1957 the two countries were involved in discussions on a wide range of nuclear matters. The growing commitment of the respective Governments towards a move back to the wartime level of co-operation were heightened by the Soviet Union's sudden and unexpected launch of the first Sputnik that year, which opened up the possibility of a serious threat to the United States from long-range Soviet nuclear rockets.

From the early 1950s scientists in both the United States and Britain had been working on missile development as an alternative to free-fall bombs. In 1954 the two countries had signed an agreement to work together in the field, though this was limited by the provisions of the 1946 McMahon Act, which made it impossible for the United States to supply Britain with missiles to launch its warheads. Some joint-programmes did develop: Rolls-Royce, for example, was allowed to build American rocket motors under licence. But the British pursued an independent missile programme – developing the Blue Streak, an intermediate-range missile powered by an American motor built under licence. Its guidance system was also American. The United States had already developed a missile with an intercontinental capability, the Atlas, and was also working on a medium-range missile, the Thor.

The Blue Streak was given the official go-ahead in 1955. It met with opposition in Whitehall, largely because it had no civil use which could – as was happening in aircraft development – offset some of the high research costs. But much of the scepticism about the need for unmanned missiles to launch the British deterrent disappeared during the abortive attempt to regain control of the Suez Canal, when the Russians made a vague threat to use nuclear missiles against Britain if it continued its military action against the Egyptians.

The launch of the Soviet Union's Sputnik 1 had been a wholly unexpected development, and led to fears in the United States and elsewhere in the West that the Soviet Union was moving ahead in technical capability. Macmillan responded by telling Eisenhower that the 'countries of the free world should try to pool their resources to meet the increasing threat', and the two leaders met in Washington a few days later on 23 October 1957. The President asked the National Security Council to approve a full exchange of military nuclear information with Britain.

Inevitably the creation of what was effectively a new nuclear alliance between Britain and the United States met with some opposition. In the United States there were those who argued that the arrangements were one-sided; that all that was in fact involved was the handing over of most of America's nuclear secrets to the British with little in return, and that the President's proposals would give the British nuclear industry commercial advantages over the United States. France had begun to develop its own nuclear programme, and there were fears that the link-up with Britain would be seen as discrimination against France. But the legislation was eventually passed in June 1958, and the formal agreement between the two countries was concluded on 3 July, bringing to an end eleven years of separate development.

The agreement had allowed British nuclear missiles, aircraft and other delivery systems to be fitted with American nuclear weapons, and permitted the exchange of all information necessary to help each country improve the effectiveness of its nuclear weapons. In addition, it permitted the transfer of technology and information that would help either country develop its own nuclear submarine fleet – in practice, this meant the United States helping Britain build up such a capability and providing the reactors for the vessels. That had already been agreed in principle between the two countries, but had been impossible under the old legislation. The United States was particularly enthusiastic about helping Britain build nuclear-powered submarines because the two navies already operated very closely wtihin NATO, and the Americans felt that if the British did develop the submarines it would improve the naval strength of the West.

One aim of the 1958 agreement was to establish a stockpile of modern nuclear weapons and missiles in Britain as quickly and as cheaply as possible. In contrast to 1943, the United States discovered that Britain had made greater progress in its research than expected, and had developed a number of techniques the United States did not possess. Although the agreement was certainly of most benefit to Britain, it was not totally so.

The apparent threat by Marshal Bulganin, the Soviet Prime Minister, to use missiles against Britain at Suez also had an effect on internal British planning.[11] Once again it highlighted the perennial British problem of keeping up with accelerating technology. Even though Britain's Hydrogen bomb was only months away from completion, it was useless if there was no effective way of delivering it to its target. Soviet missile developments meant that unmanned vehicles could be used to attack Britain, while at the same time the technology being developed could stop British bombers getting through to their targets. That was to become perilously clear in 1960 when, with the V-bombers still Britain's front-line defence system, the Soviet Union shot down Gary Powers' U2 spy plane, proving that technology existed to shoot down high-altitude planes. The V-bombers could no longer be regarded as an effective deterrent – Britain had to have missiles too.

Despite the negotiations between the United States and Britain over nuclear co-operation, the British public remained strongly committed to the idea of an independent British nuclear capability operating alongside United States forces. Furthermore, that support was shared by both sides of the House of Commons. George Brown, the Labour defence spokesman, said in 1957: 'If we still have visions of ourself as the centre, if no longer the mother of a great comonwealth of nations, and if we see ourselves influencing the circumstances in which the deterrent might be used, I do not see how we can do without it.' And the 1957 Labour Conference was warned by the former Labour cabinet minister John Strachey that abandoning the British bomb would 'make Britain the wholly dependent satellite of the United States . . . it would make a future Labour Foreign Secretary unable even to consider policies which were not approved by the State Department in Washington'.[12] This view was shared by the Conservatives. In 1955 Macmillan had said it would be foolhardy to abandon the British nuclear capability. 'Politically it surrenders our power to influence American policy and then, strategically and tactically it equally deprives us of any influence over the selection of targets and the use of our vital striking forces.'[13]

But not only did the United Kingdom need to improve its defences; it also had to find ways of keeping the defence budget under control at a time when this was beginning to give cause for concern. The 1957 White Paper, put forward by the Defence Secretary Duncan Sandys, committed Britain to major cuts in its conventional forces and directed future resources towards deterrence through nuclear weapons. In doing so it abandoned many of the aircraft industry's development projects, arguing that in the future unmanned craft would be the norm, and manned planes would be redundant.

Despite the 1958 agreement and the deployment of American Thor missiles in the United Kingdom in the same year, Britain continued to develop a whole range of nuclear weapons of its own. These included the Blue Streak missile, closely modelled on the American Atlas rocket, and an air-launched missile, Blue Steel. But the programme remained enormously expensive, and involved considerable duplication of American effort.

The ground-launched Blue Streak missile was given top priority by the Macmillan Government after Suez. With a range of some 2,000 miles, it was able to strike into Soviet territory. But it ran into difficulties because of its cost and its vulnerability. Because the missile was surface-launched it was seen to be particularly vulnerable to attack. This vulnerability was increased as the Soviet Union began deploying missiles near its Western borders. Furthermore, before it could be fired, its fuel tanks had to be filled with kerosene, which took vital minutes before its launch and made a pre-emptive strike by Soviet missiles even more of a danger. Putting the missiles into protected silos – which would make them less vulnerable to attack – would increase costs dramatically, and the United States and the Soviet Union had already developed solid-fuel motors that could be kept in a permanent state of readiness. In practice the whole project simply became too expensive.

By early 1960 Macmillan had begun to evaluate possible alternatives, and in April decided to cancel the project. But the Government still felt it politically essential for Britain to have its own nuclear deterrent, as much to help in its political dealings with Washington as for strategic reasons. Macmillan approached the Americans and asked permission to buy and modify an American-made missile, the Skybolt. This would not incur the cost of developing a system from scratch, and could also be used to extend the life of Britain's existing fleet of V-bombers. The missile could be launched from a V-bomber a thousand miles from the target, which meant the plane didn't have to go near their targets, and so were less vulnerable to air defences.

Macmillan met Eisenhower at Camp David where it was agreed that Britain could have the missile once it reached production stage. At the same meeting, Britain gave the United States permission to build a Polaris submarine base at Holy Loch in Scotland. There was no direct link between the two but it is generally accepted that the British offered Holy Loch as a bargaining counter in their efforts to get the American missile.

Although the Macmillan Government argued that Skybolt would maintain the British independent deterrent, its claims were met with scepticism by the Labour opposition. The new missile was still in the development stages, and had not been bought by the Pentagon. That, argued its opponents, left the status of Britain as a world nuclear power hanging on the fate of an untried American system. Harold Wilson, later to become Prime Minister, said the failure of the Blue Streak project was 'the moment of truth' for the British deterrent.

Skybolt had its technical opponents as well, particularly the growing lobby which felt that a sea-launched defence system would be more secure against Soviet attack. The Royal Navy had been closely monitoring the American development of the Polaris submarine-launched ballistic missile since the 1950s, and had recognized the advantages of such a system to a country like Britain. Its interest was backed in 1961 by a pressure group within the Conservative Party, the Bow Group, which argued that Skybolt should be cancelled and replaced with six Polaris submarines. It expressed the hope that the United States would be willing to allow such a purchase.

In the event the Skybolt project collapsed in the autumn of 1963. Although Britain was given little warning of the final decision to cancel the project, there were clear indications throughout 1961 and 1962 – at both official and unofficial levels, that the project was in difficulties. The Kennedy administration almost certainly failed to appreciate the political importance to Britain of the cancellation – with several alternatives available to the United States, the decision was taken on technical grounds. But to the Macmillan Government, which was going through a low ebb of popularity at home, the decision was a disaster. It had relied on the Skybolt, for without it the independent deterrent was effectively worthless.

The two leaders met at Nassau in the Bahamas in December 1962. President Kennedy offered to continue the Skybolt project if Britain paid half its development costs, but Macmillan rejected this. Skybolt had been totally discredited by the American decision to cancel it, he argued. He told Kennedy that Britain had to have an independent deterrent to maintain its self-respect, and put forward the idea that the Navy had begun pushing for so strongly – purchase of the American Polaris missile as their deterrent for the sixties and seventies. In the end the two leaders found a compromise. Britain was to have Polaris on highly favourable terms. But the British 'independent' deterrent was to be made available for inclusion in a multi-lateral nuclear force for NATO – the MLF. Britain agreed to use its Polaris submarines 'for the purposes of international defence of the Western alliance in all circumstances' apart from those cases 'where Her Majesty's Government may decide that supreme national interests are at stake'. Although that left Britain with national control of her deterrent, in practice it tied its use closely with actions and decisions taken elsewhere in NATO. Targeting is normally done through NATO, although Britain does have its own set of target data for independent use.

The Nassau agreement had other implications. The British and the Americans had set a new agenda for NATO's nuclear forces through the idea of a multi-lateral force, without in any way consulting their allies. Polaris had also been offered to the French, partly as an attempt to appear equitable, partly as an attempt to bring the newly developing French nuclear force under closer NATO and American control. The offer was rejected by de Gaulle, who was opposed to the French force becoming part of a multilateral NATO force, and hence ceasing to be under absolute French control. France also resented Britain's part in the Nassau agreement, and felt that Britain, having been so keen to join the Common Market, now appeared to be tying its future with the United States. It has often been suggested that the Nassau agreement lay behind France's veto of Britain's application to join the EEC. The Labour Government that came to power in Britain in 1964 later rejected the idea of the MLF as well.

In Britain the whole concept of an independent nuclear force came under question after the election of the Wilson Government. The Labour Party had been divided over nuclear weapons since the 1950s, and at one point differences of opinion had threatened to cause a serious rift in the Party. But by the 1960s the role of the British deterrent was under serious consideration. The doubts of Wilson and Denis Healey (Wilson's future Defence Secretary) lay not in the moral implications of nuclear weapons, but in the feeling that Britain could not afford to keep herself at the front line of nuclear technology. Before the 1964 election

Patrick Gordon Walker, the Labour Shadow Foreign Secretary, wrote that Labour did not believe that 'Britain herself should seek to make or possess nuclear weapons of her own . . . the problem that faces us is what we do when the V-bombers become obsolete. We think we should not replace them with weapons bought from America.'[14]

But though the Labour Party gave the impression in the run-up to the 1964 election that it would cancel Polaris, once in office it resolved to press ahead with the purchase. By that time the submarine construction programme was already well under way. The outgoing Conservative Government was said to have arranged the contracts for building the submarines in such a way that it would cost as much in compensation to cancel the programme as it would to press ahead with it. The Chinese had just exploded their first nuclear weapon, putting many of Britain's Far Eastern interests, and several parts of the Commonwealth, under potential risk. And Polaris was a bargain. Because its research and development was funded by the United States, it provided a cornerstone of British defence for less than 2 per cent of Britain's total defence budget.

There were also other political considerations. Now that France and China had the bomb, Britain would have more difficulty setting itself up as an example to the world in preventing nuclear proliferation elsewhere. And the nuclear deterrent still gave Britain an important bargaining position in world diplomacy and in dealing with her allies. It was the same argument as the one that had spurred the Attlee Government twenty years earlier, and had a similar impact on Wilson and his ministers, once they were in office.

Two days after the election result was announced, Wilson was persuaded by officials to carry on as a nuclear power, and soon after, a small group of ministers agreed to give the go-ahead to Polaris. Harold Wilson recalled 'I never believed that we had a really independent one. On the other hand I didn't want to be in a position of having to subordinate ourselves to the Americans.' And Wilson's Defence Secretary, Denis Healey, says the decision was political: 'The real question was whether it was worth continuing with a programme whose real value lay in the ability to have a handle on the Americans, rather than anybody else.'[15] But the Wilson Government decided to reduce the number of submarines in the Polaris fleet from five to four – weakening the deterrent by doing so because it can only be guaranteed that one of the submarines is ever permanently on station.

The first of the fleet, *HMS Resolution*, came into service in June

1968, and by 1970 all four were on operational duty. The test-firing of the missiles took place off the Florida coast. American staff remained closely involved with keeping the system operational after it came into service. But although Britain had a system that worked, Polaris effectively sealed the end of the truly independent deterrent. With British nuclear missiles made in America – and dependent on America for spare parts – it was no longer a purely national affair.

Symbolic of the way the British nuclear programme had progressed since the war was the fact that almost as soon as *Revenge* – the last of the four Polaris submarines – had begun its first patrol in 1970, the United States launched the first of its Polaris replacements, the Poseidon submarine. This highlighted the perennial problem for the British nuclear deterrent; keeping up with the United States and the Soviet Union. If the United States needed Poseidon with its eight warheads against the Soviet's new anti-missile defences, did Britain need it too, bearing in mind its much smaller force and its almost complete reliance on submarines?

The development of a successor to Polaris posed the Wilson Government with a problem. Even before the first Polaris submarine had gone on patrol Poseidon had been offered to Britain on an informal basis.[16] That left the Wilson Government with the option of making an official request if it decided it wanted the Poseidon system. But anxieties over cost, and the risk of reviving the debates that had caused so much friction in the Labour Party in the early 1960s, meant that Wilson was reluctant to do this. And there were further considerations. When Wilson applied to join the Common Market in 1967, President de Gaulle made it clear that the French reluctance would be removed if 'France were genuinely convinced that Britain really was disengaging from the United States in all major matters such as defence policy. . . .' To convince de Gaulle of Britain's change of orientation, Wilson assured him in June 1967 that the Cabinet had recently decided not to buy Poseidon. Just before the decision was announced Wilson also apparently offered to share British nuclear technology with France. But this wasn't enough. De Gaulle said he welcomed Britain's new involvement in common procurement of weapons that had been initiated by the Defence Secretary Denis Healey. But the French leader's suspicions remained, and he said he felt that Britain hadn't yet decided whether its future lay with Europe. He told Wilson that 'whether Britain liked it or not, it was linked to America' and in November 1967 vetoed the British application.[17]

Wilson's manoeuvrings with the French had backfired. The Americans took badly his assurance to de Gaulle, and the announcement by Denis Healey in the Commons that the Government would not be buying Poseidon. Wilson's talks with de Gaulle had revived American suspicions that Britain was using technology obtained in co-operation with the Americans to buy its way into favour with the French, by providing information for France's own nuclear programme. And since Britain seemed to have opted out of nuclear modernization by announcing it was not going to buy Poseidon, co-operation under the 1958 Nuclear Exchange Agreement, which provided for an exchange of technical information, was scaled down. The British had little to swap, and had no need to test nuclear weapons. This, combined with the American administration's suspicions of Wilson, resulted in a reduction of nuclear co-operation at the formal level. But they did offer some development work they had done on improving Polaris, code-named 'Super Antelope', in 1968.

In 1970 the Americans repeated their offer of nuclear co-operation to the new Conservative Government. As well as the Poseidon missiles and warheads, they agreed to continue to make available the Super Antelope project. But the new Prime Minister Edward Heath was preoccupied with European affairs, and had no immediate interest in the transatlantic nuclear relationship. He did, however, authorize expenditure of some £40 million in August 1971 on the programme to improve Polaris. The Americans agreed to help, though making no final commitment.

But even as the Government delayed its response to the American offer, international circumstances were changing. In May 1972 President Nixon signed the SALT 1 arms control treaty with the Soviet Union. And Nixon's Secretary of State Henry Kissinger, anxious that there should be no risk of damage to the continuing arms control negotiations, was against giving the British Poseidon. Informal soundings made by Heath during a visit to Washington in 1972 suggested the 1970 offer had been modified. Britain could continue to have help with the Antelope programme, and the President, if asked, would agree a transfer of Poseidon to Britain – but he preferred not to be asked. What was now on offer was the Poseidon missile without the MIRV technology.

The British nuclear weapons research centre at Aldermaston had already begun work on modernizing Polaris when it gained access to technology from the American Antelope programme, now called Chevaline. By 1972 they had found a way of making sure that the warheads could get through the thirty-two Galosh anti-missile nuclear missiles around Moscow. Ironically the two superpowers had signed the Anti-Ballistic Missile Treaty in the same year; it limited the sorts of systems that the Polaris modernization programme was designed to get through. Each side was limited to one system so Polaris could reach any other Soviet target within range, apart from Moscow. But two key factors were at the heart of the system. The British have always wanted a system that technically could hit Moscow, however implausible its use is. But the most important target is Washington, and the development of the British Chevaline programme provided a way of ensuring that Britain developed technical expertise which it could exchange with the Americans under the 1958 agreement. Chevaline is the nearest thing to an all-British nuclear programme since Blue Streak, and it kept the co-operation programme going.

But even so a third of its cost has been spent in America, £130 million of that with Lockheed. At least one contract with a British company had to be cancelled and given to an American firm to remedy design defects.[18] It was done for reasons of time and cost. Sir Raymond Lygo of British Aerospace has said that both the Government and British industry 'lacked the necessary technological and industrial base to undertake the Chevaline improvement programme without a long learning-curve and expensive reliance on United States firms'.[19]

But staff at Aldermaston say they made major breakthroughs in areas where the Americans had not done as much research. One source said recently: 'We were very pleased with ourselves over Chevaline . . . It helped us with the Americans.' Many of the ideas, such as the use of decoys were new to them: 'We've got some very clever people, still; we're very sensitive in our relationship with the United States.' Chevaline involves a new 'front end' being fitted to the Polaris missile, consisting of a sophisticated spacecraft called a Penetration Aid Carrier, which can manoeuvre in space, which has a guidance computer, sensors and two warheads. The carrier is filled with metallic balloons which look like warheads to Soviet radar. According to a detailed account given in a recent documentary film, the two nuclear warheads are also concealed in balloons to maximize the chances of deception.

When the carrier is over the target area the warhead and balloons are released, and the balloons fill up with gas. To maximize the confusion caused to Soviet radar, all the warheads and decoys are intended to come over the same target simultaneously even if several Polaris missiles are fired one after another. It is thought that the Soviet radar system would be swamped, and the Galosh anti-missiles system deployed around Moscow would be unable to find all the warheads before they had re-entered the earth's atmosphere, after which the Galosh missiles are useless. The balloons burn up in the atmosphere. The warheads are protected against the intense heat re-entering the earth's atmosphere and against the effect of a nuclear explosion from the Russian nuclear-tipped Galosh missiles. Chevaline is said to be effective until two new anti-missile systems are deployed in the mid-nineties, one of which is designed to hit a warhead when its within the atmosphere.[20] But the British Chevaline programme was dogged by delays and escalating costs. It was budgeted in 1972 at £175 million. By 1980 it had cost £1,000 million. The secrecy demanded by the Heath and the Labour Governments, and ad hoc funding until 1976, added to the financial problems and delays. Only a handful of members of the Labour Cabinet, under both the Wilson and Callaghan Governments, were told of the project. The reason for the secrecy was political. The decision was only revealed by the Conservative Defence Secretary Francis Pym in 1980 when he announced that the programme was nearly completed. He emphasized that it had been managed by the United Kingdom, 'with the full co-operation of the United States Government'.

Although the project had been hugely expensive it had put Britain into a stronger position. The Chevaline programme had brought Britain back into co-operation with the United States by providing information Britain could trade. And Britain now had something to bargain with for the next stage of its nuclear deterrent, if it decided to have one; the implied threat that if America did not provide help, Britain might go ahead and build a new generation of deterrent regardless of the cost and its impact on the conventional defence budget. Since the Carter administration was anxious for Europe to expand its conventional forces this was a good negotiating point.

With Polaris likely to become obsolescent by the end of the 1980s, James Callaghan approached President Carter at the Guadaloupe summit in January 1979 to ask if he would consider selling the American new submarine-launched missile system, the Trident C4, which was about to come into service. Callaghan calculated that while the Chevaline system might be new, the submarines themselves had been in service for up to eleven years, and were already half-way through their life. The delays over Chevaline meant it was time to start considering a replacement. President Carter said that he was prepared in principle to sell Trident to Britain, and the new Conservative Government which came to power a few months later in May 1979 found the White House in a receptive mood. Britain's bargaining position had also been helped by the deteriorating climate in American-Soviet relations – the invasion of Afghanistan on 27 December 1979 effectively killed off the chances of the SALT 2 arms control treaty being ratified by the American Senate.

The election of the Thatcher Government undoubtedly helped the negotiations over purchase of the Trident system. Thatcher regarded relations with the United States as of paramount importance. She had strongly backed the deployment of 572 American ground-launched Cruise missiles and Pershing 2 missiles in Western Europe, and gave her full support to the American boycott of the Moscow Olympics over Afghanistan. And unlike the delay in Edward Heath's decision-making over the Poseidon offer in 1970, Mrs Thatcher was determined to move quickly. There was no telling how long the offer would stay open. Trident C4 was agreed 'on a similar basis to that on which Polaris missiles were supplied under the Polaris sales agreement'. The decision reaffirmed the Anglo-American nuclear relationship.

Within a year the Government's decision to buy its new nuclear deterrent off the shelf from the United States had run into serious difficulties. In the early days of the Reagan administration the President decided to bring forward the deployment of a new generation of missile, the Trident 2 or D5 missile, and phase out the Trident 1 more rapidly than Carter had planned. The Trident 1 was an updating of the Poseidon missile, and was actually deployed in former Poseidon submarines. It weighs roughly the same, and like Poseidon has eight warheads. Trident 2 is a much more powerful missile. It has double the payload, and can carry up to fourteen warheads. It is much more accurate, and in theory could be used for first strikes against targets such as Soviet missile silos. For the relatively small nuclear force Britain required, the C4 seemed to fit the bill from a military point of view. Not only was the new generation Trident a more powerful missile, it was more expensive and required a much larger submarine. The new submarine would add 10 per cent to the cost and the missiles another 7 per cent.[21]

Although the new system was more expensive, Margaret Thatcher was determined that Britain should have the latest American technology – regardless of the protests of the three largest opposition parties. The Reagan administration was prepared to supply Trident D5. They were aware of the pressure Mrs Thatcher was under at home, particularly over the controversial deployment of Cruise missiles in the United Kingdom, and over her handling of the economy. The agreement was reached a few weeks before the Falklands conflict, at a time when Mrs Thatcher's popularity was at rock bottom. As President Reagan made clear in his letter of 11 March 1982, the Americans were anxious to ensure that Britain and the other Europeans increased their spending on conventional or non-nuclear forces. Reagan said he hoped 'the economies realized through co-operation between the two Governments will be reinforced by the United Kingdom's efforts to upgrade its conventional forces'. During the negotiations the Americans set great store on Britain's non-nuclear forces. They agreed to limit the British contribution to the research and development costs to $116 million in exchange for Britain agreeing to man anti-aircraft missile batteries outside American air bases in Britain.

Once again, however, Britain had bought American, rather than pursuing their own development programme, in the same way that they had done with Skybolt and with Polaris. Indeed, the Thatcher Government has been accused of going even further in its reliance on the United States than did the Macmillan Government. In September 1982 the Government announced that it had decided to scrap plans to build a plant at Coulport in Scotland to service Trident missiles – the Defence Secretary John Nott announced that £600 million would be saved by sending the missiles to the American servicing facility at King's Bay in Georgia. The issue was raised again in October 1987 during a briefing to reporters at Faslane, when a Ministry of Defence official appeared to say that the Trident Missiles were only 'rented' from the United States. This provoked charges that the Trident submarines were 'Moss Bros missiles' to be returned to the hirer. The Government called the reports 'an absolute nonsense' and said that the missiles on British submarines would be bought outright but would be part of a 'common stock of missiles' and that servicing would only happen every seven or eight years. The Ministry of Defence officials reportedly stressed that the United States had given assurances about long-term support for the Trident programme if Britain retained Trident after America has phased its fleet out. They said that Britain would have 'sufficient missiles in stock until alternative arrangements could be made'.

This arrangement is different from that agreed for Polaris in that Britain owns its own stock of missiles and services them itself. But even over the servicing of Polaris the British have had to rely on the Americans. A total of £437 million has been spent on fitting new motors to existing Polaris missiles to extend their life, and to cater for the new front end. The old Lockheed production line had to be opened up, and retired staff returned to work to do the job. As the watchful American Naval Audit Service found, Britain has also been relying on old Polaris spares bought at knockdown prices from the Americans. From October 1982 to May 1984 the United States sold Britain $118 million-worth of spares for $6 million – 'summer sale prices' a Ministry of Defence official crowed.[22] At present, Polaris missiles are assembled at a plant at Coulport in Scotland from parts obtained in America.

There is a significant American input into the 'front end' of the Trident missile. According to an unconfirmed report in *The Independent*, the casing, parts of the re-entry vehicle and heatshields that enter the atmosphere are from an American supplier. The 'bus' that carries the warheads through space is American made. 'Other parts, such as the cables, sockets and plugs needed for the interface between the warheads and Trident are also bought in the United States. Spending in America on the warhead parts, submarine fuel and nuclear testing comes to about £1 billion.'[23]

Both British commentators and those from the Soviet Union have pointed to the fact that the Trident missile targeting is to be done by the joint strategic staff in the United States using information from the American Navstar satellites for NATO targeting. British analysts have also highlighted the reliance on American early warning systems, such as satellites, to detect Soviet missiles. The missile warning facility at Fylingdales in Yorkshire is American, although it does have British operators.[24] They have questioned the ability of American radar in the United States to detect missiles from Soviet submarines in the Atlantic going towards Britain and therefore moving away from America.

All these technical issues boil down to one question – how can the British deterrent be said to be independent when successive British Governments have gone to such efforts to make Britain dependent on the United States. Systems such as Trident are judged as much on political grounds as on military. This is the key, according to Field Marshal Lord Carver: 'The political argument has pretty much remained the same, which is; it makes us appear, or even actually be, or be thought, particularly by the United States as an independent nation. . . .' Lord Carver told the House of Lords in 1979: 'I have never heard or read a scenario which I would consider to be realistic in which it could be considered to be right or reasonable for the Prime Minister of this country to order the firing of our independent strategic force at a time when the Americans were not prepared to fire theirs.'[25] In other words, Britain's independent deterrent is still aimed as much at Washington as it is at Moscow, albeit for rather different reasons. As Professor John Simpson, a long-time observer of Anglo-American relations, sees it: 'The United Kingdom nuclear deterrent has been, from its inception, directed towards creating a specific type of linkage with the United States.'[26]

But this policy carries potential risks. Britain's nuclear interests have always been best served at times of tension between the two super-powers. Henry Kissinger would not let Britain's request for Poseidon interfere with the SALT negotiations, whereas Jimmy Carter and Ronald Reagan were prepared to let Britain have Trident at a time when East-West relations were at a low ebb. There must, therefore, be some doubt about the continuing availability of Trident to Britain at a time of negotiations between the two superpowers on long-range nuclear weapons.

Those doubts suddenly came to the fore after the summit between Ronald Reagan and Mikhail Gorbachev in Reykjavik in October 1986. During that meeting the Soviet leader proposed that all ballistic missiles should be scrapped, and that steps should be taken towards a nuclear-free world. Apparently Reagan accepted the proposal, though the summit later broke down over the question of the American Strategic Defence Initiative. The news provoked outrage among America's allies, who felt they hadn't been properly consulted, and particularly from Mrs Thatcher who felt the Iceland talks had put the Trident programme into jeopardy. British officials made clear the depth of the anger, and the rift was hurriedly patched up at a meeting at Camp David a few weeks later. And spokesmen from both countries have emphasized that Britain's Trident programme will not be affected.

But the Soviet Union has made it clear that if a 50 per cent cut is achieved, there must come a point when the British and French deterrents are put on the negotiating table – particularly as the two countries are planning to have a total of 1,200 warheads on eleven submarines between them by the mid-1990s. Exactly at which point this happens is not clear. Soviet officials say privately they may allow it to go some way down beyond a 50 per cent cut before they want the French and the British to come in. But in some circumstances there could be international pressure of the sort put on the West Germans over the Pershing 1a missiles during the negotiations over the INF Treaty in 1987.

The key question is whether a future American administration will feel that American interests are being served by continuing to help Britain with its American nuclear deterrent. Because Britain's nuclear forces are intricately tied to the United States, it is much harder for Britain to resist American pressure than it is for the French, for example. Certainly, Mrs Thatcher has made clear her determination to retain Trident. But Foreign Secretary Sir Geoffrey Howe warned in 1983, 'never say never'. If the continuing improvement in East-West dialogue leads to further breakthroughs in arms reduction, pressure from the United States may eventually force Britain to give up its nuclear capability. Joint operating of facilities, such as the Trident missile servicing agreement, only serves to highlight the British dependency on the United States.

This point has been made by the Journal of the Defense Preparedness Association in January 1988. Their London correspondent said:

'The real underlying concern about this unique "missile pool" arrangement lies in the belief shared by many informed observers that we are entering an historic phase when the strategic interests of Europe and the United States are diverging . . . since this arrangement is by contract and not a sovereign treaty it can be argued that its strategic nuclear deterrent is not, in the final analysis, truly independent.'[27]

5

☆☆★☆☆

THE INTELLIGENCE
CONNECTION

Whether the wartime exchange of British experience for American
resources really paid off is a matter open to argument. What is really
beyond doubt is the decision in favour of co-operation doomed the
British services, in the long run, to junior status.

Kim Philby, *My Silent War.*

THE second pillar of the Anglo-American relationship is the connection between the two countries' intelligence communities. During the Second World War Britain was the clear leader of the intelligence effort. However, since then the roles have been reversed.

Inevitably, because of the secrecy that surrounds the intelligence community, it is impossible to paint a full picture of the way the relationship works. But the considerable amount of information published in recent years has made it possible to trace the evolution of the intelligence connection and the shift in the balance of power.

The links between the British and American intelligence services go back to the very first days of the War. The channels had been opened by President Roosevelt who took the extraordinary step of writing secretly to Churchill on his appointment as First Lord of the Admiralty. The letter was sent on 11 September 1939, only eight days after Britain had declared war, and over two years before the United States entered the war.

The letters between 'Naval Person', as Churchill called himself (or 'former Naval Person' when he became Prime Minister in May 1940) and 'POTUS', as Churchill called Roosevelt (President of the United States) continued during the war. Churchill himself sent about one thousand letters. Roosevelt and Churchill were both fascinated by intelligence, and in his first letter, Roosevelt invited Churchill to keep him in touch with anything he ought to know by sealed letter in the diplomatic pouch. Churchill sent Roosevelt a message on average once every thirty-six hours. 'No lover ever studied the whims of his mistress as I did those of President Roosevelt,' Churchill later admitted.[1]

The letter set off a chain of events described by a former CIA Deputy Director of Intelligence Ray Cline, as just short of 'benign covert operation', in which the British persuaded Roosevelt to set up the sort of integrated intelligence system through which the British intelligence community could co-operate best with the United States. At that time, apart from the FBI, the United States had no real intelligence capability: 'Gentlemen do not read each other's mail,' said the Secretary of State Henry Stimson as he shut down the Black Chamber code-breaking unit in 1929.[2]

At the forefront of Britain's intelligence operations was William 'Little Bill' Stephenson, Churchill's favoured intelligence representative. Stephenson, whose wartime exploits have been well publicized through his codename, as *A Man Called Intrepid*, was appointed, with Roosevelt's approval, as head of British Security Co-ordination (BSC) in New York in May 1940. He worked under cover of a British Passport Control Officer. The BSC covered all the British intelligence services, the Secret Intelligence Service (SIS or MI6), the Special Operations Executive (SOE, which was disbanded after the war), the Security Service (MI5), and the Government Code and Cipher School (the forerunner of the modern GCHQ signals intelligence centre).

Stephenson was a Canadian millionaire businessman, and First World War fighter ace. He was known as 'Captain Machine Gun' from his days as a former amateur lightweight boxing champion. With an introduction from his old friend Gene Tunney, the American world heavyweight boxing champion, to avoid official channels, Stephenson attempted to build up a relationship with J. Edgar Hoover, the FBI chief. Although Roosevelt instructed the FBI to co-operate discreetly with Stephenson, co-operation was limited because of Hoover's suspicion of the British and because the FBI's role was restricted to counter-intelligence.

Stephenson's main ally was William 'Wild Bill' Donovan, seized upon by the British 'like a shining Knight', according to Ray Cline.[3] The men were two of a kind, both successful in business but looking for a return to action. Donovan was a national figure because of his exploits against Mexican bandits in 1916, as a war hero in France in 1918, and later as a candidate for the Governorship of New York. He had become a successful lawyer on Wall Street and had also acted as Roosevelt's favourite intelligence man, who had nicknamed him 'my secret legs'. Stephenson used his contacts with Hoover and Roosevelt to arrange for

Donovan to visit London in July 1940, a few weeks after Dunkirk. British intelligence had intercepted reports from the American Ambassador in London Joseph Kennedy, suggesting that Britain was finished. The British had discovered leaks to the Germans from the Embassy, including some of the secret Naval Person letters. A junior diplomat Tyler Kent was caught red-handed.[4]

Donovan became the willing object of an intensive lobbying campaign co-ordinated by Sir Stewart Menzies, chief of MI6, to convince Roosevelt that Britain had the will to defeat Hitler. The aim was to secure American co-operation in intelligence and military equipment in return for revealing details of Britain's technical prowess. Donovan was shown some of Britain's most highly prized secrets, such as the use of German spies as counter-agents, the 'Doublecross' system, and the new invention of radar. He was also given full access to the chiefs of British intelligence and the leaders of the war effort. He was taken to meet King George VI, and also met Churchill, now Prime Minister, in his wartime bunker.

The campaign succeeded. Immediately on his return, Donovan impressed upon Roosevelt the bias of Kennedy's reporting and the need for urgent American help.[5] Stephenson sent a cable to Churchill on 8 August stating that Donovan was 'doing much to combat defeatism [in] Washington by stating positively and convincingly that we shall win'.[6] Within a few days Stephenson cabled: 'Most immediate. Fifty destroyers agreed last night.'[7] The elderly destroyers were given in return for leases of American air and naval bases in the Atlantic and Caribbean. While the destroyers were of little military use they represented the first step to formal co-operation. It was followed later by measures such as the Lend Lease Act of March 1941, and the use of American spotter planes in the hunt for the German battleship *Bismark* in May 1941.

It also marked the beginning of co-operation on intelligence, with the first formal agreement being signed in November 1940. The British codebreaking centre at Bletchley was in the process of breaking German codes using a working version of the German encoding machine called Enigma under the code name Ultra. But to break the code of the intercepted signals they needed to work out how to set the machine each time. For this they needed help with computing, and the information about the details of America's success in breaking the Japanese codes known as Purple. As Stephenson told Churchill: 'We can offer our secret intelligence in return for help. It has to be done at the President's level. There have been intelligence breakthroughs that would advance our own efforts. The President would have to authorize disclosure. There are the means to produce in America the sophisticated equipment we need for intelligence weapons.' But the full reason why Britain needed the equipment was to remain a closely guarded secret. In January 1941 an American team brought two Purple machines over to the British codebreaking centre at Bletchley.[8] Full details of the Ultra system were only handed over by Britain in May 1943 when the formal agreement on codebreaking co-operation was signed. Co-operation on signals intelligence still continues today on the basis of the principles first established in 1943. Australia, Canada, and New Zealand soon were brought in as a second tier.[9]

Britain remained the most influential of the two nations in intelligence terms throughout the war. Having begun the process of getting American aid, it still had to achieve its second goal, the establishment of a single integrated intelligence system in the United States. Donovan himself had been convinced that the United States needed this after seeing for himself in his second visit in the winter of 1940 the SIS, and the newly formed Special Operations Executive (which co-ordinated British covert operations in action in the Mediterranean, North African and Balkan theatres).[10]

The British believed a centralized system would be easier to deal with than a fragmented one – particularly if Donovan was its chief. But Stephenson warned London that Donovan was not sure he wanted the job of running 'the agency that we envisage', and Donovan later accused Stephenson of having 'intrigued and driven him to the job'.[11] Stephenson and the MI6 staff sent to the United States helped Donovan compile reports advocating the creation of a new agency. This met with much opposition from the FBI and the military, who saw their roles being diminished as a result. To maximize the chances of success, Donovan had to convince the Americans of the threat facing them at home. Fears of a German fifth column conspiracy within America were manufactured by the British with the help of sympathetic Americans such as Donovan. He pushed this line in private briefings, and put his name to lurid newspaper articles and a pamphlet, *Fifth Column Lessons for America*, compiled with British help. President Roosevelt himself joined the propaganda war on 27 May 1941, warning of 'the Trojan Horse, the fifth column that betrays a nation unprepared for treachery'.[12] In the same speech he committed the United States to 'armed patrols to ensure delivery of needed supplies to Britain'.[13] Soon after, Stephenson cabled London: 'After months of battle and jockeying in Washington . . . our man is in position.' And on 11 July 1941 Donovan was formally appointed by Roosevelt as Co-ordinator of Intelligence. The British role at the time was summed up by Desmond Morton, a senior MI6 officer and a long-term informant of Churchill: 'To all intents and purposes American security is being run for them at the President's request by the British . . . It is of course essential that this fact should not be known in view of the furious uproar it would cause, if known to the isolationists.'[14]

Stephenson himself endorsed this: 'It is fair to say if our friend [Donovan] had not been able to reply on BSC's assistance, his own organization could not have survived.' Training and equipment for Donovan's staff were provided by the BSC. In June 1942 the COI was replaced by the Office of Strategic Services (OSS) which divided the world into British and American zones. The pattern of co-operation has continued to this day, although there has been a complete reversal of power in the intelligence relationship. The American intelligence service was substantially reformed in 1946 with the formation of the Central Intelligence Group (CIG). A year later this became the Central Intelligence Agency (CIA), with a specific brief to fight the Cold War.

Donovan was thought by many of his colleagues to be too pro-British and, after the death of his mentor Roosevelt in 1945, he was excluded from the top positions in the post-war restructuring. He returned to his legal practice. Britain's role remained powerful for a time, but she gradually learnt that she had to play second fiddle. There was some resentment at the British assumption that they should continue to run all the spies, while the Americans provided the money. But since liaison work between the intelligence agencies provided as much as 70 per cent of reports there was little the Americans could do.[15]

After the war Britain had also done some limited restructuring of its intelligence network, closing down the Special Operations Executive and transferring its covert functions to MI6. It co-operated with the CIA's new covert action department in a number of operations – with disastrous results. Among MI6's first attempts at covert operations was the operation to topple the Albanian dictator Enver Hoxha by infiltrating a small group of British-trained Albanian agents into the country. The British were only able to finance the operation with American help. A high-level delegation was sent to sell the idea that the Soviets would only be persuaded to stop their expansion if the West took action. The CIA accepted the proposition eagerly.[16] The first attempt, a seaborne landing in October 1949, failed to set off a revolt, and further joint operations with the CIA in 1950 and 1951 were even less successful.

The British gave up at the end of 1952, but the Americans tried again in 1953 when their agents ran into a trap organized by the Albanians 'like lambs to the slaughter' as Hoxha himself boasted.[17] It ended with a show trial in 1954 – the agents captured were shot or, in one case, sentenced to 'suffer death by the cord'.[18] Attempts to ferment unrest in the Ukraine and Latvia were also unsuccessful. It later became clear that the operations had failed because they had been betrayed by Soviet spies in the British intelligence system. Kim Philby had become MI6 Liaison Officer in Washington a few weeks after the operation had begun in 1949, and was also a member of the joint US–UK Special Policy Committee which planned the operations.

Post-war intelligence co-operation had already been damaged by the discovery in 1950 of the nuclear spies Alan Nunn May and Klaus Fuchs, who gave the Soviet Union the vital information they needed to build an atom bomb. They were uncovered through information given by a Soviet defector to the United States and by American analysis of Soviet wartime radio signals.[19] The intelligence connection was further damaged by the news of the defection in May 1951 of the head of the American Desk in the Foreign Office, Donald Maclean, who had been co-ordinator of atomic co-operation in Washington while First Secretary at the British Embassy. He fled to Moscow with Guy Burgess, a former Second Secretary at the Embassy in Washington.

But what was most disturbing to the Americans was their suspicion that Kim Philby was also a Soviet spy. The CIA Director General Walter Bedell Smith sent an ultimatum to London: 'Fire Philby or we break off the intelligence relationship.'[20] Philby was recalled from Washington, officially pensioned off and paid £4,000 in instalments (though he was later rehired). Philby had been at the heart of Anglo-American intelligence co-operation. His role as liaison officer was 'comparable with being Ambassador and executive officer combined'. He had full access to the CIA; he drank Martinis with just about everyone who was anyone in the CIA.[21] One CIA officer told the *Sunday Times* team which uncovered Philby's past: 'How much did Philby know? The sky was the limit. He would have known as much as he wanted to find out.'[22] There is little doubt that it was Philby who had betrayed the operations against Albania, the Ukraine and Latvia.[23] Philby also would have had access to information from the FBI, to signals intelligence, and to diplomatic exchanges. American suspicions which had begun while Philby was in Washington poisoned relations for a time. 'The wartime alliance,' said Tom Braden, a senior CIA officer, 'that I had always considered the Rock of Gibraltar was full of suspicions and worry and concern.'[24] The revelations added to the Americans' sense of Britain's decline as a major power. For Allan Dulles, who had worked with MI6 during the war and who became Director of the CIA from 1953 to 1961, the traitors represented the moral and political decline of a country being beyond its means and cracking apart.[25]

MI5's failure to uncover and arrest the traitors, its failure to pass on vital clues to the FBI and its clumsy attempt to justify its failure alienated the FBI. On 11 June 1951 the Director of MI5 Sir Percy Sillitoe flew to Washington, along with a senior counter-intelligence officer Arthur Martin, disguised as his chauffeur. Sir Percy took with him files which had been doctored to remove the evidence that MI5 had suspected Maclean for many weeks but failed to investigate properly.[26] But the CIA and FBI Directors Bedell Smith and J. Edgar Hoover spotted the flaws straightaway.[27]

Despite all the tensions, intelligence co-operation continued. Firstly, the evidence against Philby wasn't totally conclusive – CIA operations had continued against Albania after 1951 despite Philby's involvement in planning earlier operations. Secondly – and most importantly – the CIA still needed British help. It could co-operate usefully with others, the French for example, in a series of tripartite security conferences with the British.[28] But the Americans were appalled by French security lapses. As Ray Cline sees it: 'There was no other service with which to collaborate. The Germans were penetrated more badly. The Israelis had a limited service of high quality. If we were to have any serious collaboration, we had to have it with the British.'[29] And Britain still had its uses. One chief of covert operations Frank Wisner once told Philby: 'Whenever we want to subvert any place we find the British own an island within easy reach.'[30]

The British had also technical expertise. Peter Wright has made great play of this in his book, *Spycatcher*. Well before he himself revealed it, it was known that it was Peter Wright who analysed the Soviet remote-controlled microphone found in 1952 in the great seal hanging above an American Ambassador's desk in the US Embassy in Moscow.[31]

And while co-operation on operational intelligence was damaged, co-operation over the sharing of national intelligence analyses was actually intensified. Both the British Joint Intelligence Committee and the CIA office of National Estimates compile their own assessments of current intelligence issues, or produce reports after special conferences on specific problems, for example the extent of the Soviet guided missile programme in September 1952. The American Joint Chiefs of Staff had agreed in 1948 to the limited release of American intelligence reports to the British after 'thorough re-editing'.[32]

In October 1951, at the height of the recriminations following the defections of Burgess and Maclean, a senior officer from the CIA's Office of National Estimates was posted to London to maximize co-operation with the British counterpart, the Joint Intelligence Committee (JIC).[33] The Liaison Officer Ray Cline, who was fully involved in the process of producing analyses known as assessments, says: 'The British allowed me to participate in the process from the ground up, and I became a working member ex officio of the Joint Intelligence Staff; that's where the work gets done.'

This openness was, of course, in British interests, partly to compensate for American annoyance, and partly to keep the United States actively engaged in countering the perceived Soviet threat. The co-operation couldn't have been closer, said Cline: 'I often used to be in their offices. They'd say: "This has a code sign which means its not for Americans, but I can't be bothered to lock it up!". . . . The British were extraordinarily open. They provided not only most of their highest-level joint intelligence estimates but also supplied the CIA Station Chief with most of their clandestine MI6 reports.'[34] [35] The CIA was understandably less forthcoming in return.

For intelligence analysis, where interpretation is crucial, comparing notes and sharing judgements is part of the process. Analysis has been given increasing emphasis in the intelligence communities of both countries, particularly with the advent of signals and other forms of electronic intelligence, which will be considered later in the chapter. As a result of the shift in emphasis, co-operation between Britain and the United States has continued at the analytical level, even if at the operational level it has been more variable. According to Ray Cline, 'the exchange of "finished" i.e., evaluated and analysed reports with London continues to this day as does an informal liaison exchange system on the analytical level'.[36]

Some joint covert operations continued, though with the United States the senior partner. In 1951 the Iranian Prime Minister, Dr Mohammad Mossadeq, nationalized the Anglo-Iranian Oil Company, the forerunner of BP, which had a monopoly of Iranian oil. A team of MI6 agents were dispatched to Tehran to engineer the downfall of Mossadeq. When Iran broke off diplomatic relations in October 1952, and expelled the British Embassy staff, making it impossible for the British to carry out an operation on their own, Britain tried to persuade the Americans to take part in a joint operation.[37] John Foster Dulles, the Secretary of State, did not need a great deal of persuasion. But in return, the British delegation sent to Washington had to accept America's choice of Prime Minister, General Fazlollah Zahedi, whose pro-Nazi past was well known.[38] The operation, variously codenamed Operation Boot and Ajax, which had been planned by the British, was carried out by Kermit Roosevelt, the CIA's Middle East chief, and a cousin of the late President.

The coup was to prove a triumph for American commerce, the Anglo-Iranian Oil Company was not restored by the new Government. Instead, an international consortium operated the now state-owned National Iranian Oil Company. BP was only given 40 per cent, the same share as the United States. And though the Shah always felt a particular debt to Britain, Iran, dominated by Britain for so long, now became part of the American sphere of influence. There were growing tensions in the Middle East, as MI6 developed increasingly unrealistic covert plans for action in Syria, and Egypt to shore up their faltering position in the region.[39] They had also resisted American plans in 1951 for wartime intelligence co-operation in the Middle East involving, according to documents in the United States National Archives, a 'steering committee probably including French and Turkish numbers, in which event there are implications, on which the British Secret Service is not prepared to commit itself'.[40]

Co-operation with the CIA had continued in Central Europe as MI6 hatched a plan to monitor all Soviet communications in Vienna, which was still under four-power control, by tapping into Russian land-lines in operation Silver. It provided vital intelligence on Soviet policy on the East–West border areas at the height of the Cold War. The operation was started in 1949 by the British who had opened a shop selling Harris Tweed as a cover. However, the shop proved so popular with local shoppers that it became a major distraction! The CIA were told about the operation as they began their own attempt in 1951.[41] Co-operation continued in Berlin in 1953 with Operation Gold. In both these operations the Americans did not tell MI6 that they had discovered how to capture echoes of the Russian signals before they had been encrypted, and could read them in the original text. They certainly had reason to keep this secret, for Operation Gold was betrayed by a Soviet spy in MI6 before it had even started. George Blake, an MI6 officer in

West Berlin, had warned the Soviets of the building of a tunnel under
the boundary between East and West Berlin to tap Soviet Army cables.
The Soviets left the tunnel in operation until April 1956 when it had been
in use for eleven months. But Blake's betrayal and the compromise of all
the information gathered was not revealed until he was finally unmasked
in 1961. That lead, like many others, was provided by the Americans. In
this case it came from Michal Goleniewski, a KGB informer in Polish
intelligence who had defected to America in 1960. Goleniewski's
evidence also led to the eventual unmasking in January 1961 of the
Portland Spy Ring which had been passing on British naval secrets on
the detection of Russian submarines from the Underwater Weapons
Establishment from Harry Houghton, a disaffected worker. He was
discovered as a result of the evidence provided by Goleniewski.
Houghton's controller, Gordon Lonsdale and the radio operators, Helen
and Peter Kroger, were rounded up.

Evidence from two other Soviet defectors to the United States led to
the final unmasking of Kim Philby in 1963, though he managed to escape
to Moscow from Beirut after making a partial confession. But evidence
provided by the two Soviet defectors, Igor Gouzenko (who had
defected in 1945) and Anatoli Golytsin (who came over in 1961), was to
throw into turmoil the counter-intelligence sections of CIA, the FBI, as
well as MI5.

The Director-General of MI5 Sir Roger Hollis flew to Washington in
1963 to reveal there was evidence that his own deputy Graham Mitchell
(who had just retired) was a long-term Soviet agent.[42] The affair added
to the feeling in the American intelligence community that the British
could not be trusted. As in the late forties and early fifties, there
seemed to be a never-ending stream of disasters.

The FBI had also passed on evidence of another Soviet agent – an
American Michael Straight – who had been approached at Cambridge
University in 1937 by Anthony Blunt to become a Russian spy. Despite
his refusal, Straight was repeatedly put under pressure to work for the
Russians. He remained silent, until facing security vetting for a job in
1963, he confessed all to the FBI. The confession allowed MI5 to obtain
Blunt's confession that he had been a Russian agent throughout his
period in MI5 during the war.[43]

To add to American misgivings the Minister for War, John Profumo,
had been forced to resign in 1963 in the scandal over the revelation that
he shared his mistress, Christine Keeler, with a senior officer in GRU,
the Russian military intelligence. Profumo resigned after lying to the

House of Commons about the affair.

The Americans had never fully forgiven the British for the disasters of the early fifties. Maurice Oldfield, the MI6 liaison official in Washington from 1960 to 1964, told a colleague: 'I took a bet with myself that the names of Burgess and Maclean would be mentioned within a month of my arriving in Washington.' He was shown a memorandum from the Joint Chiefs of Staff stating that 'little or no action has been taken to prevent repetition of these mistakes'.[44] Oldfield was able to defend MI6, but the United States Navy was very critical of the Royal Navy for the failings over the Portland Spy Ring even though the discovery of the Ring was one of the few British counter-intelligence successes.

But it was MI5 which bore the brunt of American criticism, with strong pressure in the CIA for a re-examination of the relationship. Claims that the CIA actually plotted to take control of MI5 have been denied by CIA sources. But there is no doubt of the scale of upheavals in Washington. As Maurice Oldfield put it: 'The situation is much more like Alice in Wonderland than anything Lewis Carroll could have thought up. There must be several candidates for the role of Mad Hatter.'[45]

This was the period known as 'sick-think', as the CIA counter-intelligence Chief, James Angleton, combed the CIA for Soviet spies.

As the CIA itself was convulsed by hunts for Soviet penetration, the paranoia and soul-searching crossed the Atlantic. Angleton claimed in 1963 that the Labour Party leader Harold Wilson may have been working for the Soviets.[46] He cited evidence from his favourite defector Golytsin, that Hugh Gaitskell, Wilson's predecessor as Labour Leader, had been murdered by the Soviets. Angleton's paranoia has been blamed for initiating the intrigue within the British intelligence system.[47]

During the sixties and seventies, MI5 in London was embroiled with inquiries into Soviet penetration, leading, according to some reports, the Director General of MI5 Sir Michael Hanley to reveal at an intelligence conference of the United States, Britain and the other Commonwealth members, between 8 and 10 May 1974, that his predecessor, Sir Roger Hollis, may also have been a Soviet agent.[48] Hollis, like Mitchell before him, was later cleared by an official inquiry.[49] The CIA was also bitterly divided over the extent of Soviet penetration in its own ranks but with the dismissal of James Angleton by the CIA Director William Colby in 1974, it subsided within the CIA. However, as Peter Wright's book *Spycatcher* has demonstrated, the issues are still alive in Britain.

The fact that Americans had gone through a similar period of 'sick-think' helped to save the intelligence relationship. Another mitigating factor had come in 1960. The thousands of documents provided by the spy run jointly by Britain and America, Colonel Oleg Penkovsky of Soviet Military Intelligence (GRU), gave the Americans an extraordinary advantage in the Cuban missile crisis. The documents handed over by Penkovsky revealed the Soviets' backwardness in long-range nuclear missiles.[50] This allowed President Kennedy to threaten the Soviet leader Nikita Khrushchev and to force him to back down and agree to remove the medium-range missiles from Cuba. Despite ingenious plans to smuggle Penkovsky out in a caravan, or by submarine, he was arrested in October 1962 at the height of the crisis, and shot as a traitor. Although there have been some doubts expressed about Soviet planting of disinformation, Ray Cline, who was directly involved, has called Penkovsky 'probably the most successful penetration in the post-war period'.

The documents which Penkovsky mined from the archives like a research librarian allowed American analysts to compare the information with pictures from new spy satellites (the first was launched in 1961) or from United States U2 spyplanes. 'So', says Cline, 'analysts could say "that's an MR4 or MR3, that's the cherry picker that they lift it up with", and we know that we've got the details on it. That's an enormous asset.'[51]

Cline says Penkovsky's role was deliberately played up after his death to conceal the value of the first of the new satellite sources. And the plaudits earned over Penkovsky helped the relationship because the balance of the intelligence relationship was tipped even further in the direction of American leadership by the satellite photography. They were and still are the only Western nation to have their own high quality capability. 'It was only', says Cline, 'because of our tradition of close collaboration with British intelligence, in cryptoanalysis and espionage, and general exchange of finished intelligence that we felt we should share with the British in the U2 and the satellite processes.'[52]

Britain's recovery from the nadir of 1963, and the potential breakdown of the relationship, has been assisted in recent years by the recruitment of a number of Soviet agents. Not only have they provided valuable information which can be traded with the Americans, but they also suggest that the era of penetrations has come to an end if it can be assumed they would not have come to Britain unless they thought it was safe. Oleg Lyalin, a member of the KGB Department Five, which is responsible for assassinations and sabotage, co-operated with Britain while working under cover at the Soviet Trade Mission in London. He defected in August 1971 after having been arrested for drunken driving.

In 1982 Vladimir Kuzichkin, a KGB officer who had been posted in Tehran during the Iranian revolution, defected to Britain. The Americans were particularly worried about Russian influence in Iran, which they feared was growing rapidly. Kuzichkin brought two trunks full of documents about the KGB and the Iranian Communist Party, the Tudeh Party. During his debriefings in a safe house in Sussex he was able to provide a detailed insight into the KGB's activities in Iran. A list of several hundred Soviet agents or sympathizers in Iran was passed to the Iranians in October 1982, at the CIA's behest, after much agonizing by the British. The Tudeh Party was banned, 1,500 members were arrested and a number were executed. [53]

But the most important case is that of the defection of Oleg Gordievsky, the KGB's chief, or Rezident, in London in 1985. He feared he had come under suspicion, while on leave to the Soviet Union in July, so he called in a promise that MI6 would help him if he was at risk. He was secretly 'exfiltrated' – spirited out – of the Soviet Union. A story was put about that he had left by motor-boat while at a resort on the Black Sea. But a recent report suggests that he was smuggled in a diplomat's car into the British Embassy in Moscow, while the KGB were overstretched handling a student congress. He was taken to Finland hidden in a van used to carry diplomatic freight, which is exempted from customs checks. His arrival in Helsinki was concealed by the presence of an unusually large team with the Foreign Secretary, who was attending the Conference on Security in Europe from 30 July 1985. It was a major coup for MI6. [54]

Gordievsky had been working for British and Danish intelligence while at the Soviet Embassy in Copenhagen between 1966 and 1970, and from 1972 to 1978. He came to London as head of the KGB political section in 1982, after a four-year spell in Moscow and became acting Rezident in 1984, after the identity of his predecessor Arkady Gouk had been exposed during the trial of Michael Bettaney, the disaffected MI5 officer who had posted secret documents through Gouk's door.

Cord Meyer, a former CIA station chief in London, believes that, as Rezident, Gordievsky would have had an 'absolutely unique insight into identities of British or other nationalities working for the KGB throughout the British Isles, and you can imagine what a treasure trove that would be for any self-respecting intelligence agency'. [55]

He would have given, says Meyer, a 'really complete grasp of Soviet penetration'.[56] So Meyer believes that Gordievsky provides evidence that the British intelligence community was no longer penetrated. Gordievsky is also reported to have identified several British citizens who spied for the Soviet Union.[57] American analysts, such as Ray Cline, warn that it's never possible to be certain of a defector's veracity, but he accepts Gordievsky's value and says: 'While Penkovsky penetrated the archives, this guy was penetrating the KGB and reporting back. He was a Philby in a sense.'[58]

The (then) CIA Director William Casey flew to London before the Geneva summit between President Reagan and Mikhail Gorbachev in November 1985 to get a personal briefing on Gorbachev from Gordievsky (who had helped organize the Gorbachev visit to London in December 1984).

In February 1985 Gordievsky was brought to Washington for debriefing by all the American agencies. But in American Press briefings a few months later the Americans gave him a 'markedly lower' level of attention than the British had done,[59] although American officials conceded that 'MI6 had an international reputation for high professionalism on handling spies'.[60]

During this time, the American service suffered a number of setbacks. One Soviet defector Vitali Yurchenko had returned to the Soviet Union in a blaze of publicity claiming to have been kidnapped by the CIA. A CIA officer, Edward Lee Howard, defected, blowing a number of operations in Moscow. And revelations were coming of other major security breaches in America.

The information given by Gordievsky and Kuzichkin provided some return for the vital American intelligence given during the Falklands War in 1982. The United States even moved a photographic satellite to cover the Falklands Islands even though it shortened the satellite's endurance.[61] However, according to one leading American analyst Professor Andrew Burrows, for much of the war, 'weather conditions during the conflict precluded such coverage'.[62] As well as signals intelligence from the United States' listening posts in South America, and the breaking of Argentinian codes, the real intelligence breakthroughs came from traditional human sources.[63] Argentine officers and officials who believed in American declarations of neutrality provided 'a steady flow of intelligence to the CIA station and the American military attachés in Buenos Aires, who forwarded it to Langley and onto the State Department and the White House. It was then only a matter of who could beat a path more quickly to the British,' according to the

Washington Post reporter Bob Woodward (of Watergate fame).[64] The CIA station in Buenos Aires is reported to be in the same block as the Argentine High Command and able to listen to High Command discussions through agent penetration and electronic eavesdropping.[65]

Despite the earlier counter-intelligence disasters, relations are still close. An adviser to President Carter on intelligence says: 'I must say I was impressed by the British on the whole. They were very "seat of the pants". They had very good people, but very few resources.'[66]

The British services have constantly had to make their far smaller resources go further. According to Miles Copeland, a former CIA officer:

'The British station is almost identical except that it is smaller, better covered and better integrated into the Embassy to which it is assigned. Also it is poorer, its budget normally being about a third of the budget of its American counterpart. For this reason, it is in most parts the duty of the station chief to use his superior prestige and cunning to persuade his CIA colleague to join with him in Anglo-American operations for which he supplies the brains and the CIA colleague supplies the funds.'

This has caused annoyance on occasions. Robert Lamphere, a former FBI officer, complained that 'MI6 had the reputation of skilful horsetraders with whom you trafficked at your peril'. They often held back titbits for the next trade.[67] But the smaller size is not always a disadvantage. According to Frank Snepp, a retired CIA officer, MI6 staff are less specialized and have wider knowledge of tradecraft, and the British operator is 'probably better trained in languages . . . able to move from one area of the world to another with relative ease'.

Economic intelligence is one area where the British are said by experienced American analysts to be particularly valued. 'Generally speaking, our intelligence people felt the Brits have got it better organized than we have,' says Ray Cline. Another former CIA officer David Atlee Phillips agrees, but says that nowadays 'the CIA are as good as the Brits'. Analysis of economic trends, such as the oil price or the state of the Soviet economy, are now one of the most vital parts of current intelligence assessments. It's clear that assessments are compared and exchanged on a two-way process.[68]

Such was the level of information still being passed on to the British by the CIA in the late seventies that the Director, Admiral Standfield Turner, apparently felt that the British had a virtual stranglehold. But his successor, William Casey, on being briefed on Turner's views, dismissed them saying he 'liked the British. What else?'[69]

A description of the work of the CIA in London has been published by two academic specialists on intelligence, Professors Desmond Ball and Jeffrey Richelson. They claim that the CIA maintains forty staff in London, based largely at a special wing in the United States Embassy.[70] Other reports put the total at seventy. They operate from five cover offices, including the Political Liaison Section, which is headed by the station chief. This is responsible for liaison with MI6. The Joint Reports and Research Unit provides analysis and swaps intelligence assessments on economic, scientific or general strategic issues with the Joint Intelligence Committee in the Cabinet Office, Whitehall. It is the largest office with a staff of about thirty.[71] Communications for the Embassy are provided by the Area Telecommunications Office, which has a staff of thirteen. Staff from the Foreign Broadcast Information Service exchange transcripts of foreign radio and television programmes with the BBC Monitoring Service at Caversham in Berkshire. The transcripts cover items such as news broadcasts, interviews and speeches, and are included in the Summary of World Broadcasts published daily by the BBC.

The CIA is said to have other offices near the Embassy for debriefing, and a radio communication centre at Croughton near Banbury.[72] Some CIA officers work in a special liaison office in the signals intelligence section at the Embassy. There are also FBI liaison officers in London, as legal attachés who work with MI5 and staff from the Defence Intelligence Agency, which works with Defence Intelligence staff at the Ministry of Defence. The British agencies have liaison teams based in the United States.[73]

The post of CIA Station Chief is a plum one. Cord Meyer, who held the post between 1973 and 1976, says 'short of being near top of the Government in Washington, I know no vantage point that offers a wider and at the same time more specifically detailed view of the forces at work behind the scene on world stage'.[74]

Meyer says he got on well with the heads of British intelligence such as Maurice Oldfield, the MI6 chief. 'He, my wife and I would go out to the theatre and have dinner afterwards at Rules.'[75]

During Meyer's period in London from 1973 to 1976 there were repeated stories in the Press that the CIA was involved in covert action. Meyer however claims: 'Our co-operation was governed by strict ground rules that forbade the recruitment of each other's nationals as agents and ruled out any kind of covert intervention.'[76]

Although allegations for covert action have been made repeatedly, the evidence for this is much less than in other countries within Europe. CIA manipulation has been documented in Italian elections, for example, with $10 million being spent in 1948 to boost the campaigns of moderate political parties. By the 1958 election the budget had risen to $25 million.[77]

One reason for the lack of evidence for covert action in Britain is that, unlike the other countries, Britain does not hold inquiries into the operation of its intelligence systems. Secrecy and pressure on the media, as over Peter Wright's *Spycatcher*, or the BBC radio programme *My Country Right or Wrong*, has reduced the flow of information. Another reason for Britain's relative immunity may lie in its closeness to the United States. It has never had a government which has defied American interests consistently. The occasions that a British Government has challenged the United States are relatively few, and those have been short-lived. Even the Suez crisis lasted only days, largely as a result of American economic pressure. But with the close co-operation between the intelligence services in the two countries, there seems to be little reason why the CIA would need to carry out its own operations that might imperil the relationship. As the American intelligence specialist Jeffrey Richelson says of the claims of covert action: 'I doubt it, so much to lose, so little to gain.'[78]

But there has been some evidence of covert CIA operations in Britain, particularly at the height of the Cold War. The most famous example is the Congress for Cultural Freedom [CCF], which was pledged to 'defend freedom and democracy against the new tyranny in the world'. This was revealed as a CIA front by the *Guardian* in 1967. Tom Braden, who was in charge of the CIA programme, which he described as 'a vast project targeted on intellectuals . . . the battle for Picasso's mind if you will,' confirmed in an article entitled 'I'm glad the CIA is immoral' that both the CCF and *Encounter* had a CIA agent within them. Braden wrote that in one year the CIA contribution was $800,000 million to $900,000. A CIA subsidy for *Encounter* magazine came out of the money paid to CCF, according to Braden. But he wrote, 'only one of the people running it knew it was paid for by the CIA'.[79]

A number of leading Labour right-wingers attended CCF conferences and international seminars during the fifties when the Congress was an important forum for intellectual debate in Europe. They included Anthony Crosland, who organized a number of its seminars, and Denis

Healey, but there is no suggestion that they knew about the CCF's paymasters.[80] When the CCF was unmasked in the late sixties another CIA front was established, Forum World Features (FWF) news agency. It was aimed not at intellectuals like CCF, but at directly influencing public opinion. A CIA internal memo written in 1968 obtained by Granada Television and published in *Time Out* in 1975 claimed that 'FWF was created from the residue of the Forum Service, an activity of the Congress for Cultural Freedom from which the CIA withdrew its support in 1966'. Below was added: 'Run in the knowledge and co-operation of British Intelligence.'[81] The FWF was used to transmit CIA and British propaganda throughout the world, as the memo said: 'In its first two years FWF has provided the United States with a significant means to counter Communist prop[aganda] and has become a respected features service.' FWF was taken by newspapers worldwide, including thirty in the United States.[82]

Brian Crozier, the Director of FWF, has claimed that CIA involvement ended in March 1966.[83] He has challenged documents published in *Time Out* said to show CIA support for FWF and The Institute for The Study of Conflict, which he also founded. He says that the Institute is neither 'owned nor financed nor controlled by the CIA or any other intelligence service'.[84]

FWF was wound up in 1975. Of the controversy while he was in London, Cord Meyer says: 'It died pretty quickly because Forum World Features didn't continue so there was nothing to shoot at.'[85]

Meyer has denied press allegations that the CIA penetrated trade unions, and of CIA operations against the IRA. He says this latter claim 'was like aiming a pistol at you'. He took measures to avoid IRA attacks, dashing from the kitchen door of his house in London to his car as it was being driven on the move.[86]

Individual journalists and international news agencies were used to plant CIA stories, not only for world-wide consumption but also because news agencies in the United States were said to be off-limits to the CIA, so the way to ensure material reached the American media was to provide it to the overseas news agencies that they took.[87]

More recently there have been allegations in Britain that the CIA has worked to prevent trade between Western Europe and the Soviet Bloc, particularly in high-technology goods. CIA agents are said to have periodically raided companies based in Britain in its efforts to ensure that restrictions on strategic export controls (discussed in chapter 12) are fulfilled. The allegations were raised in Parliament by the Democrat

MP Paddy Ashdown, but have been denied by the Government.

Whatever the vicissitudes in human intelligence relations, co-operation on signals intelligence is the most secret aspect of the intelligence alliance and the most intense.

Under the UK–US Security Agreement (UKUSA) of 1947, which replaced the wartime agreement, the British accepted that their wartime dominance of signals intelligence and cyphers, the famous Ultra code-breaking, was over. Under that agreement, the United States was called the First Party, and Britain, Australia, Canada and New Zealand the Second Parties. The five countries have a host of other agreements on intelligence co-operation, with the United States National Security Agency (NSA) firmly in charge. Indeed in 1954, according to documents in the United States National Archives, the British 'did not agree to' attempts by the Americans to take charge of both ends of the links 'so that the United States would have control of both terminals of the GCHQ-NSA communications'.[88]

The agreements cover all the details of security, coding and the division of the world. The result is that GCHQ and the NSA work together as a multinational eavesdropping system, though there are many items the NSA does not pass on, even to GCHQ. As part of the bargain GCHQ monitors communications in the Soviet Bloc as far as the Urals and Africa, as well as the Far East from its outstation in Hong Kong. There are even joint operations in places such as Ascension Island, or Diego Garcia.

Relations between GCHQ and NSA are said to run more smoothly than those between the other intelligence agencies on both sides of the Atlantic. 'Between us', wrote the GCHQ Director Sir Leonard Hooper to his NSA opposite number Lt General Marshall Carter in 1969, 'we have ensured that the blankets and sheets are more tightly tucked around the bed on which our two sets of people lie, and like you, I like it that way.'[89]

Together with satellite photography, information from electronic intelligence is now the most important intelligence source. The Special United States Liaison Officer based in London, known as the SUSLO, is also a very senior official from the National Security Agency which runs the United States' signals intelligence system. The NSA, formed in 1952, is responsible for intercepting communications world-wide. To provide day-to-day liaison with the NSA's British counterpart, GCHQ (Government Communications Headquarters), there are said to be at least sixty NSA and United States Navy staff working at its headquarters in Cheltenham. GCHQ also has a UK Liaison Officer in charge of the liaison office based at the British Embassy in Washington. And at the NSA's headquarters at Ford Meade in Maryland the GCHQ has its own suite of offices identified by a large royal crest and the E11R legend on the door.[90]

The British liaison offices are much smaller, partly because their resources are fewer and also because Americans have used their position as senior partners to make London the focus of liaison to control British knowledge of what the United States' agencies are doing.

Co-operation is often intense. Work on certain types of traffic is shared. A former NSA worker has revealed recently the scale of co-operation in the era when such traffic was still sent by radio signals. If the Americans were getting poor reception at their station in Britain for commercial traffic, then at Kirknewton in Scotland they would ring a control centre at Cheltenham and say, for example, that Bucharest to Moscow on 'such and such a frequency is not good, can you help us?' The control party at GCHQ would receive information every half hour on whether the stations it controlled were working to capacity. So if a call came in, they could find 'another station in a different location which wasn't covering as many stations as they could' to help the Americans out.[91]

The United States has a system of signal intelligence-gathering facilities operating from Britain. These are used to monitor the Soviet Union and Eastern Europe – to intercept military, commercial and government or diplomatic communications by phone, radio, telex links and to intercept radar and other electronic signals. With modern technology able to make codes unbreakable even by the most powerful computers, emphasis has shifted to such signals which are not coded, though the sheer volume of such signals has required selective monitoring.

One of the biggest NSA facilities in Britain is at RAF Chicksands near Bedford, a former RAF wartime signal interception centre. It was given to the USAF in the early fifties, and is used to eavesdrop on the Soviet Air Force. It also provides one of the NSA's biggest relay centres of intercepted signals from listening stations in Britain and Europe. The traffic relayed is said not only to include Eastern Bloc military communications, but also diplomatic traffic from NATO countries, particularly France. Congress was told that 'the information gathered is not shared with NATO nations'.[92]

The NSA's biggest outstation is at Menwith Hill outside Harrogate. Code-named Steeplebush, it is said to be the largest satellite centre in the world. It extends over 562 acres and nearly 1,200 people work there, two-thirds of them American.[93] It currently has eight satellite tracking dishes, and eight giant golf-ball-shaped domes.

In September 1987 plans were announced to double the size and build another series of domes, and radio masts as part of the 'expansion of operations facility'.[94] This comes after an earlier expansion programme in which £110 million was spent on an 'expanded mission' of satellite surveillance.[95] The exact purpose of the current expansion plan is not officially revealed, as Menwith Hill is one of the most secret facilities in Britain, but there is speculation that it is related to new satellite systems.

Menwith Hill's exact functions have never been confirmed, although it is officially described as a communications relay centre. It links to the NSA headquarters communications from United States satellites, including American electronic intelligence satellites such as Jumpseat, and other satellites in an orbit which allows them to hover over the northern and polar regions of the Soviet Union, intercepting Soviet signals traffic.[96] In 1966 it took over the functions of the station at Kirknewton, Scotland, intercepting ordinary commercial telex and cable traffic in the Eastern Bloc which is now transmitted by satellite rather than by radio signals. GCHQ staff share seats in some areas alongside NSA staff. So close is the working relationship that according to one former worker: 'When the Brits would put down their headphones for their 10 a.m. teabreak the Americans would simply cover their positions.'[97] Menwith Hill is also said to intercept signals from Soviet satellites.

But the facilities at Menwith Hill are said to go much further, and include monitoring and analysing communications in Britain and Western Europe. According to the British journalists Duncan Campbell and Linda Melvern,[98] it is linked directly into the heart of the British telephone system. They have identified high-capacity cable connecting it to a nearby microwave tower, which they say, allows the NSA to mass-tap into thousands of lines between Britain and Europe as well as transatlantic calls and all telex and telegram traffic. However, this is disputed by some independent American observers. James Bamford, a specialist on the NSA says: 'Domestic British communications would have little interest to the NSA, which used Menwith Hill primarily to eavesdrop on Europe and the Soviet Union by way of SIGINT satellites.'[99] Jeffrey Richelson, an intelligence specialist, says if such bugging is done at all 'it certainly is tangential to the main mission'.[100] In 1980 the Government issued a 'limited and highly specific denial' that Menwith Hill intercepted transatlantic incoming or outgoing calls, or British domestic calls, apparently leaving open the question of interception of calls from Europe.[101]

But there is little doubt that Britain and the United States have co-operated in giving one another access to the traffic of their own major telecommunications companies. Copies of cables sent by the nationalized company, Cable and Wireless, were sent to GCHQ by van and later made available to NSA liaison staff either unprocessed or as summaries. In the fifties, two-thirds of long-distance communications were by cable.[102] However, processing was a laborious task.

Since then, computer technology has made much easier the analysis of current traffic which is sent now by telex, computer links, or phone. GCHQ and NSA have some of the most powerful computers in the world. The agreement to share data and the new technology has, according to James Bamford, allowed the NSA to 'ransack the entire United Kingdom telex and cable systems to locate a reference to Jane Fonda, Muammar Qadaffi, oil or drugs, IBM or British Petroleum'.[103]

To cater for the development of transatlantic traffic by satellite in the late sixties, the NSA and GCHQ built receiving dishes on each side to intercept the signals.

Two satellite dishes were built in Bude in Cornwall in 1970 to coincide with the new Intelsat III communications satellite. One of their functions is said to be to intercept commercial signals coming to the Goonhilly Downs commercial satellite receiving dish. Sir Leonard Hooper, the then GCHQ Director, told the NSA Director Marshall 'Pat' Carter that in persuading the Government to provide the money to build the dishes in Cornwall, he had 'leaned heavily on you and sometimes taken your name in vain – when I needed something at this end'. Sir Leonard joked that the first two dishes should be called Pat and Louis, the first names of Carter and his deputy Louis Tordella.[104]

It has been a two-way process. GCHQ had access to similar traffic from the American commercial cable companies under the NSA's Shamrock programme which aimed to get round the ban on domestic mass interception by obtaining all the international cables sent by the three main American cable companies. It was curtailed in 1976.[105]

A United States Department of Justice report in 1975 revealed the scale of exchanges as part of the NSA's illegal Minaret programme in which 6,000 American citizens were monitored between 1967 and 1973.

GCHQ played a key role in providing information, for according to the report, 'Minaret intelligence was obtained *incidentally* in the course of NSA's interception of aural and non-aural (e.g. telex) international communications, and the receipt of GCHQ acquired telex and ILC (commercial) cable traffic.'[106]

The United States also intercepts signals and from its allies – including Britain, according to some reports. An unpublished Congressional report from 1977, quoted by the *New York Times,* claimed that the 'NSA monitor the traffic of specific countries, including Great Britain our closest ally'. The report quoted a former employee who claimed knowledge of a 'team of men whose only job was to read and process intercepted British communications.'[107]

William Friedman, the greatest of American codebreakers, is said by his biographer to have come to Britain in 1957 to mollify colleagues at GCHQ after the United States broke British and French codes during the Suez crisis the year before. And a disaffected former American signals intelligence operative said in 1973: 'Our Chicksands installation monitors all their communications, and the NSA unit in our Embassy in London monitors the low level stuff. They are all working with machines we gave them.'[108]

However, there have been some clashes between GCHQ and the NSA despite the generally good relations between them – for example, over the payment of royalties for cipher machine research. Britain wanted to maximize the return to private contractors. Raymond Tate, the NSA official responsible from 1973 to 1978 says: 'I've had thousands of hours of arguments on this subject. Traditionally the Brits and Americans have had a very close relationship. Over the years it's maintained the closeness although there have been some very distinct bumpy roads; part of the time I was there it was very bumpy.'[109]

But the biggest crisis came over the arrest of Geoffrey Prime, the former GCHQ translator who spied for the Soviets for fourteen years. He gave them the intercepts from the highly secret Rhyolite electronic spy satellites. The cost of the damage caused by the leak of such information from a source at the heart of the intelligence signals operation has been estimated at $1,000 billion, according to one NSA source.[110] The row provoked a great debate in the British press about Prime's impact on American co-operation. 'We have a long way to go before the Americans will really trust us again,' one newspaper editorial wailed. There were reports that the Americans feared that more spies remained undiscovered at GCHQ.

But the United States was going through its own series of spy scandals. Equally secret information on the actual design of the Rhyolite satellite had been sold to the Soviets by Christopher Boyce, a worker at the company TRW, which built them. Boyce was caught in 1977, the year Prime ceased to work at GCHQ.

The fact that the American intelligence community has also been penetrated by a number of traitors has counter-balanced the damage done by Prime. And the idea that the Prime affair has cut co-operation is 'nonsense', according to the American writer James Bamford. 'As weak as security was at GCHQ, it was a fortress compared to the NSA. The NSA was simply much better at hiding how much, and how badly it has been penetrated.' The Prime affair provided a means of putting pressure on the British, he says.[111]

American pressure has been reported to be the reason that led to the Government taking the controversial decision to ban union membership at GCHQ in 1984. They are also said to have pushed for greater security measures, including the use of the so-called lie detector. It has also been suggested that the decision to begin developing Britain's own electronic spy satellite, Zircon, followed a reduction in the amount of secret information being passed on by the Americans.[112] GCHQ officials reportedly wanted to reduce their dependence on American satellites. But as with other prestige symbols, such as nuclear weapons, there was also a feeling that if Britain had its own spy satellite it would have more clout in its relationship with America. The original Zircon programme is said to have been cancelled in February 1987 after £70 million had been spent because Mrs Thatcher had decided to buy more up-to-date American satellite equipment.[113] In fact, according to American analysts, the project was always an Anglo-American operation, with British companies building the satellite with American technology.[114] Jeffrey Richelson has claimed that a British-owned spy satellite could be launched as early as 1989. Other countries are also developing their own satellite systems. The French, for example, are developing the Helios photographic system for launching in 1993.[115]

The furore over the Zircon satellite in 1987 highlights the essentially junior role that Britain plays in the intelligence relationship. Unlike some other aspects of the relationship, time – and in this case technology – has reinforced America's dominance. 'Dependence is so great and co-operation so close,' says the writer Chapman Pincher, 'I am convinced that the security and intelligence chiefs would go to any lengths to protect the linkup.'[116]

6

☆☆★☆☆

WHO PRESSES THE BUTTON?

It is inconceivable we should refuse United States aircraft and pilots the right to defend their own people.

Margaret Thatcher, on her controversial decision to allow the United States to use British bases for its raid on Libya.

THE debate over the nuclear relationship between Britain and America has been at its sharpest in the last few years. At issue is the presence of American bases on British soil, and the controversy over the arrival of Cruise missiles at Greenham Common in 1983, which has been further fanned by the use of four of the other bases in the raid on Libya on 14 April 1986. The United States keeps an estimated 1,300 nuclear warheads in Britain, two or three times the number thought to be in Britain's own nuclear arsenal. [1]

The American nuclear weapons include the 119 Cruise missiles declared at Greenham Common and Molesworth in the INF Treaty signed by Ronald Reagan and Mikhail Gorbachev in December 1987. In addition, there are an estimated 600 freefall bombs, about 126 nuclear depth charges and about 500 warheads for American Poseidon missiles. They are stored at six locations throughout Britain. [2]

The doubts over the degree of Britain's control over the use of these weapons were rekindled by the American raid on Libya. Although the aircraft attacking Tripoli and Benghazi were only carrying non-nuclear bombs, the ensuing furore over the use of British air-bases brought into question once again the calculated ambiguity of the understanding between the two countries about the control of American nuclear weapons in Britain – reached nearly forty years ago.

The first American bombers were stationed in Britain during the Berlin crisis in 1948, when a fleet of sixty B-29 bombers arrived in East Anglia 'for a short period of temporary duty'. Britain accepted the American request with so little objection that the United States Secretary of State George Marshall asked Foreign Secretary Bevin whether he had 'fully considered the implications'. [3] The Commander of the B-29s said: 'Never before in history has one first-class Power gone into another first-class Power without any agreement.'[4] One Soviet publication remarked that 'The British Isles had now become an aircraft carrier'. The Defence Secretary James Forrestal noted in his diary in July 1948, that the bombers' presence 'would accustom the British to the necessary habits and routines that go in the accommodation of an alien, even though an allied power'. He added: 'Once sent they would become somewhat of an accepted fixture, whereas a deterioration of the situation in Europe might lead to a condition of mind in which the British would be compelled to reverse their present attitude.'

This was a recurring concern. The Air Force Secretary wrote to Forrestal's successor, Louis Johnson, two years later over plans to replace the B-29s with B-36s: 'I know [the British] well enough to know that sometimes they can be very slow, and this strategic counter-measure is something which cannot afford to be held up while the British Cabinet is debating about things.'[5]

In 1949, B-29s modified to take atom bombs had been sent to Britain. Britain's acceptance of American nuclear weapons confirmed its dependence on the United States for defence. The formation of NATO in April 1949 had cemented the military links between the two countries, but it was the nuclear ties that had the greatest implications for the bilateral relationship.

The question of how much control Britain should have over America's use of atomic weapons stored in Britain was left unresolved until 1951. The Quebec Agreement of 1943, which had given Britain a veto, had been abandoned at America's urging in 1948 and there had been no replacement agreement. So Britain had no formal control over the use of the American B-29s even though they were based in Britain. Furthermore, Britain felt the Americans were being selective over the information they gave about the aircrafts' use and nuclear capacity.

The issue of a veto came to a head on 30 November 1950. Asked at a press conference about the use of the nuclear bomb in the Korean War, when the Allies were being pushed back, President Truman commented: 'There has always been active consideration of its use.' The *Washington Post*, which had also stated that the President had said 'he didn't want it used'[6] reported: 'British officials were described as shocked and astounded by the statement which was interpreted in London as meaning General Douglas MacArthur had been given a free hand to use the atomic bomb against the Chinese Reds.'[7]

In the House of Commons, where a foreign affairs debate was being held as the news of Truman's comment came in, Roy Jenkins recalls that 'a mood of near panic set in'.[8] In the furore, Prime Minister Clement Attlee made it clear he would read the riot act to Truman. Despite the White House's immediate attempts at clarification, Attlee announced a visit to Washington at once. But there were some reasons behind Britain's concern. In August 1950, the Secretary for the US Navy had been sent as Ambassador to Ireland for calling for pre-emptive strikes, and the Commandant of the Air College was retired for declaring that the Air Force only awaited orders to drop its bombs on Moscow. And an opinion poll in the *Washington Post* showed 45 per cent of Americans in favour of using the bomb.[9]

Truman's Secretary of State Dean Acheson said that Attlee made great efforts while in Washington a few days later to get President Truman to sign an agreement between the two countries on the control of nuclear weapons. He chose his moment when the two leaders went off for private discussions in Truman's study on the last day of the talks, 7 December. Acheson said he was horrified to hear Attlee come out afterwards and remark: 'We have had a good talk about the bomb. We want to say in the communique that neither of us will OK the bomb without prior consultation with each other.'[10] The previous day, Truman told Attlee that he 'would not consider the use of the bomb without consulting with the United Kingdom,' but as the official American history puts it: 'The Prime Minister asked whether this agreement should be put in writing, the President replied no, it would not be in writing, that if a man's word wasn't any good it wasn't made better by writing it down.'[11]

So Attlee thought he'd made a major breakthrough at the final talks. Attlee's precipitated American officials into furious activity, and Acheson later boasted he 'unachieved' the agreement.[12] He says that he had as a precedent an incident the previous morning when a formation of geese had set off a false alert on the early warning radar, and he had been instructed to 'inform' Attlee, but not advise him.[13] That was all Acheson was prepared to concede in the communique. Acheson said he 'pointed out that over and over again the President had insisted that no commitment of any sort limited his duty and power under the law to authorize use of nuclear weapons'.[14] Attlee had no alternative but to concede this point in the communique; with the British Ambassador Sir Oliver Franks acting as scribe, and kneeling on the floor – 'the first time', remarked Truman, 'that a British Ambassador has knelt before an American President'.[15] All the final communique eventually promised was that the United States would 'keep the Prime Minister informed at all times', the paragraph being deliberately placed so it was not clear if it refered to Korea or Europe, according to the official United States papers.[16]

Despite this, Attlee declared in the Commons a few days later on the basis of the private assurance that he had received 'perfectly satisfactory' pledges from Truman that he regarded the American 'atomic bomb as in a sense a joint possession of the United States, United Kingdom, and Canada, and he would not authorize its use without prior consultation'. This wasn't the exact American understanding, but then, as Acheson's special assistant Lucius Battle put it: 'Frankly I suspect [the agreement] had been left deliberately fuzzy.'[17] Fuzzy or not, the so-called Attlee–Truman accord has been cited by successive Prime Ministers to justify their assertion that Britain does have a veto over the use of all the American bases in Britain. Yet there was no fuzziness as far as the *Washington Post* was concerned. In its report that next day the *Post* said that one of Attlee's chief objectives 'was to obtain from Truman a promise that Britain would be consulted before any decision was made. It was noted here yesterday that although Mr Truman said he would keep Mr Attlee informed, he reserved for himself the right to make a final decision about the use of the bomb.'[18]

Attlee's statement to the House didn't satisfy Churchill, who only found out from the communique that the Quebec agreement on full consultation he had reached with Roosevelt in 1943 no longer prevailed. He was determined, both in opposition and then as Prime Minister from October 1951, that the situation should be remedied.

In January 1952 Churchill visited President Truman in Washington, and the two leaders signed a communique, the product of lengthy discussions over the previous year. This reaffirmed the earlier understanding and said that 'the use of these bases in an emergency would be a matter for joint decision by His Majesty's Government and the United States Goverment in the light of the circumstances prevailing at the time'. This phrase has remained the only form of words governing the use of the United States bases in Britain to this day.

The communique, which was put together by the British Ambassador Oliver Franks, was designed as a diplomatic formula to bridge the gap between the two sides. It skirted around the issue of whether Britain still had a veto. 'There was still a little ambiguity there', says Lucius Battle 'that served everybody's interests and everybody's needs.'[19] It has never been completely clear whether the United States could or would live up to the implications of that communique. Jack McFall, an Assistant Secretary of State, successfully introduced a resolution stating that 'talks were not in any sense negotiations toward final and binding decisions'.[20] In 1951 the Joint Chiefs of Staff advised that 'the United States must be prepared to use atomic weapons if and when necessary from any and all bases which may be available'.[21]

Kennedy's Defence Secretary Robert McNamara has said the agreement is certainly not tantamount to giving Britain the right to veto American use of its own weapons. 'I think consultation means a discussion . . . with the party having the final authority – in this case the United States – making the final decision.' Furthermore, the United States constitution prohibits any agreement that takes away the right of the President to use any American weapon in the national interest.

The other issue that was deliberately left unresolved was exactly what 'subject to circumstances prevailing at the time' actually meant. 'No piece of paper, however well intentioned,' according to Paul Warnke, an arms control adviser to President Carter, 'is going to make a real difference at a time of crisis. The person . . . the country that physically controls the weapon is going to make the decision.'[22]

However, in the late 1950s the Americans did concede joint control of one missile, Thor. The negotiations were remarkably quick by diplomatic standards; they began in December 1956 and the agreement to deploy the missiles was ratified by Macmillan and Eisenhower in Bermuda three months later. It provided for the missiles to be supplied free of charge by the United States, and for the RAF to provide all the logistical services and facilities for them. All the warheads were American controlled, and they would be stored under United States control until orders came for them to be used. At the same time, the two countries agreed to co-ordinate the targeting of their nuclear forces, and Eisenhower sanctioned the release of the information about American weapons that would allow the two countries' nuclear bombers to carry each others' weapons.

Thor missiles have been the only American weapons on British soil with an unambiguous dual-control system. The missile was operated by British forces while the warhead was controlled by the Americans. An American officer had a key for the warhead and a British officer had a key to set the launch procedure for the missile. But even then there was confusion, and the Prime Minister Harold Macmillan was embarrassed by the comments of the commander of the first Thor Squadron, Colonel Zink, who Macmillan wrote in his memoirs, 'put his foot in it on a grand scale' by announcing to the Press in February 1958 that he had 'full operational control'.[23] Zink was firmly corrected by the Pentagon.

The Colonel Zink affair was one of a number of embarrassments which Macmillan had to face over the American bases. Denis Healey challenged him over the status of the new base for American Polaris submarines at Holy Loch, thirty miles from the towns of the Clyde Valley. American use of Holy Loch was part of the quid pro quo for Skybolt.

Macmillan announced the imminent arrival of the Polaris submarines on 1 November 1960, at the height of the controversy over nuclear weapons. The issue had nearly split the Labour Party at its Conference at Scarborough, and the CND was mobilizing support in huge numbers. Macmillan himself admitted in the House of Commons that it was impossible to reach an agreement 'on all fours' with the bomber agreement as the submarines would patrol in international waters. He was he said 'perfectly satisfied that no decision to use the missiles will ever be taken without the fullest possible previous consultation'. The American State Department reacted with surprise: 'There might not be time for consultation,' said their spokesman Lincoln White. 'No commitments had been made,' he added.[24] The Foreign Secretary Lord Home was forced to concede that consultation 'in case of emergency' could not be certain. And a week after his first statement Macmillan himself said that consultation 'might be impossible in circumstances of a surprise attack on the West'. But in trying to reassure MPs he raised further questions. In his first statement he had said: 'It was not possible to make an agreement on all fours with the bomber agreement.' Now he insisted that Britain had 'exactly the same control' over Holy Loch as over the bomber bases. If that is the case, it would seem to confirm that the obvious caveat in 1952 understanding on the 'circumstances prevailing at the time' means the agreement would not apply in an unforeseen nuclear crisis.[25]

Although the 1952 agreement is now nearly forty years old, it remains the only tangible arrangement between the two countries over the use of nuclear weapons – however vague the wording may be. The issue of control of American missiles came to the fore once again in the early 1980s following NATO's decision to deploy a new generation of American medium-range missiles in Europe. Cruise and Pershing 2 were intended to match the Soviet SS20 missiles but to many Europeans they symbolized a new era of United States control over their defence. Within Britain there was particular anxiety over who actually controlled the missiles, especially in view of the vague nature of the earlier undertakings.

When the first Cruise missiles arrived at Greenham Common in October 1983, the Government rejected the idea of dual-key control like the Thor system because of the enormous cost – £1 billion. Instead, Mrs Thatcher was forced to rely on the formula agreed by Churchill and Truman. Characteristically, she had no doubt about the ambiguities. In February 1983 she told journalists: 'I am satisfied that those arrangements would be effective. A joint decision on the use of the bases or the missiles would of course be dual control. Got it?'[26] she added. But the *New York Times* claimed two months later that Mrs Thatcher wanted the Americans to make an unambiguous statement pledging that the missiles would never be used without British consent, or a clause to that effect to the 1952 Agreement.[27] Richard Perle, the hawkish Assistant Defence Secretary, publicly dismissed the idea three days later saying he didn't think it was 'necessary to change existing procedures'.[28] But this didn't stop Mrs Thatcher. A month later she maintained that the 'existing agreement means that no nuclear weapons would be fired or launched from British territory without the agreement of the Prime Minister. That is categorical.' President Reagan attempted to help her out in a TV interview by saying: 'I don't think either one of us will do anything independent of the other . . . er . . . this constitutes a sort of veto doesn't it?'[29]

But in another TV interview, shown three days later, the Defence Secretary Caspar Weinberger refused to elaborate whether there really was a veto. The reason for this is clear. As one of his predecessors James Schlesinger had stated, the position is that, 'such consultation procedure does not imply any actual inhibition on the capability of the United States'. And as the NATO guidelines on consultation, known as the Athens Guidelines, state clearly: 'The United States President retains the right to use American nuclear weapons without prior consultation.'[30]

The hollowness of the formula designed to cover up Britain's lack of a veto means that, whenever the issue arises, the Prime Minister is inevitably embroiled in a political controversy. This was true even during the Libyan raid, although there had been consultation between Mrs Thatcher and President Reagan's envoy General Vernon Walters. The leader of the Liberal Party David Steel argued strongly that the Attlee–Truman accord was very much out of date. It had never been published, and it should now be revised, published and approved. 'If

damage is not to be caused to the NATO Alliance,' he said, 'there must
be no doubt as to the conditions under which the American bases in this
country are used.'[31] But it is this very ambiguity which both allows a
British Government to make assurances which it knows a United States
administration can neither give nor deliver.

The peacetime control of nuclear weapons is also enveloped in
secrecy. Several accidents involving American nuclear weapons have
been reported in Britain. In 1980 it was revealed in an American
newspaper that a B-47 bomber had crashed at Lakenheath on 27 July
1956 and, according to the official report quoted, the 'ensuing fire
enveloped a storage igloo containing several nuclear weapons in storage
configuration'. Inside the igloo were three B6 atom bombs, containing
several tonnes of conventional explosive and, also stored in the igloo, an
estimated fifty kilograms of plutonium in the nuclear capsules. USAF
officers later claimed that if the conventional explosive had gone off
there would not have been a nuclear explosion, but the spread of
plutonium particles would have caused a 'desert' over that part of East
Anglia. And although American families were evacuated, no information
was given to local villagers, or the police.[32] A cover story was fed to the
local Press. A year after this accident was made public, a Poseidon
missile was apparently accidently dropped as it was being removed from
an American submarine at Holy Loch, and fell seventeen feet. It was
armed with ten warheads which contained a particularly sensitive
conventional explosive. If it had gone off the conventional explosive in
the warheads could have spread radioactive particles for miles.
Attempts to keep the accident secret failed and the news spread
through the local community.[33]

This pattern of secrecy was repeated elsewhere. A former member
of an RAF emergency team at the St Mawgan base in Cornwall claimed
in *The Independent* that British servicemen were barred from entering
the area near the American nuclear weapons store during a fire alarm.
The store at St Mawgan is thought to hold sixty nuclear depth charges.
Ministry of Defence sources told *The Independent* that the incident in
which the firemen were threatened with machine guns 'would be almost
impossible today'.[34] A minister assured MPs that 'there has never been
an accident involving damage to or release of radioactivity from nuclear
weapons' in Britain.[35] Documents revealing American contingency plans
for accidents state as an assumption that 'United States control will be
re-established as soon as possible over nuclear weapons regardless of
the accident location'. The plans only allow for co-ordination with the

host country; the host nation is expected to provide support facilities. The plans, by the United States European Command allow for at least 500 Americans to be in place for thirty days.[36] The plan tells United States personnel what to do in the event of a nuclear weapon accident, coded 'bent spear' – if not particularly serious, or 'broken arrow' – for a full-scale disaster alert. The plan warns of opposition from 'dissident individuals, radical elements or hostile forces', drawing attention to the United States Rules of Engagement for the United Kingdom of 'deadly force'.[37] The British Government has denied any loss of sovereignty in a United States nuclear weapons accident, saying that 'it is clearly understood in the arrangements that the United Kingdom has sovereign rights over its territory and territorial waters'. The Chief Constable of South Yorkshire, Peter Wright, has said that the United States contingency plans relating to control of American weapons if an accident happens 'have no effect in this country'.[38]

Other documents show that the United States has been developing its capability to cope with nuclear accidents in sixteen countries including Britain. It now has Nuclear Accident Response Teams at twelve bases in Britain, including five locations where American nuclear warheads are stored – equipped to deal with accidents and with devices held by terrorists.[39] The United States has encouraged its allies – including Britain – to build up their Accident Response capability, and the Ministry of Defence has confirmed that the British teams from the Nuclear Accident Response Organization hold regular joint tests of contingency plans.[40] A secret Pentagon report – obtained under the Freedom of Information Act – revealed that in 1984, during a joint exercise codenamed 'Cinder exercise Kerria', Americans came to a British 'field test of the United Kingdom diagnostic capabilities against an improvised nuclear device'; it demonstrated new ways of locating homemade nuclear devices which might be held by terrorists. Since 1976 the United States has had a special team using sophisticated detection devices to find nuclear weapons which might be held by terrorists.

In 1985, according to the report, two exercises were held, one of which was called operation 'Premier Task', to 'familiarize organizations with their role in responding to a nuclear weapons accident involving United States weapons in the United Kingdom.' These were 'command post exercises' to train the overall organization of the safety measures. One exercise, whose name is still classified, lasted four days and simulated an accident in England. Staff based in both Britain and the

United States were involved.[41]

Americans have been to most British exercises in the three series, code-named Sharp Foil, Franchise, or Senator. The last reported Senator exercise was held in 1981 at Swynnerton in Staffordshire; there have been claims that radioactive dust was spread dangerously.[42] British staff have had training at the United States Interservice Nuclear Weapons School in New Mexico. The courses include a simulated nuclear weapons accident using radioactive material, and teams in protective clothing go in search of 'hot spots'.[43] There has been a controversy over whether there has been nuclear contamination at the training sites in Britain, with soil at the training centres said to be noticeably radioactive. The Government has denied this, saying that the doses are extremely low.[44]

However, the American military presence is far greater than just its nuclear forces. It maintains a huge network of bases and supply facilities in the United Kingdom, as well as a wide range of intelligence-gathering facilities. Unofficially there are said to be 150 facilities of all kinds, ranging from bases to housing estates to access to certain ports.[45] The official British Government figure for American bases and military facilities is sixty-six.[46]

There has been a considerable expansion over the past eight years. The number of service personnel has gone up by a third to 31,500. (There are 26,000 dependents.) The increase has been caused by the arrival of Cruise missiles, two new types of planes, and the expansion of new facilities such as aircraft repair workshops and contingency hospitals.[47]

Britain has about a third of America's total aircraft commitment to Europe, including 292 combat aircraft, and 30 other aircraft.[48] They are based at seven main operating bases in South-East England. All the bases are called RAF Bases, although they only have one RAF officer, a Squadron Leader, who deals with local liaison. The only agreement covering the operation of the bases is the Ambassadors Agreement of 1950, which dealt only with the cost of preparing the bases in that year. Another secret memorandum was signed in 1974; it covers the use of other RAF bases by the Americans in wartime.[49]

The United States keeps many of its shorter-range aircraft at forward bases in West Germany, and its longer-range aircraft in Britain.[50] The most important are the 150 F-111s based at Upper Heyford in Oxfordshire and Lakenheath in Suffolk. The F-111s at Lakenheath fly under the slogan: 'The mission of the 48th Tactical Fighter Wing in peace is to train for war. Don't you forget it!'[51] The F-111Fs at Lakenheath, and the F-111Es at Upper Heyford can carry three nuclear bombs, or conventional weapons as they did in the raid on Libya in April 1986. They were supported then by EF-111s equipped with electronic jamming equipment from Upper Heyford. It is said that the jamming equipment cannot be used near Britain as it would also black-out civilian radar, and television transmissions.[52]

Among the other aircraft, are 108 A-10 Thunderbolt 11 aircraft nicknamed 'tank-busters' which provide ground support for troops on the central front in Germany from Alconbury in Cambridgeshire, and Bentwaters and Woodbridge in Suffolk.[53]

Woodbridge is also the home of the 21st Special Operations Squadron. It has MH53J helicopters specially equipped for clandestine operations, and C130 Hercules transport aircraft specially adapted for low flying and night vision.[54]

The adjacent base at Bentwaters is the new home for the 'aggressor squadron', whose guards have been photographed wearing Russian fur hats.[55] This is presumably to add authenticity, as the pilots are trained in Russian air combat techniques to train in mock combat against American and allied pilots, using cameras instead of guns, and electronic tones instead of missiles. The squadron is being equipped with twelve F16C 'fighting falcon' aircraft, as the squadron moved from its old base at Alconbury.[56]

Alconbury is still the base for reconnaissance planes with 13 TR1s, the modernized version of the U2 spyplane. The TRI's main function is detecting radar installations. It flies high up along the German border and is able to detect radar signals and record military activity deep into the Warsaw Pact territory.[57]

There has been intense speculation in the Press whether any of the ultra secret F19 'Stealth' fighters have come to Britain. They are made of special materials which makes them almost invisible on radar. Officially its said they have not been based here, but some observers believe they may have come to Britain to train. Their pilots are reported to have trained in Britain in 1984 and 1986 on other aircraft.[58]

There is also speculation about the possible stationing of the new highly sophisticated F15 Eagle aircraft, and the long-range bomber, the FB-111 in Britain in the early nineties. In the short-term, it seems likely that another nuclear-capable 50 F-111s will be based in Britain, following the agreement to abolish ground launched Cruise and Pershing 2 nuclear missiles.[59]

Mildenhall in Suffolk is the headquarters of the Third Air Force which controls the USAF bases in Britain. It provides half of the United States air transport capacity in Europe, and it has about fifteen C130 Hercules transport aircraft, and about fifteen KC135 refuelling tankers. (There are another eighteen KC135s at Fairford in Gloucestershire.) Mildenhall is also used for transiting transporters, C141 Starlifters and C5 Galaxies. As well as its transport role, Mildenhall has four EC135H aircraft, codenamed Silk Purse, converted 707s, which act as command centres in a crisis – for example, if the command bunkers in Germany were overrun or unusable. Mildenhall also has a reconnaissance function. A detachment operates two SR71 Blackbird signals and electronic monitoring aircraft. The Blackbirds can fly at over 2,000 mph at very high altitudes and are used to monitor signals from Soviet radar and anti-aircraft installations in the Soviet Union. RC135 spyplanes based in America also use Mildenhall. The RC135 is the work-horse of the United States signals gathering aircraft. It flies from Mildenhall over the Baltic and Barents Sea off the Soviet Coast picking up signals which cannot be easily intercepted by satellite. [60]

The United States has co-operated closely with the British over reconnaissance since the 1950s, and from the time RB-45 Tornadoes flew with joint RAF–USAF crews. [61] They flew up to 1,600 miles into the Soviet Union. With the advent of the U2 spyplane in 1956, the Americans attempted to bypass the restrictions on the number of flights they could carry out. Each American flight had to be authorized by the President, and the CIA wanted to increase the number by getting British pilots to fly some missions, authorized by the British. [62] It is said that one in five of the U2 missions over Soviet territory were flown by British pilots from bases in Britain, Cyprus or Turkey. The U2 piloted by Gary Powers shot down in May 1960 was from a base in Turkey, but there was a less publicized diplomatic row a few months later over the shooting down over Soviet waters of a British-based RB47 aircraft on an intelligence mission in July 1960. The Soviets warned of 'this provocative act of the American Air Force operating from British territory'. [63]

During the Suez crisis in 1956 an American-piloted U2 from Turkey photographed an RAF raid on Cairo military airport as it was going on. The RAF sent the CIA a telex saying 'warm thanks for the pix. It's the quickest bomb damage assessment we ever had.'[64] The reconnaissance missions also use British bases at Akrotiri in Cyprus and on the island of Diego Garcia.

Among the other USAF facilities are the best-known American bases

in Britain: the Cruise missile bases at Greenham Common and Molesworth. The USAF also has access to two stand-by deployment bases,
and twelve bases shared with the RAF in wartime, known as co-located
bases. They would be used jointly, or the RAF aircraft would have been
moved forward to continental Europe. The USAF plans to send an
additional 1,500 aircraft to Britain in wartime.[65]

There are a number of other bases, including four forward-operating
bases for long-range B-52 bombers, storage and repair facilities, and
four training ranges. The USAF has a number of communications
facilities, ranging from radio relay stations to the electronic intelligence
centre at Chicksands in Bedfordshire, or the satellite control centre at
Oakhammer in Hampshire. In 1986 an agreement was reached to
change one of the most famous symbols of American presence in
Britain; the golfball-shaped radars at Fylingdales missile early warning
centre in Yorkshire to be replaced by cube-shaped radar arrays.
Fylingdales is operated by a largely British staff.

The USAF has by far the largest number of facilities in Britain. By
contrast, the United States Navy and the Marine Corps have only about
4,000 staff in Britain, based at eight different locations. The largest base
is at Holy Loch in Scotland, the centre for the ten American Poseidon
nuclear submarines where 1,800 people are assigned. The two naval
nuclear weapons stores are at Machrihanish, also in Scotland, and at St
Mawgan in Cornwall. They are used by American and allied anti-
submarine aircraft and to store sixty-six nuclear depth charges each.[66]
Machrihanish is also the base of the American SEALS Special Forces
Group who carry out commando raids and sabotage in wartime. Twenty
people are assigned to the Special Warfare Group. Of the other naval
facilities in Scotland, Thurso in the far north of Scotland is a communica-
tion centre and Edzell near Tayside is operated by the Naval Security
Group and the National Security Agency. It is part of the 'Classic
Wizzard' network, operating ocean surveillance satellites monitoring
Soviet shipping movements.[67]

The other ocean surveillance centre is at Brawdy in Wales. It is
officially termed an oceanographic research centre but is in fact part of
Project Caesar, which plots Soviet submarine movements through from
ports on the north-east coast, from the Arctic Sea into the Atlantic. It
consists of hundreds of miles of cables with underwater sonar sensors
between Northern Scotland, Ireland and Greenland.[68] The sensors pick
up sounds given out by Soviet submarines and these are then monitored
to chart the course of the submarines through the Atlantic with

sophisticated electronics and computers.[69]

Information from centres such as Edzell and Brawdy, as well as from ships and aircraft, is relayed to United States Naval Headquarters in Grosvenor Square in London, near the US Embassy which was used by General Eisenhower as his wartime command centre. Seven-hundred-and-fifty people work in the building which houses the Fleet Ocean Surveillance Information Centre (FOSIC), which collates all available information.[70] But such is the close co-operation between the Royal Navy and the United States Navy that according to information first inadvertently released by an American defence contractor, the Royal Navy has established its own Joint Ocean Surveillance Information Centre (JOSIC)[71] and is spending $47 million on new computer equipment to access the United States Navy's upgraded Ocean Surveillance Information System which channels the data on Soviet activity. It is not a NATO system.[72] New equipment, which doubled the number of information displays, was due to be delivered to the Naval Headquarters in August 1987 as part of the modernization of the second floor command centre.[73] Both this and JOSIC are part of the Worldwide Military Command and Control System (WWMCCS) which links all major American military commands throughout the world to the United States Command Authority, which is ultimately in the hands of the President and can order the use of nuclear weapons. According to press reports, WWMCCS has been plagued with defects and false alarms, and a billion dollars has been spent to remedy them.[74]

The Royal Navy has also bought equipment to access another United States Navy communication system not assigned to NATO, the American Submarine Satellite Information Exchange System (SSIXS). It provides very-low-frequency radio communications links for speech or teleprinter communications between British submarines and British aircraft carriers to allow closer co-ordination between the British and American navies.[75]

Under the new American maritime strategy, the United States aims to challenge Russian submarines in their home waters – and, although it's not NATO policy, Britain has been working closely with the United States on this strategy. To be effective it needs the co-ordination of British and American attack submarines. SSIXS goes some way towards this, but Rear Admiral Frank Grenier, the man in charge of British submarines, says new systems will have to be designed to allow British and American submarines to communicate with one another and so make them more effective, working together in packs, rather than individually, in what he described as the 'battlefield under the ice'.[76]

Co-ordination of a different sort is carried out over the patrol patterns of Britain's Polaris strategic submarines, which are always cleared with the American representative at the Royal Navy Polaris Command Centre at Northwood in Middlesex. The aim is to co-ordinate patrols, or to prevent 'mutual interference'.

Naval activities in the Northern Atlantic are effectively run by the two countries: the Supreme Commander Atlantic is always American; the UK Commander controls the Eastern Atlantic and Channel in NATO operations.[77] The United States also operates its own communications links in Britain, separate from British or NATO communications, which include the system known as the Minimum Essential Communications Network, which is intended for last-ditch communication in wartime. There are also separate systems of microwave radio links. The United States has been developing a new communications system, the DEB, Digital European Backbone facilities. It provides secure communication links between American facilities in Europe and replaces existing land-lines. Work on the fourth stage was due to begin in 1988. Plans for ten communication centres in Britain and seventeen repeater towers to relay the signals have been revealed in congressional testimony.[78]

In 1983, the United States began work on a new European command headquarters in High Wycombe for use in wartime. It is quite separate from the NATO command structure and is described as 'a survivable European Command and Control Centre'. It would replace the main United States command centre which is based in West Germany. The new centre is a refurbished RAF bunker, and is protected against chemical and biological warfare and nuclear radiation.[79]

The United States Army facilities in Britain are fewer in number but nonetheless vast. The Burtonwood supply depot covers five square miles, has two million square feet for storage of equipment for American troops brought over at short notice. Another depot at Caerwent stores 25,000 tonnes of munitions in 400 buildings for United States Army theatre reserve stocks. The Army and other services have a total of eighteen other storage depots.[80]

Thus the United States has a huge presence in the United Kingdom with no formal treaties covering them, and with their own alternative communications centres. American forces are partially immune from British laws – under the 1952 Visiting Forces Act all service personnel are exempt from being tried in British courts if the offence 'arose out of and in the course of his duty'. This implies, for example, that an

American serviceman on guard duty who shot a British protestor would not be charged unless the United States authorities agreed. British police have to hand over Americans to United States military police who can charge the person or send them back to the United States. Off-duty offences are exempt if they involve only American property or only Americans are involved. And the Home Secretary confirmed in 1952 that any British civilian who failed to comply with a United States military subpoena to attend an American military court was liable to be jailed under the (British) Army and Air Force Acts.[81]

One area of intense speculation has been over the contingency plans for wartime agreed with the Reagan administration in the early eighties. The United States has negotiated agreements with the NATO 'host nations' to provide extra facilities for American forces in wartime. The agreement signed with West Germany in 1982 was published. By contrast, the British equivalent, which dates from the 1973 US–UK Lines of Communications Arrangement and was updated in 1983, has been kept secret – a factor resulting inevitably in speculation and official denials. It is thought that the plan would involve the huge logistical task of 100,000 Americans arriving at west coast ports and airports. A reserve division of 18,000 would arrive through Liverpool to be equipped from prepositioned stores at Burtonwood. The forces would be transported on to the continent via south and east coast ports such as Poole, Southampton, Felixstowe or Hull, using military and civilian transport facilities.[82] Rear Admiral Eugene Carroll, a former Director of Operations for United States European Command, has claimed that 'quotas' of British civilian labour are required under the plan.[83] MPs were told in March 1986 that 'the United Kingdom has agreed to take steps to try to ensure that its requirements for civilian manpower support are met. Detailed planning in support of the arrangements is classified.'[84] Ministers have acknowledged that civilian labour is needed for transport and casualty handling, and the electricity supply industry. According to official Pentagon reports, both the British and Americans have signed bilateral agreements with the Netherlands for the onward movement onto the continent.[85]

Under the plan for US–UK Lines of Communications Arrangement, the contingency plans are reviewed automatically every two years.[86] They have gone through several drafts and there are details on financial arrangements which have been the subject of intense negotiations with the Ministry of Defence in the early eighties, and thirty detailed technical understandings have been reached.[87]

One issue that has come under scrutiny is the plan for coping with casualties. There have been press reports that, in wartime, 40,000 NHS beds would be cleared to prepare for American casualties.[88] Ministers have revealed that there are plans for 'interim medical care for US military casualties in National Health Service hospitals'.[89] But in response to questions about the clearance of entire hospitals, they say: 'No United Kingdom Hospital is designated for the exclusive use by American military casualties.'[90] In Congressional testimony, American officials say that they have asked for 'extensive medical support', but a US Navy official has stated that 'the Government of Great Britain is not capable of providing the level of support for the numbers of estimated naval casualties that would be incurred in a European war'.[91]

The United States is building in Britain at least ten hospitals only for use in World War Three, with stockpiled equipment ready for use by medical teams flown in from America. They have taken over a number of redundant British hospitals and barracks. Most of the USAF's 500-bed hospitals are completed. The US Navy is building a 1,000-bed hospital at Kirknewton, and the Army is establishing a hospital at Winston barracks near Lanark, also in Scotland.[92]

Britain's secrecy about the wartime planning has provoked speculation about the scale of the operations, and the scale of American control. A leaked draft of the status of forces plan seemed to suggest that the American Commander would have unlimited powers including law and order.[93] But Lord Trefgarne, the Minister for Defence Procurement, told the House of Lords in May 1986 that 'there are no amendments to the US–UK agreement providing for American forces to quell disorder by British subjects.'[94]

The failure to publish or debate the British plan leads to understandable doubt and controversy, though in fact it is likely that under the Visiting Forces Act no extra powers are needed.[95]

The American anxiety about the Labour Party's defence policy is largely founded on concern about the future of its key installations in the United Kingdom. Not only are the bases in Britain crucial to NATO's conventional strength and to its strategy of nuclear deterrence, but they are also a key part of America's own defence system. Labour has never indicated that it would close all American bases in Britain; but the threat towards the nuclear bases alone was enough to ring alarm bells in Washington, and to contribute strongly to the kind of partisan interest in British politics seen in the past few years.

Furthermore, the extent of the United States defence network in the

United Kingdom is one reason why Britain remains of paramount importance to Washington. Although it should be emphasized that the military network in Britain is probably no more crucial than that in West Germany – it makes Britain an important ally as the staging post, but not the key ally.

It is extraordinary that the two countries have not agreed a formal structure for control of the bases. And it is still more surprising that there has been relatively little debate about the situation, particularly given the low opinion the British as a whole have had of American leadership in recent years. This lack of debate is probably largely due to ignorance. The average Briton certainly has little idea of the scale of the American military presence in Britain, and of the informal nature of Britain's control.

But the real significance of the American military presence in Britain is that it is another indicator of the fact that Britain, like her European allies, remains highly dependent on the United States for her defence.

7

☆☆★☆☆

THE EUROPEAN DIMENSION

A growing number of the American people feel abused by our allies.
They feel that we spend a much greater portion of our wealth on the
common defence; that we have too large a number of soldiers
stationed on their territory; and that the allies use the money they save
on defence to subsidise their trade, creating our enormous deficit.
While these perceptions may be overdrawn, they reflect a real and
profound public sentiment.

Representative Pat Schroeder[1]

THE defence of Britain has to be seen within the context of NATO,
which means looking at it from the European perspective. For the
United States, Britain is now just one of the European members of the
Western alliance, and not even the most important; this is West
Germany. Officials in Washington, while pointing this out, are anxious to
add that relations with Britain are the closest of all the NATO allies, not
just because of long-standing links and the language ties, but also
because of the increasing divisions within the alliance, with the growing
assertiveness of West Germany, and France's determination to maximize its independence. Britain has long been, in American eyes, a useful
means of influencing the other European allies, but successive British
Governments' reluctance to get wholeheartedly involved in defence or
economic co-operation within Europe has frequently been a source of
annoyance in Washington.

Britain's role in Europe is still being debated within the Government
nearly forty years after NATO's formation. The problems and solution
are seen from fundamentally different perspectives within Government
circles. For Mrs Thatcher, close American relations are vital, so the
issue is to avoid developing links within Europe which might annoy the
United States and be seen as undermining the relationship with
America, while still taking sufficient steps to persuade the Congress
that Europe is doing enough to defend itself. For those who are more
European orientated, such as Michael Heseltine the former Defence
Secretary, and to an increasing extent the Foreign Office, the task is to

develop European co-operation as a substitute for what will probably be
diminishing American involvement, without hastening the day that the
United States can feel it can leave Europe to fend for itself.

The problem is that the structure of NATO has scarcely evolved
since the early fifties from its original pattern of American orientation.
Up to half of the American defence budget, and a third-of-a-million
servicemen and women are directly committed to Europe. The sheer
scale of the contribution has preserved a strong American influence.
The Supreme Allied Commander Europe (SACEUR) is always a senior
member of the American command structure, and while the NATO
Secretary General is always a European, the political decision-making
process is American centred. This is because the key decisions NATO
has to make in the Nuclear Planning Group and other political committees are generally over the deployment of American nuclear weapons.
And the key working committees which look at the policy options, the
High Level Group and the Special Consultative Group, are chaired by
American officials, and their working staff are American.

The sheer scale of American involvement is increasingly questioned
on both sides of the Atlantic. For the United States, the question is
whether Europe is doing enough to help itself by building up its
non-nuclear forces to reduce the dependence on nuclear weapons, and
in the American conventional contribution. For Europe, Britain included, the problem is whether America will continue to commit its
troops to Europe, and above all, whether the American nuclear
guarantee is still valid. And underlying these issues is the question of
the extent of American political control, and in particular whether the
United States is prepared to devolve political power along with the
responsibility it wishes to share.

The current debates stem directly from the way alliance has evolved.
Since the late forties, America's hope has always been that Europe
would develop its own integrated defence under American tutelage.
United States administrations have frequently been more enthusiastic
over European co-operation than those in Europe themselves, particularly Britain. The aim of the European Recovery Plan, announced by the
American Secretary of State George Marshall in June 1947, was not just
to bail out the shattered European economies, but as he himself said, it
also had as 'ultimate objective closer integration of Western Europe'.[2]

Britain, then the strongest country in Europe, was concerned about
the risks in co-operating with politically unstable European countries as
a Cabinet committee warned in 1947.[3] The economies of France and

Italy were rapidly deteriorating, and there were fears about the role of
the Communist parties in both countries. But the Cabinet committee
concluded that Britain was strong enough to control bodies such as the
Organization of Economic Co-operation, which was to be the focus for
Marshall Aid. The Foreign Secretary Ernest Bevin also wanted an
American presence in continental Europe, which was something that
the United States was reluctant to have.

The Marshall Plan had indicated a major shift in American foreign
policy, that it was now willing to engage itself economically and
politically, in contrast to the policy of isolationism after the First World
War. Military involvement was another question. In Congress, the
'Great Debate' over the United States' role in the defence of Europe
was long drawn out, as a number of leading Senators were reluctant for
the United States to make a major commitment. At the ratification
hearings on the North Atlantic Treaty held by the Senate Foreign
Relations Committee in April 1949, Dean Acheson, the American
Secretary of State, assured the Committee that there was 'absolutely
no intention to send substantial number of American troops to Europe in
any eventuality short of war'.[4] Acheson says he made a mistake in
assuring one senior committee member Senator Hickenlooper, that the
answer to his question about substantial American troop involvement
was 'a clear and absolute "No" '. Acheson later wrote: 'Even as a
short-range predicition this answer was deplorably wrong. It was
almost equally stupid. But it was not intended to deceive.'[5]

The Truman administration was already practising the form of
diplomatic footwork between Congress and the Europeans that has
become a standard part of the repertoire of every subsequent administration, according to the Congressional analyst Stanley Sloan. This
involves reassuring the Europeans about the American commitment,
while at the same time, 'justifying to Congress the increasingly
expensive price-tag attached to the entangling alliance that NATO has
become'.[6]

A year after Acheson's assurances, the administration asked for
approval of a plan to appoint General Eisenhower as NATO's first
Supreme Allied Commander Europe and to dispatch four extra American Army divisions to Europe, making six in all. It had been precipitated
by the invasion of South Korea by North Korea in June 1950. It was
feared, as Chancellor Adenauer of West Germany put it, that 'Stalin has
the same plan for Europe as Korea'. The plan was approved as Senate
Resolution 99 in April 1951, which added a condition that 'the European

allies were making a realistic effort on behalf of European defence'.[7] President Truman made it clear that 'a basic element in the implementation of this decision is the degree to which our friends match our actions'.[8]

One way for the Americans to ensure their action was matched was to bring in the West Germans to provide the extra manpower and resources required. However, this was resisted by the French Government, because of their opposition to German rearmament. They wanted extra controls over the Germans. The French put up an alternative plan for a European Defence Community (EDC), which included proposals for a European Army, controlled by a European Defence Minister.[9] It would include all the German forces and a proportion of the French forces, and with possibly some British involvement. The Americans embraced the idea with enthusiasm; Secretary of State Acheson declared: 'The European Defence Community and NATO are completely interconnected. Neither is complete without the other.' But Acheson's vision of a partnership between America and Europe was rejected by the Europeans themselves. The British were reluctant to get involved. They saw no role for themselves in continental Europe, preferring a transatlantic relationship. Churchill called the idea a 'sludgy amalgam'.[10] He was prepared to act 'as a splendid godfather who took the French and Germans to the Altar', said Sir Frank Roberts, Private Secretary to the Foreign Secretary Sir Anthony Eden. But there was no question of direct British involvement.[11] This left the French in the position of having to control the Germans alone, a position which they didn't relish. There was also widespread public opposition in France to loss of full control of any of their forces, and when a vote was eventually taken in the French National Assembly in 1954, the EDC was rejected.

The collapse of the EDC had critical implications for NATO. It killed all prospect of developing an integrated European defence. While this may have been unrealistic, it had the added effect, says the Congressional analyst Stanley Sloan, of 'institutionalizing a political imbalance in the transatlantic alliance – a structural flaw which today poses the most serious challenge to NATO's continued political viability'.[12]

Even before the EDC finally collapsed, the British were preparing an alternative plan. The Foreign Secretary Sir Anthony Eden had had the first idea in the bath one Sunday morning.[13] They had to keep the ensuing plan secret to avoid annoying the Secretary of State in the new Republican administration, John Foster Dulles, who was an even more ardent supporter of the EDC than his predecessor, Acheson. The

British document was held in the safe of Eden's Private Secretary.[14] It proposed expanding the membership of the 1948 Brussels Treaty (France, Britain and the Benelux countries) to include Italy and West Germany to form the Western European Union (WEU). From Britain's point of view this had a vital advantage over the EDC; it involved no transfer of sovereignty, and it kept each member-country's armed forces separate, with their own equipment, individual defence ministries, and arms equipment industries. To achieve agreement to the plan at the London Conference in September 1954 after the collapse of the EDC, Britain had had to agree to keep four British Army divisions and a tactical air force in Germany. The Foreign Secretary Sir Anthony Eden called it a 'very formidable step for us to take. You know that ours is above all an island story. We are still an island people in thought and tradition.'[15] The plan was accepted, the occupation status of West Germany was lifted, solving the immediate problem of German rearmament, and West Germany entered NATO a year later. But the fragmentary nature of the alliance had been institutionalized.

The failure to integrate forces under the EDC and the fragmentary nature of NATO contributed to the dependence on nuclear weapons. While the debate over the EDC had been going on, growing fears about the Soviet Union's intentions at the height of the Cold War had led to a new assessment of the military strength of the Soviet Bloc. British and American intelligence estimated the Soviet Bloc's forces at 175 divisions, while NATO had about 45 divisions. According to General Andrew Goodpaster, who was on the Supreme Commander's staff, the estimates failed to take the difference in quality into account and he says it created 'a gap of our own making, a paper gap'. He recalled that the military were much less worried than the civilian planners and politicians. They felt that the West could put up quite an effective defence, particularly as the Soviets could not rely on Romanian or Polish divisions.[16] The issue of how to count the military strength of the Soviet Union and its allies has dogged NATO to this day.

At the NATO conference at Lisbon in February 1952 NATO set itself a target of increasing its forces by 1954 to ninety divisions, including reserves. The Korean War had put a major strain on the economies of France and Britain, which were both spending 10 per cent of their GNP on defence. A NATO Council meeting in 1953 reported that the NATO countries had increased spending three-and-a-half-fold since 1949.[17] And it soon became clear that it was impossible to meet the extra burden demanded by the Lisbon force goals. With the lessening of the tension following the end of the Korean War in July 1953, and Stalin's death a few months earlier, the situation seemed less threatening.

Within eighteen months of the Lisbon Conference, NATO abandoned its goals, and the United States went instead for a solution, which is still favoured to deal with political and military problems – the nuclear fix. This decision further reinforced Europe's reliance on the United States.

In October 1953 the American Government declared it would be prepared to use short-range theatre nuclear weapons in any major conflict in Europe. A year later, the United States went further, declaring it would use nuclear weapons to counter any form of aggression, conventional or otherwise. As John Foster Dulles explained: 'such weapons must now be treated as in fact having become conventional.'[18]

It was also relatively easy for the United States to adopt this concept. It had a large bomber force in Europe capable of dropping nuclear weapons on the Soviet Union, and had begun to deploy short-range nuclear weapons in large number in Europe. In contrast, the Soviet Union had no assured way of reaching the main targets on the United States' mainland with nuclear weapons. So it was possible for the United States to provide a nuclear guarantee effectively risk free. The proposal to adopt the 'New Look' nuclear strategy was presented to NATO's political committee, the North Atlantic Council, as a virtual *fait accompli*. It was enshrined in a NATO strategy document approved in December 1954, which provided for the use of nuclear weapons in 'massive retaliation' against a Soviet advance. It also accepted the use of short-range nuclear weapons within a battlefield. The idea of a contained nuclear war had been endorsed by President Eisenhower, who declared that 'the tactical use of atomic weapons against military targets would be no more likely to trigger off a big war than the use of twenty-ton "block-busters" '.[19] This decision allowed governments in Europe to maximize the level of resources put into economic development and social welfare policies. A NATO report argued nuclear weapons meant that troop levels on the Central Front could be cut to a third of the levels of 1951. All the weapons were American held; they included nuclear-capable artillery, and Corporal and Honest John short-range missiles. It wasn't until 1957 that it was agreed that American tactical nuclear systems would be provided to the European allies. The British Army on the Rhine received its first American warheads for Corporal missiles in 1959 and 1960, and some of the other European allies got American nuclear capable systems thereafter.[20] Then, as now, the allies' warheads were stored and controlled by the Americans.

Britain had endorsed the new strategy – even before the United States – in a Global Strategy Paper in 1952 which foreshadowed the ideas in the 'New Look' plan. Britain was developing its own nuclear deterrent. The British Army on the Rhine had been trained to fight a nuclear war by 1958, well before they were fully equipped with nuclear weapons. And, in the 1957 Defence White Paper, cuts in conventional forces were explicitly linked to nuclear deterrence.[21] The White Paper proposed cutting British forces in West Germany, and provoked much criticism from other members of NATO.

Britain's acceptance of a defence strategy reliant on nuclear weapons added to the sense of fatalism among NATO members about the prospect of providing an effective non-nuclear defence for Europe. The NATO Governments felt there was no alternative to the American nuclear guarantee, and by 1961, 3,500 American theatre nuclear weapons had been deployed in Europe.

But that fatalism was increasingly under challenge during the late fifties, and the concept of massive retaliation enshrined in the New Look strategy was being questioned. Leading defence analysts, such as Dr Henry Kissinger, and Denis Healey in Britain, attempted to develop coherent strategies for the use of tactical weapons in a limited nuclear war. But these were short-lived – estimates in 1955 suggested up to five million Germans would be killed or wounded in a nuclear battle.[22]

A strong anti-nuclear movement built up in West Germany, and the Campaign for Nuclear Disarmament (CND) became a significant force in Britain. At the same time, in the United States, the development of a Soviet long-range bomber in 1954, and the first medium-range missiles in 1958 and the launch of the Sputnik in 1957 had challenged the assumptions that the United States had relative immunity. If the Russians could launch Sputnik, it would not be long before they could develop long-range missiles that could reach the American mainland, as a response to an American use of nuclear weapons. Although the documents provided by the spy Oleg Penkovsky showed British and American intelligence analysts that Soviets were having problems developing their missile technology, the potential Soviet capability had a direct impact on American thinking. The claim of a Soviet missile advantage had been a major factor in John Kennedy's presidential election campaign in 1960. Robert McNamara, the Defence Secretary in the Kennedy administration, abandoned the idea of a gap, but he agreed that the New Look strategy had to be replaced.

General Maxwell D. Taylor, the United States Army Chief of Staff, had called in 1959 for a strategy he termed 'flexible response', which involved conventional forces large enough to meet a Soviet conventional advance, with nuclear weapons only being used at a late stage. This was attractive to McNamara, whose deputy Roswell Gilpatric confessed he had 'never believed in a so called limited nuclear war. I just don't know how you build a limit into it once you start using any kind of nuclear bang.'[23] And if there was no such thing as a limited war, it meant the United States itself would become directly involved in an unwinable nuclear war in response even to a conventional attack in Europe. This became known in the early sixties as MAD – mutual assured destruction.

This was comforting for the Europeans, particularly for the West German Government, as it meant that the United States was directly tied into the defence of Europe. It seemed to guarantee that a war in Europe would never happen because of the consequences. The tactical weapons in Europe acted as a 'tripwire' to America's own nuclear forces. But it was scarcely comforting for the Kennedy administration. Robert McNamara made a speech to NATO foreign and defence ministers in Athens in May 1962, which was described by an American analyst as 'unprecedented in candour, unusually blunt in its argument and coldly logical in its structure'.[24] The British Prime Minister Harold Macmillan thought the speech was put forward with 'equal vigour and clumsiness'.[25] McNamara declared that Washington was not prepared to use its nuclear forces in Europe in response to a Warsaw Pact conventional attack as a trigger to nuclear war. As McNamara had described it himself: 'We in effect proposed confining nuclear weapons to only two roles in a NATO context: deterring the Soviets' initiation of a nuclear war, and as a weapon of last resort.'[26] In other words, he proposed raising the threshold when nuclear weapons would be used. McNamara's 'cold logic' meant that the European allies would have to build up their conventional forces. 'You can't imagine the depth of feeling and acrimony that developed,' he recalls.[27]

Over the next five years the European allies consistently rejected the logical consequence of the strategy as outlined by General Taylor: increases in conventional forces. Taylor argued that the only way to provide a credible defence against a conventional defence was to build up non-nuclear defences. McNamara later conceded that 'the substantial raising of the nuclear threshold as was envisaged when "flexible response" was first conceived, has not become a reality'.[28]

This failure to increase the European conventional forces contributed to misgivings in Washington over continuing the American presence in Europe.

The West Germans were worried about the economic strains of any conventional build-up, and they also feared it would decouple America from Europe by removing the certainty that American strategic nuclear weapons were tied into the defence of Europe. It also contributed to the French withdrawal from NATO's command structure in 1967, and de Gaulle felt that McNamara had confirmed his suspicions about American unreliability. The Germans, because of their position as the central front, had no chance of opting out, but their growing economic power made them the most important European member of NATO, and their views were becoming more forceful.

Britain, which was going through another period of defence cuts under the Wilson Government, did not want any increase in conventional forces, and adopted the role of intermediary between Washington and Bonn. Sir Arthur Hockaday, a senior official at the Ministry of Defence, was the chairman of the NATO Working Group, which devised the document number 14/3 that became known as flexible response. This is full of phrases associated with a political compromise; it described the strategy as being 'based upon a flexible and balanced range of appropriate responses conventional and nuclear to all levels of aggression'. As Sir Arthur puts it: 'One of its great merits in terms of getting the new strategy accepted at the time was that it was so flexible that anybody could interpret it in almost any way he so wished. In a sense that is one of its defects.'[29] But it was calculated ambiguity. This ambiguity is often said to be the best way of keeping the Warsaw Pact guessing about what the West would do if attacked. But Simon Lunn, a British analyst, puts it more directly: 'This ambiguity permitted the accommodation of conflicting American and European interests, but it did not represent their reconciliation.'[30] But Sir Arthur Hockaday justified this, saying that NATO's strategy 'was so delicately constructed as a bureaucratic construction, it was rather like a wasps' nest; you poke your finger a bit and the whole thing might crumble.'[31] But the compromise left problems in store for NATO in future.

Flexible response remains NATO strategy today. But the acrimonious debate had left lingering doubts both in Europe and the United States over the American contribution to the defence of its allies. These doubts in America were further exacerbated by the unwillingness of the Europeans to co-operate in the way the Kennedy administration had wanted. Kennedy had made a 'Declaration of Interdependence' on 4 July 1962, Independence Day, but one which still envisaged a strong American influence over the conduct of the alliance.

Implicit in the concept of flexible response, with its idea of carefully calculated responses at a series of levels, was the need of a centrally controlled strategy with the lowest appropriate level of force used at each stage. Those within the administration strongly advocating a strong European dimension were also pushing for nuclear weapons to be kept under American control, and had opposed the transfer of American weapons to European allies, notably Britain and France. At issue for both Britain and France was the question of their own independent nuclear deterrent. The British Prime Minister Harold Macmillan persuaded President Kennedy at Nassau in the Bahamas in December 1962 to sell American Polaris nuclear missiles, to the dismay of the Europeanists in the administration. Not only did they object to duplication of effort, they also believed that it discouraged Britain from taking steps towards European co-operation. As Under Secretary of State, George Ball saw it, the Nassau Conference 'encouraged Britain in the belief that she could by her own efforts, so long as she maintained a specially favoured position with the United States, play an independent great power role, and thus it deflected her from coming to terms with her European destiny'.[32]

As part of the deal at Nassau, the Americans had floated the idea of British Polaris missiles becoming part of a Multilateral Force (MLF): twenty-five ships with eight Polaris missiles each with a multi-nation European crew under the control of an American, NATO's Supreme Commander in Europe. It was thwarted by French outright opposition, British reluctance, and a lack of will in Washington.

The Nassau agreement had confirmed to de Gaulle his view of the British as being dependent on the United States. He had himself turned down an offer of Polaris missiles, choosing to develop the French nuclear weapons separately. Within weeks of the Nassau Conference, de Gaulle announced his veto of the British entry to join the Common Market at a carefully staged press conference. He also announced his rejection of the MLF and the American offer of Polaris. Within a further six months he had withdrawn the French Atlantic fleet from NATO and thus beginning the process leading to France's withdrawal from NATO's command structure.[33] The only advance in European co-operation was the Franco–German Treaty in 1963, in which France formalized its rapprochement with West Germany, which de Gaulle believed would provide France with an alternative source of strength to the Atlantic Connection.

NATO did reach a consensus over one question – relations with the Soviet Union. Following a report by the senior Belgian politician Pierre Harmel, NATO leaders agreed that the alliance should also pursue détente. However, the lessening of tensions had an impact on alliance relations.

The failure to develop wider European economic and defence co-operation and the watering down of the original flexible response strategy left the NATO alliance still dependent on the American nuclear guarantee, and left the guarantors more and more certain they were being taken for a ride.

There were growing pressures on Europe to spend more on its own defence. A report by the Senate Foreign Relations Committee in 1963 asked: 'Is it not unreasonable to insist that the continuance of the present costly level of our military commitment in Western Europe be contingent upon a substantial increase in the Western European commitment to NATO.'[34]

By 1966 the issue was becoming the subject of increasing debates in Congress. Senator Mike Mansfield, the Senate Majority Leader, felt that European economic recovery made its continuing dependency on the United States unnecessary, and so he introduced legislation calling for a reduction of American forces in Europe. He also hoped that the prospect of troop cuts would push Europe into developing the 'twin pillar'. A number of factors had contributed to Mansfield's dissatisfaction. He believed that the United States was over-extended, embroiled as it was in the Vietnam War, a war of which the allies made no secret of their misgivings. Another bone of contention was the growing number of trade disputes with the Common Market.[35] The lessening of East-West tension as détente with the Soviet Union got underway, and the ongoing arms control negotiations, also meant that Mansfield and his supporters felt that Europe didn't need as much protection from the Soviets as it once did. Mansfield's amendments declared: 'The present policy of maintaining large contingents of United States forces, and their dependents on the European continent, also contributes further to the fiscal and monetary problems of the United States.' Although all the Mansfield amendments from 1966 to 1974 were defeated, they left a lasting impact.

The Nixon, Ford and Carter administrations all made efforts for Europe to become more self reliant without wanting any change in the political relationship. At the time that Britain eventually joined the Common Market, with Edward Heath as Britain's first staunchly pro-European Prime Minister, the Nixon administration attempted to make the Europeans toe the line. Henry Kissinger's Year of Europe speech in April 1973, launched inappropriately from New York, made clear the difference in interests. He declared that the United States had 'global interests and responsibilities' while 'our European allies have regional interests'. Kissinger was clear that a more united Europe would be more likely to challenge American dominance of the alliance, and he wanted to forestall the challenge. Kissinger's speech was received unenthusiastically in Europe. The French President Georges Pompidou told him sarcastically: 'For Europeans every year is the year of Europe.'[36] The tensions were highlighted over the 1973 Middle East war, when Edward Heath refused to allow the use of British bases for the American resupply of Israel, and the United States only informed Britain and the other allies of a nuclear alert after it had been called. President Nixon warned the allies, it was time to 'sit down and determine that we are either going to go along together on both the security, economic or political front, or we go separately'.[37]

The Europeans were also developing doubts about the American commitment to Europe. In the mid-seventies, the West Germans, and the new British Labour Government were particularly concerned about the continued validity of the American nuclear guarantee. Although flexible response remains NATO strategy, the strategy of extended nuclear deterrence has never totally reassured the European allies of the American commitment to their defence. It has been called by one leading British commentator Lawrence Freedman, 'an inadequate con-ventional defence, backed by an incredible nuclear guarantee'.[37] The remarks by a number of American politicians, from the time of McNamara, had precipitated fears that with the continuing build-up of Soviet nuclear weapons, it was becoming unrealistic to expect the use of American long-range nuclear weapons for the defence of Europe. In 1971 President Nixon had asked: 'Should a President in the event of a nuclear attack be left with the single option of ordering the mass destruction of enemy civilians in the certainty that it would be followed by mass slaughter of Americans?' Henry Kissinger made the point publically in a speech in Brussels in 1979: 'Our European allies should not keep asking us to multiply strategic assurances we cannot possibly mean or, if we do mean, we should not want to execute because, if we execute, we wish the destruction of civilization.'[38]

In the late 1970s these doubts about America's nuclear commitment also came out into the open. The West German Chancellor Helmut Schmidt argued in a famous speech in London in 1977 that the forthcoming Strategic Arms Limitation Treaty (SALT 2), by regulating a rough parity between the two superpowers' long-range nuclear arsenals, effectively neutralized their strategic nuclear capabilities, thus undermining the American nuclear guarantee.

The Carter administration was at first reluctant to take any measures to allay the European fears, partly because of furious rows with Schmidt over whether to deploy a new short-range warhead known as the neutron bomb. But once set a problem, the high-level committees within NATO attempted to find a solution. The answer: another technological fix – ground-launched Cruise and Pershing 2 missiles in Europe, which could reach the west of the Soviet Union, and which, it was thought, would visibly link American nuclear weapons to the defence of Europe. But, to many ordinary people in Western Europe, the decision by NATO Governments in December 1979 to go ahead with deployment of 572 Cruise and Pershing 2 missiles seemed to increase the nuclear threat to Europe, as the new missiles seemed more usable than the other nuclear weapons in Europe. The heightened tensions after the Soviet invasion of Afghanistan on 27 December 1979, and the election in November 1980 of Ronald Reagan to the White House – in his most combative phase during the election campaign and then as President – added to the sense of European insecurity. These doubts went far beyond the peace movements, as opinion polls suggested a majority of people were against Cruise deployment, and in 1982 there were huge demonstrations from the peace movements throughout Europe. But despite the public pressure, NATO Governments continued to deploy the missiles in five countries.

Public disquiet receded with the mellowing of Reagan's rhetoric, and Mikhail Gorbachev's acceptance of the American 'zero option' proposal to remove the Cruise and Pershing 2 missiles if the Soviet Union removed its SS20 missiles led to the signing of the INF Treaty in December 1987. While trumpeting the Treaty as proof that a resolute approach had brought Soviet concessions, in private, many within the nuclear elite were apprehensive. They believe the removal of the missiles will take away an important linkage between Europe and the United States' nuclear deterrent.

The proposal to update the short-range nuclear arsenal and build up medium-range nuclear systems not covered by the Treaty is intended to allay some of those fears. But in West Germany it has caused even greater problems across the political spectrum. The new short-range weapons are designed for use on the central front, which inevitably means the two Germanies. With the slogan 'the shorter the range, the deader the Germans' a West German spokesman had highlighted the German dilemma. Opposition has come from the right and left in West Germany to the modernization plan, and the centre right Coalition Government has been at pains to slow down any formal announcement of the deployment of new systems on its soil. The debate has highlighted the lack of consensus on the use of the 4,000 short-range weapons in Europe, since the abandonment of New Look policies, and concepts of limited nuclear war. It is not clear how they would be used as part of a graduated nuclear response. Their function has always been to counterbalance the perceived Warsaw Pact numerical advantage in conventional forces.

Coinciding with German angst about modernizing short-range nuclear weapons, came a semi-official report from a Pentagon Commission apparently advocating the selective use of nuclear weapons – not, said the report, 'as a link to a wider and more devastating war' as in current strategy, but 'as an instrument for denying success to the invading Soviet forces'.[39] This section of the report, 'Discriminate Deterrence', by a group of veteran American strategic analysts, including Dr Henry Kissinger and Dr Zbigniew Brzezinski, was immediately repudiated by the Pentagon, but not before it had caused a stir in Europe, particularly West Germany. The report's advocacy of selective nuclear strikes, tactical as well as long-range, reawakened fears of a limited nuclear war. The authors' defence that they were attempting to make deterrence credible by making the use of short-range nuclear weapons more plausible, cut across European Governments' preference for a nuclear weapons strategy that balanced logic and credibility against the risk of heightening public fears. As one American commentator put it: 'In Europe the people who make nuclear decisions know what they want. They think nuclear weapons are fine. They like them the way they are. They like politically unusable nuclear weapons. Those, they say are the best kind.'[40]

The biggest potential rift came over President Reagan's willingness to trade away American nuclear missiles at the Reykjavik Summit in October 1986. Without any consultation, the President seemed willing to give up the very weapons that were supposed to guarantee Europe's security. The Summit only foundered over Reagan's determination not to make any concessions over his vision of a 'Star Wars' missile defence – a technology indeed that might protect America but not necessarily Europe. The outrage it caused among European Governments was partially assuaged by Mrs Thatcher's hasty visit to Camp David when she persuaded the President into agreeing a communique that papered over the crisis and reaffirmed nuclear deterrence. It was the second rescue performed by Mrs Thatcher at Camp David; a year earlier, by making full use of her personal relationship, she had got the President to agree to a formula that apparently toned down the plans for deployment and testing of a 'Star Wars' Strategic Defence Initiative.

President Reagan's announcement of his Strategic Defence Initiative in 1983 highlighted his doubts over the morality of nuclear deterrence as a means of defence, and the unease in the United States that its territory had become exposed to nuclear devastation since the Soviets had built up their nuclear arsenal. It raised long-standing doubts in Europe about the nuclear guarantee, especially if, as it first seemed, the United States – but not Europe – might have a shield against nuclear weapons. The subsequent scaling down of the 'Star Wars' plan has allayed fears in Europe. But the trauma over Reykjavik has not been easily forgotten by European Governments. As one West German official put it: 'We are in a post-Reykjavik world which implies much more danger.'[41]

The nuclear guarantee is only one of the areas of recent disagreements between Europe and the United States. The crisis, over Europe's determination to push ahead with co-operation with the Soviet Union in the project to pipe gas from Siberia to Europe, is just one of a number of trade issues involving technology exports and co-operation that have bedevilled relations. Differences of perspective over, for example, the Libyan raid (backed only by Britain), or over the Middle East, where the European Community (EC) has attempted alternative policies, have sometimes led to open clashes. There are often competing interests: Western Europe, because of its proximity to the Soviet Union, sees the need to build up trade relations. For the United States the situation is much more adversarial. The tendency of the Reagan adminstration to see nearly all international issues as symptoms of East-West tensions, resulted in radically different perspectives, as Europe has tended to take a more pragmatic view. The American offer to escort Kuwaiti oil tankers through the Gulf in 1987 was precipitated by earlier Soviet offers of help to Kuwait. Fear of American backlash if they did nothing, prompted five European Governments to send minesweepers as a group after the American operation plunged into near disaster when an American-flagged tanker hit a mine.

Doubts in Europe about American leadership are widespread. As a senior French foreign ministry official has put it: 'The Western alliance is in a situation comparable with that of the Catholic Church before the Second Vatican. We are there in all our glory but the number of our believers is going down. The liturgy is becoming obsolete. And the authority of the Pope is being challenged.'[42]

But the real pressure for a reduction of the American presence in Europe comes not from Europe, but from the resurgence of unilateralism in the United States. The cost of the American contribution of a third-of-a-million men and women in Europe, and reinforcements in the United States, large numbers of aircraft and tanks, as well as nuclear weapons, has come under intense scrutiny. A range of estimates on the cost of the contribution to NATO put it at between 45 and 60 per cent of the defence budget of $300 billion. If Japan is included, the cost has been put by one leading Congressional critic at $171 billion. It is impossible to make a precise estimate.[43]

While the United States was prepared to pay the costs when Europe was economically devastated, it is now raising increasingly the point originally raised by Senator Mansfield; that Europe is not paying a fair share for its defence. The United States spends 6.7 per cent of its wealth or Gross National Product on defence, averaging $1,150 per person, while the Europe average is 3.3 per cent; West Germany is only paying 3.1 per cent or $453 per capita, while Britain is one of the highest spenders, at 5 per cent of GNP, or $488 per capita. Japan is the principal target, since it only spents 1 per cent of GNP.[44]

To American eyes, the United States with 240 million people is supporting 366 million Europeans within NATO countries, which together have a GNP almost as large as the United States.

The current round of criticism was sparked off by the failure of the allies to increase defence spending by 3 per cent a year, as agreed in 1978, and also by the way the existing resources are being spent. This has in particular infuriated the most influential Senator on defence issues, Sam Nunn. He has targeted the failure to develop a coherent non-nuclear defence. He said it's 'absolute foolishness to continue to have a very large part of our military budget going to reinforce NATO from the United States in a crisis if the forces get to Europe at a point when the Europeans are given out of ammunition.' 'At that stage,' he says, 'you either go nuclear, you negotiate peace or you surrender.'[45]

He warns against any assumption that American troops currently in Europe are 'nothing more than a tripwire to our nuclear power'. If that happens, Nunn warns, 'it seems to me that the number of those forces is not very relevant'.[46]

In 1984 Senator Nunn and fellow-Democrat Senator William Roth proposed an amendment to remove 90,000 troops from Europe unless NATO improved its capability for conventional defence. They said that the allies had to take steps over five years to ensure NATO had enough ammunition to fight for thirty days, and to make other improvements. The amendment declared that NATO must 'lengthen the time period that Western Europe can be defended adequately by conventional forces without the necessity of resorting to the early use of nuclear weapons in the event of a non-nuclear attack'.[47] Senator Nunn defended himself against charges of being an isolationist, saying his amendment 'is not a petition for divorce . . . This is a petition for the alliance to carry out its vows that have been made over and over but have since not been carried out.'[48] The punitive part of the amendment was narrowly rejected, but, like the Mansfield amendments of the 1960s, it has had a considerable influence on Congressional thinking. Senator Nunn, now the chairman of the all-powerful Senate Armed Services Committee, has been the proponent of further legislation which has pushed for improved co-operation in buying and making military equipment to develop a coherent non-nuclear defence.

Senator Nunn's criticisms go to the heart of the failure to develop the conventional side of Flexible Response strategy. Senator Nunn believes that: 'If you told the people of Europe that in the first few days of a war, NATO – because of not having sufficient conventional forces in the right places – is going to have to use nuclear weapons before the Soviet Union and Warsaw Pact use them, in other words we're going to have to initiate a nuclear war in order to defend ourselves, I think you'd probably get four-or-five to one rejection of that. But nobody tells them that. We're all hiding behind symbols like the American troops.'[49]

Pressure for troop cuts has been growing within Congress, and there are parallels with the situation in the time of the Mansfield amendments in the late 1960s and 1970s; superpower tensions have diminished but yet trade disputes with Europe are increasing, and the rise in United States military spending has caused major economic problems. The budget deficit for 1987 was $150 billion, and the national debt stands at a staggering $2 trillion.[50] If spending is to be brought into line, agonizing negotiations are required between Congress and the administration

over budget cuts. The whole question of burdens has become a major
political issue in 1988. Already there have been calls for cuts in troop
numbers.

The leading campaigner for a fairer sharing of the burden is Representative Pat Schroeder, who has chaired a special panel on the issue
for the House of Representatives Armed Service Committee. She
views the issues in stark terms, and the panel attacked administration
officials for attempting to defend 'some pretty dismal figures'. She has
long seen this as a major political issue and predicted: 'The next
President will have to come to terms with the fact we are not stuck in
the 1950s.'[51] In the 1988 presidential campaign, George Bush pledged:
'We must ensure that they carry their fair share of the loan.' Michael
Dukakis warned: 'The allies must do more to bear their fair share.'[52]

A significant reduction in the size of American contributions to
Europe appears inevitable – and the only question that remains is when.
The leading British analyst of Congress and United States troops Phil
Williams says that 'all that is required for the emergence of a serious
congressional campaign for troop reductions is the emergence of a
senior figure prepared to pursue the issue and weld the various groups
into an effective coalition'.[53]

Although there is no such figure at present, as Sam Nunn's proposals
have been specifically tied to improvements in conventional forces. But
what makes the current situation different from earlier phases, is that
pressures are also coming from outside Congress.

The Defence Secretary Frank Carlucci announced cuts in planned
spending of $33 billion in February 1988. One of Carlucci's predeces-
sors, Harold Brown, has said that 'what Carlucci cut is just tiny
compared to what will have to be done'. Carlucci himself has estimated
that he and his successors will have to cut $200 billion to $300 billion of
planned expenditure over the next five years. That is equivalent to the
total defence budget for a single year. Carlucci's figures assume that
Congress allows spending to rise at 2 per cent above inflation. And he
says that even with this rise, it would involve a 'very intense major
reorganization of the defence programme'. Carlucci's plans may under-
estimate the scale of the problem since real increases in expenditure
will not be acceptable to many members of Congress. According to Les
Aspin, the Chairman of the House of Representatives Armed Services
Committee, the cut in the defence budget will be nearer $422 billion
over five years.[54] Under the Gramm–Rudman legislation, cuts in
planned spending are mandatory to cut the budget deficit.

So the major tasks of Defence Secretaries from now on will be to decide how to spread the cuts. It is unlikely that Europe will be spared.

The budget deficit is only one of two major problems affecting the American economy. The trade deficit is the second, and the American contribution to NATO has been attacked as a contributory factory, being effectively 'a subsidy to European industry', claims Professor Melvyn Krauss in his book *How NATO weakens the West*. As a result of 'freeloading', says Krauss, Europe can spend less on defence so 'it has had extra resources to develop highly efficient industries which can outcompete American industry'.[55] Not only that: European industry's keenness to sell high technology goods to the Eastern Bloc regardless of American wishes, only improves the defence capability of the Warsaw Pact, and adds to the United States costs.

The United States' economic problems have a direct impact on the economies of Europe. The instability, highlighted in the stock market crash of October 1987, and the collapse of the dollar in 1988, and the long-standing inflow of foreign capital to finance the United States' deficit, mean that 'a kind of systematic justice permits the United States to manipulate the world monetary system so the rich allies pay at least indirectly the costs of their own defence', says David Calleo, a long-time observer of alliance relations.

However, such a system is very inefficient economically, and the burden it puts on the world economy is severe. As a result, says Calleo, 'the NATO relationship, central to post-war structures has gradually become a critical mechanism for its disintegration'.

David Calleo argues that America is still attempting to act as if it is as powerful as it was in 1945. He says 'under NATO's present arrangements, the Europeans have been militarily underdeveloped while the United States has been militarily overextended'.[56] He believes the fundamental challenge to American foreign policy had been the relative decline of American power in relation to the rest of the world, and that the attempt by the United States to regain its old supremacy under Reagan appears 'more and more self defeating'.[57]

This theme has been taken up by a British-born Professor at Yale, Paul Kennedy, in a book which had a great deal of impact at the start of the 1988 presidential campaign. Kennedy believes the United States is facing the same choice as Britain faced in 1900: what he calls the 'imperial overstretch'. Professor Kennedy says: 'Decision-makers in Washington must face the awkward and enduring fact that the sum total of the United States' global interests and obligations are nowadays far larger than the country's power to defend them.'[58] Although it may be going too far to make too close a parallel with Victorian Britain, and Kennedy says nothing is inevitable, it seems true that however well the American economy performs, the United States will decline relatively as other economies develop. This fact will undoubtedly have a direct impact on the transatlantic relationship.

The United States is focusing on areas outside Europe where it does more and more of its trade. Trade with Japan and the rest of Asia has risen dramatically in recent years while trade with Europe has declined. Slowly, the United States is becoming more orientated towards the Pacific rather than the Atlantic. Many American neo-conservatives believe the United States should reconfigure its force so it can be more effective in the Third World, where they believe Soviet Bloc activity is not being challenged adequately. The fact that European Governments have been so critical of such actions – for example in Central America or the invasion of Grenada – reinforces the conservatives desire to cut the costs of European contribution.

A debate has raged over the apparent decline in American power. The Carter and Reagan administrations' crises over Iran have highlighted American frustration that the United States is no longer as powerful as it was in the immediate post-war era. President Reagan's attempts to show that America can 'walk tall', to conceal the relative decline in dramatic gestures such as the Libyan raid or Grenada invasion, have been very popular at home. But the impact of the defence build-up in strengthening the United States' position in the world has been more than offset by the weakening of the economy.

The burden-sharing debate is being fostered by those whose interests do not normally coalesce: liberal Democrats and neo-Conservatives.

This represents a reaction to the perceived decline of American power. It is a development from the Reagan administration's policy of pretending that the relative decline hasn't happened. This time it is said to be the fault of others. The myth is being perpetuated that only if America cuts its European contribution will it then have restored its position.

Although there is little doubt that the American commitment has allowed Europe to depend on the United States, it is also true that it has provided considerable advantages for the United States. As Charles Krauthammer, the American political analyst sees it: 'We pay our money, we get our Empire: a front-line 4,000 miles from home, access to the world's most advanced economies, and control of the most coveted real estate on the globe. Empire has its costs. It may not be worth the price. But it is hardly forced on America by foreigners.'[59]

The mounting pressure for troop cuts is recognized by officials in London, Bonn, and Brussels. Limited troop cuts, they say, do not necessarily make a major impact on West-European defence capability. The numbers have gone up and down over the years. The political impact depends on the way the cuts are made. When the INF Treaty was being negotiated, the Reagan administration tried to reassure European Governments worried about the potential loss of the missiles by saying that America's real commitment was not missiles but flesh and blood – the United States forces in Europe. They have become a political symbol. The political consequences will depend on how reductions are made. If they come as a result of a Congressional Resolution demanding punitive cuts as the shock to wake up the Europeans, demanded by some, the political impact will be severe. If, however, they were the product of negotiations within the alliance, or as a result of arms control talks, the impact is much less.

The NATO European Governments believe they have a case. They point out that as a group Europe spends $110 billion – a third higher in real terms than in 1971 – and provide 90 per cent of the manpower, and 85 per cent of the tanks and 80 per cent of the aircraft in peacetime. After allowing for American reinforcements in a crisis, 60 per cent of the ground forces and half of the air forces would be European.[60] But the European allies accept that greater co-operation is essential, firstly to forestall punitive action, and also so that they are in a position to substitute for any American withdrawal.

Since 1970 a gradual process of procurement co-operation and standardization has been under way with the establishment of the Eurogroup. The process, which is central to the development of European procurement co-ordination, is described fully in following Chapters.

Attempts to integrate ground forces have moved more slowly. The most progress has been made by the West Germans and the French (who are not in the overall command structures). In September 1987, 20,000 French troops trained in a joint exercise called 'Bold Sparrow' in West Germany. Since then a mixed Franco–German brigade of 4,000 soldiers is being set up in the south of West Germany. Although the numbers are small, the Germans regard it as the best way of increasing French involvement in NATO. But Mrs Thatcher made it clear she believes Franco–German co-operation could create sub-structures which could undermine NATO. This is hardly surprising. Franco-German co-operation has been seen by the French, at least, as an alternative to Atlantic links, which is anathema to Mrs Thatcher. However, the Franco–German co-operation has been generally welcomed in Washington. A working party chaired by Senator William Roth, and including Senator Sam Nunn, for the North Atlantic Assembly, proposed in May 1988 that a European Division, built on the basis of the Franco–German brigade, should be established. The Division should be the nucleus for 'more extensive joint European forces', and the report stresses 'the active involvement of Great Britain in the future evolution of European Defence co-operation is essential politically and militarily'.[61]

The report also called for an annual European security assessment. This issue is the toughest for the European members of NATO to determine. NATO's current strategy dates back to the decision to rely on nuclear weapons in the early fifties based on a worst-case assessment of the Soviet threat. NATO now faces a similar period of decision. It has to consider not just the size of the Warsaw Pact forces but make an assessment of the nature of the Soviet Union's intentions. Official Western figures have traditionally attributed to the Warsaw Pact a large advantage in conventional forces. Under Stalin, and then Khrushchev with his threat to 'bury' the West, the situation seemed clear.

Now is it much less certain. It is undeniable that Mikhail Gorbachev's arms control initiatives have led to a lessening of tensions. No-one could have predicted the sheer scale of Soviet–American rapprochement since 1985. However, opinions are still divided about the extent to which Mr Gorbachev's many peace overtures will be translated into action. This reflects not only doubts about Gorbachev's intentions, but also the uncertainty about his ability to carry through policies for the long-term.

It is also unclear how the growing instability in Eastern Europe seen in 1988 will affect East–West relations. Zbigniew Brzezinski, President Carter's National Security Adviser, has described Eastern Europe as being in a 'pre-revolutionary state'. While that may be going too far, there is no doubt that sustained unrest in any of the countries followed by repressive counter-measures would have a major impact on East–West relations, because of the rising expectations.

The Moscow Summit in May 1988 at which Gorbachev repudiated Khrushchev's threat to 'bury' the West, and Reagan withdrew his 'evil empire' epithet while walking with Gorbachev in Red Square in Moscow, radically changed the rhetoric of Superpower relations. While voices such as that of Frank Carlucci were soon heard calling for caution, at the time of the Summit it seemed that the perception of the threat might change significantly.

Although it will take some years for the new talks on conventional weapons to reach fruition, the prospects of large-scale reductions have never been better. The talks could lead to cuts in the numerical imbalances perceived by both sides. This would transform the debate within the West from the question of burden sharing to a question of whether such a large burden need be carried at all. If it were possible to negotiate away the imbalances, and agree a balance at a lower level, then it is possible too that the European members of NATO could sustain such a force level on their own without American involvement. This could involve a cut in defence spending, or more likely, bring the extra costs of raising the nuclear threshold out of the realm of impossibility. And the question that would be raised within Congress in such a climate is whether American military support was really necessary for Europe. It would also transform the relationship with the United States, and it would result in a much weaker relationship within the alliance.

One of the asymmetries that will have to be considered is that of military doctrines. NATO's doctrine is defensive, with selective strikes planned only to hit an attacker's supply lines. The Warsaw Pact doctrine is defensive in intention, but offensive in capability. But Soviet spokesmen are talking of concepts of 'sufficient defence' or 'reasonable sufficiency'. What exactly they mean is not fully clear, but implicit is the idea of major cuts on the basis of overtly defensive strategies, including the existing Soviet proposal for zones free of offensive weapons along the East–West border and the limiting of certain weapons, such as tactical nuclear weapons. Such ideas are only a step away from some of the ideas for alternative defence strategies that have been put forward by the Left within Europe for a number of years.[62]

This is something conservative Western European governments would find difficulty in accepting at present. In the view of Stephen Shenfield, a British specialist on new Russian defence thinking: 'Perhaps it is the fear of uncontrollable political change which in part explains both the dogged resistance that the new thinking is evidently meeting in the USSR and the deep unease with which the Western élite are reacting to the shifts in Soviet Policy.'[63]

But it is not just doubt over political change that could lead to a more cautious assessment of conventional balance. Regardless of conventional cuts that might be achieved in the long run, NATO will have to modernize its conventional forces, to keep them up to date and to raise the nuclear threshold from its current dangerously low level. But these goals will not be easy to achieve; extra American resources won't be forthcoming, and nearly all the European allies' defence budgets are not projected to increase in real terms. The demographic situation in West Germany means that there will be a growing shortage of manpower. And highly sophisticated weapons often touted as a technological solution would place an added economic burden. So greater co-operation is essential to maximize existing resources. As well as moves towards an integrated weapons procurement system to improve conventional forces, proposals are being made to co-ordinate Anglo-French nuclear systems. Co-operation on a new stand-off missile to be fired from aircraft has been slow. As ever, the British have been torn between the idea of co-operation with their traditional friends in America, or changing the habits of two generations, and doing it jointly with the French. Suggestions for common patrolling of nuclear-missile submarines have been treated with scepticism by the French, who are determined to maintain their independence. But the French have hinted that their nuclear protection might be extended to include West Germany.

Suggestions for a European nuclear deterrent based on the French and British systems have been made. Sir James Eberle, the Director of the Royal Institute of International Affairs in London, believes: 'If we are going to keep a nuclear programme going in Europe, then it makes very good sense politically, militarily and economically that we should do it in partnership with the French. That's the skill of the game, building a European pillar without knocking down the American one.'[64] The idea of a Franco–British axis to a European nuclear deterrent is shared by analysts in Paris, such as Pierre Lellouche at the French Institute of International Relations. He has taken the idea of a European pillar even further: 'At the end of the road, in a decade or so, you have a confederation of European countries. They would pool their forces under a joint command. They would have nuclear coverage, between 1,000 and 2,000 warheads. They would be allied to the United States but in a different, equal relationship.'[65]

Such an approach presents clear problems. Firstly, neither the French or British Governments have been particularly enthusiastic.

Intense debate within the British Cabinet on the issue of co-operation with France surfaced in January 1988, according to informed reports.[66] Such a deterrent would supplement rather than replace the American nuclear umbrella. But with the Soviet Union still having so many more nuclear weapons, such a deterrent would have severe problems of credibility.

But it would be of more importance in terms of political links with Washington. The relationship between Europe and America is as much in question as the East–West connection. And while greater European co-ordination is regarded universally as the solution, it's by no means a panacea.

If Europe co-ordinates its policies more closely and is more self reliant, there is a potential for greater clashes with the United States; if the two sides take differing views on an issue, the Europeans united as a group would have more clout. As one official told a Dutch parliamentarian who asked about the official American view on defence co-operation: 'Of course we support European defence co-operation, just so long as they don't go off in the corner and gang up on us.'[67]

Dr Henry Kissinger recognized this over twenty years ago when he predicted: 'A united Europe is likely to insist on a specifically European view of world affairs – which is another way of saying it will challenge American hegemony in Atlantic policy. This may well be a price worth paying for European unity: but American policy has suffered from an unwillingness to recognize there is a price to be paid.'[68] The differences in outlook between the two parts of the alliance have increased since the sixties. It is not just that the generation brought up after the war does not share the same perspective as the generation of leaders that fought in the war together, but also that their interests are dividing.

The decision by NATO European Governments to revive the Western European Union in 1984 – which body had been moribund for 20 years – irritated the United States at first. The Assistant Secretary of State for European affairs, Richard Burt, laid down, in characteristically undiplomatic language, the terms under which he was prepared to assent to its revival. In 1985 the State Department sent cables to its Embassies in Europe to discourage the WEU members from developing a common position on SDI, the American Star Wars programme. The WEU members then backed down; since then the WEU has lost momentum.[69]

There has been intense co-operation between Washington and the European capitals on issues deemed by the State Department to be relevant to Europe, such as the INF Treaty or conventional arms control talks, but the areas of consultation are specifically limited.

The debate within Congress has concentrated on attributing blame and demanding greater effort from Europe. The issue of devolution of power as well as responsibility is only beginning to be addressed; and the implications of greater European unity as spelled out by Dr Kissinger have not been addressed so far. In the 1950s, such was the disparity in relative power that there was no question that Europe would remain subservient to the United States. In the 1960s the 'Atlanticists' in the United States did not accept that a price had to be paid for encouraging European co-operation, as suggested by Dr Kissinger in 1966. And when in office, he himself dealt with the problem in 1973 by ignoring the issue and by making it clear that Europe was expected to be subservient to the United States. So the question posed by a French writer, 'if the United States gradually pays the fiddler less and less, why should it keep calling the tune?', is still only now being considered.

There are some signs of a slight change in attitudes. A week after the Washington Summit in December 1987, President Reagan declared: 'For these four decades NATO has too often seemed an alliance between a number of partners and one very senior partner. Well now,' the President added, 'the alliance must become more and more an alliance among equals – indeed, an alliance between two continents.'[70]

Stanley Sloan has proposed what he called a 'new transatlantic bargain' involving policies of 'defence, détente and devolution'.[71] The idea of a re-negotiation of the transatlantic relationship is taken up in recent reports such as that by the North Atlantic Assembly, but while it spells out the imperative for co-operation in a new relationship, it does not address the question of devolving power to West Europe.

The American analyst David Calleo criticizes what he calls the 'instinctive resistance to devolution. Most defend the present hegemony. Of those who do not, most seem to believe the United States should quickly or slowly disengage completely. These views in effect are two sides of the same unilateralist coin: if the United States cannot determine what a coalition does, it should not mix with it.'[72]

It is by no means clear if European co-operation will be the start of a new relationship within the alliance, or whether it will provide the vehicle for increasing disengagement.

8

☆☆★☆☆

THE BATTLE
FOR THE
DEFENCE MARKETS

*Britain must give up pretending that she is in the same league as the
United States and the Soviet Union when it comes to developing whole
families of sophisticated new weapons.*

Eric Lubbock, Liberal MP,
after the cancellation of TSR2 in 1965.

THE sheer size of the United States economy gives its industries an
enormous advantage over competitors in Britain and other industrialized countries. That has been particularly true for the defence
industry which, since the war, has seen its world position decline
dramatically – in what is now a very high cost area it has reached a state
where it needs international collaboration to survive.

If Britain was going to be able to compete on its own with the United
States in the most important defence and industrial markets, then the
1950s were the time for the foundations of future success to be laid.
During those years British technology was as up-to-date as any in the
world. The engineers working in Britain's research laboratories were
capable of producing the most modern aircraft and selling them at a
competitive price, even without the huge resources available to their
American counterparts.

However, success could only be achieved if products were competitive and time and resources well managed. In the most important areas,
notably the aerospace industry, Britain wasted the opportunity to win a
sizeable share of lucrative markets.

In the first few years after the war the key defence export markets
sold unused and second-hand wartime equipment. Those markets were
dominated by Britain and the United States, the only two countries with
defence industries that had escaped large-scale destruction at the end of
the war. By 1955 British sales of weapons systems alone had reached

almost £4 billion. In contrast, the Americans gave away most of their military exports to important allies.

Such earnings were nothing short of a godsend to an economy recovering from near bankruptcy, and they also provided the means for defence contractors to continue intensive researching of new products. Although a large proportion of the immediate post-war sales had been warships – by 1955, forty-seven had been sold to overseas buyers – the aerospace industry emerged as the key both to defence export earnings and to the development of the most up-to-date defence technology. In the same decade Britain exported some 800 aircraft – planes such as the Gloster Meteor, English Electric's highly successful bomber, the Canberra, and the Hawker Hunter.

But by the mid-fifties the boom years were drawing to a close. Poor decisions were taken within a British defence industry and defence establishment and the market itself began to change and become far more competitive and cut throat. There was also a change of emphasis on the part of America. In the immediate post-war years American military aid had been crucial in creating a stable United States sphere of influence, and then in securing a bulwark against the spread of communism. But it soon became clear that not even the size of the American economy could go on sustaining such a huge transfer of money overseas. One obvious way to redress that flow of money was to commercialize American arms exports, and to ensure that only those allies who couldn't afford to pay for weapons got them without charge. In the late fifties the Pentagon established a new division called Military Assistance Planning to implement this. It was headed by Henry Kuss, whose aggressive promotion of United States arms over the next decade was to play a huge role in driving the British out of their most lucrative markets and sending their defence industry into retreat.

The new mood in the Pentagon was redoubled with the arrival of the Kennedy administration and its Defence Secretary Robert McNamara. He was a former Ford executive, and set about comercializing the Pentagon still further, expanding its money-spinning export trade, and ensuring that the American arms industry was highly efficient and competitive in the key overseas markets. There was a second motive for the sales drive. The Berlin crisis in 1961, following the construction of the wall between East and West Berlin, had proved that there was still a very definite need for effective defence in Europe. Yet there was a lack of standardization and defence equipment in NATO; each country had weapons systems and ammunition totally incompatible with those of allies who might, in time of war, only be fighting a few miles away. McNamara saw the sale of United States arms throughout NATO as the obvious solution. American equipment was built with the most up-to-date technology and was – at least in the eyes of the Pentagon – quite simply the best in the world. Not only would it lead to greater standardization, but it would also help to ease the growing American balance of payments problems caused by its heavy overseas commitments. With the balance of payments deficit running at around $3 billion – an unprecedented level – because of this the huge American expenditure on defence had to be tempered.

The administration launched an internal inquiry into how such changes might be brought about, resulting in the establishment of a group within the Pentagon to promote American arms sales overseas. It was called the International Logistics Negotiations (ILN) and Henry Kuss was appointed to run it. It became a highly successful sales department for the American defence industry and from 1962 onwards started achieving results: the value of arms sales, previously much smaller than the value of arms included in aid programmes, rose to an average of $2 billion each year, twice the level of the free military aid. The British defence industries now had to compete with huge American companies equipped with vast research programmes, an enormous captive domestic market and a Government agency with a brief to sell their goods throughout the world. And American competition had to be overcome, and sales won, in order to fund new research efforts and to produce the kind of revenue needed to justify development of the latest high-technology defence systems.

At the same time the United States began to buy less foreign defence equipment; throughout most of the 1950s Britain had, in fact, sold the Americans more weapons than it had brought from them. As the American corporations began to market more aggressively in Western Europe, extracting huge orders from countries like Holland and Germany for planes such as the ill-fated Lockheed Starfighter, so the Pentagon's own procurement departments began to review the source of their supplies. In 1962 the United States introduced a fifty per cent preference for home-produced systems into its procurement policy – that is, making any foreign competitor undercut its rivals by half before it could secure a contract. British companies such as Tube Investments, which had previously made significant sales of equipment to the Pentagon, saw their business disappear overnight.

By the early sixties, therefore, Britain needed a modern, highly effective range of aircraft and other defence equipment which could compete with the Americans on an equal basis. Their equipment was technically as good as that on the drawing-boards of the big American corporations; but the British defence industry simply failed to live up to the challenges that faced it.

There were too many contractors and vested interests competing for research resources. In 1955 there were still twenty-one companies in Britain designing aircraft, many of them far too small to play a significant role in producing the high-technology jets of the future. Whenever the military issued an operational requirement for a new aircraft, it was standard practice for several firms to submit a design. Within the context of an economy the size of the American one, that would have been normal business practice; but for Britain to have several relatively small aircraft makers fighting with each other to design a plane that none of them could afford to sustain without heavy Government funding was an appalling waste of resources. That fact was eventually recognized by the Government in 1959 when it forced the aircraft division of Vickers and General Electric, two of the strongest firms, to merge, creating the British Aircraft Corporation. The other major contractors also merged to form the Hawker Siddeley group. But it was too late. The product rivalries of the fifties and the waste of much good research effort was to severely handicap the industry in later years.

In addition the defence industry was handicapped by latent rivalries between the services. The Navy would issue an operational requirement not dissimilar to something being sought by the RAF, but because of their rivalry the Admirals and the Air Marshals would seldom sit down to discuss their joint requirements and agree on a plan to save research costs and unnecessary duplication.

Few of those in positions of authority at that time realized the implications; throughout the fifties and early sixties millions of pounds were poured into research projects, only for it to be decided at a later date that Britain really couldn't afford them. What was needed was the concentration of resources on single or small numbers of very carefully researched projects, aimed at a clear market, and once launched, seen through to the end. But because of the nature of the industry there were always alternatives from other companies with their own lobby pushing for them. Instead of co-operating and concentrating on designing a British plane, capable of taking on the world, companies like Bristol Aviation concentrated on designing the Bristol plane, able to take on the rival de Havilland or the Vickers plane. It was an appalling waste, and left the United States dominant in areas where only a few years earlier the British had been their equals.

The problems were compounded by the inability of the British to market their products on anything like the same scale as the Americans – and indeed other European countries with far less developed defence industries. In 1962, for example, the British Government had three supply attachés and a counsellor working in this field in their Embassy in Bonn. By contrast the French had a staff of thirty, led by senior military officers, with a detailed brief to promote France's defence systems, and the Americans had what was called a Military Assistance Advisory Group, with a staff of some 200, headed by either a General or an Admiral.[1]

The American corporations each had a network of representatives throughout Europe, all with generous expense accounts. Even the American Government was said to provide lavish hospitality for potential customers. A delegation of West German Defence Ministry officials to California were reported to have been given envelopes full of 'out of pocket expenses' and were assured that every comfort – including female company – was available free of charge.[2] The issue was raised in Parliament in December 1962 by the former Labour Minister Emmanuel Shinwell, who alleged that American trade organizations in Europe had won orders for arms sales 'obviously because of some private inducement of a financial character'.[3] He demanded an inquiry but the idea was rejected by the Government. Instead the British continued to take their delegations to local guest houses, and to eschew the colourful publicity material and hard-sell techniques used by the Americans. It may have been more honest and more honourable, but the orders went elsewhere.

After the election of the Wilson Government in 1964 the British became more outspoken in their hostility to the American sales drive. In March 1965 Patrick Gordon Walker, who had served for a few months as Wilson's Foreign Secretary, told an American audience that there was 'considerable resentment' about American hard-sell techniques in Europe. 'Arms are sold by states or governments,' he said, 'and it cannot be right or good if there is a cold war within our alliance.' It was not in America's interest to become the monopoly producer of major arms in the alliance.[4] But that was precisely the intention in the United States. In 1962 the *Sunday Telegraph* reported that in the late 1950s the Pentagon's description of the transatlantic arms relationship was 'interdependence'.[5] By the 1960s it had become 'complementarity' – in other words the allies should make weapons to complement, not compete, with the United States. Robert McNamara used to refer to sales to Europe as 'satisfied customers getting military hardware of high quality at low rates'. And he was only too happy to boast of the amount Kuss's organization was saving the American taxpayer. In 1965, when the Wilson Government talked of sales to the Pentagon to offset the costs of major arms purchases from America, Pentagon officials gave little public or private support to the idea, dismissing it as internal political 'window-dressing'.[6]

The failure of the long-range fighter-bomber, TSR2 – the great hope of the RAF in the early sixties – remains the most potent symbol of the sudden decline in the British defence industry from the mid-fifties onwards, and of the opportunities that might have existed had different decisions been taken. The original plans for the plane were drawn up in 1955 when the RAF began to look ahead to an eventual replacement for the Canberra bomber. It was notable as the only major military aircraft development project which escaped the 1957 Defence White Paper. The RAF argued that a versatile, high-speed bomber was vital to Britain's defence – not only as a key component of the strategic deterrent, but also to do what ballistic missiles could not, that is serve as a conventional weapon to support forces on the ground and mounting long-range attacks behind enemy lines.

Had it ever been put into service, TSR2 would have gone far beyond anything ever built by the British aerospace industry before. It was intended to fly at twice the speed of sound at high altitudes, and faster than any other aircraft at low altitudes. Its range, a combat radius of 1,200 miles, meant it could hit targets in the Soviet Union.

However, from the start it was a classic illustration of the problems in the defence industry. And it was to demonstrate that, without firm resolve in international markets, the British would never be able to compete with the American corporations and the revived Pentagon sales machine of the late fifties and the sixties. The TSR2 (short for tactical strike reconnaissance) project was technically superb. Its chief test pilot said it was the smoothest plane he'd ever been in, and praised its versatility.

But it was an RAF plane, and the Navy were building one too, though much less versatile and with a much lower performance. When the original operational requirements for TSR2 were put together by the RAF in 1955, the Yorkshire firm Blackburn were already well under way with the design of the Navy plane, which eventually entered service as the Buccaneer. But the two services could have agreed upon a common design for the shell of the aircraft and adapted it to meet their own needs. This would have saved both time and money and would have produced a bomber able to compete effectively abroad.

But instead the RAF went ahead with their own plane, while the Navy, which had wanted the RAF to buy theirs, tried as hard as possible to undermine it. Indeed, throughout its development the TSR2 was dogged by the ever-present Buccaneer, which was pitched at a much lower price. The early orders for the RAF plane were delayed because the Buccaneer lobby continued to try to persuade the politicians and civil servants that their plane was a better buy. It was time that would eventually prove of great importance when an American rival to TSR2 emerged in the early sixties.

From the start the British Aircraft Corporation, which was formed simultaneously with the granting of the order, needed a lucrative and prestigous export sale to defray some of the development costs of TSR2 (rumoured by the early sixties to be going well over budget) and to give the enterprise a credibility that a wholly domestic project could never have. This would also have provided vital ammunition against the Navy, and appeased the Treasury, who were becoming increasingly alarmed over the amount of money being put into major defence developments. The most likely export order was a sale to the Australian Air Force, which was extremely concerned about the increase of the military power of both China and Indonesia. For a few months in 1960 there was even talk of American co-operation with the development of the plane, and talks were held with Boeing about a possible licence agreement for the plane to be built at Seattle.[7] But given the climate within the Pentagon, a purchase of such a major aircraft was never on the cards. That made it even more crucial to secure the Australian sale. From the start the Australians were kept fully aware of the development of the plane and prospects for securing that order seemed good.

But the divisions within the British services and events across the Atlantic were to dash those hopes. In 1962 the Pentagon gave General Dynamics a contract to build a plane very similar to the TSR2 in its original operational requirements. The contract was to prove one of the most controversial in American defence history. The total budget for the new plane was $6,500 million – more than the entire British defence budget, and the contract for the plane, the TFX, later the F-111 – provoked huge controversy.

Congress was violently opposed to the Pentagon decision, chiefly because Boeing had put in a bid for a similar plane at a lower price. McNamara was accused of treating the Congressmen like he treated junior Vice-Presidents at Ford. Indeed, the hostility rose to such a pitch that at one meeting on Capitol Hill the Defence Secretary was reduced to tears. Both the Pentagon and General Dynamics badly needed a fillip for their project, and they, like their British counterparts, saw a sale to the Australians as the way to secure it. They resolved to undercut TSR2 at any price.

In the summer of 1963 the Australians were offered TSR2 for £2.1 million each – a substantial discount. But within weeks the TFX had been offered by the Americans at an even lower price. And again the service rivalries within the British defence establishment surfaced to help frustrate the hopes of the designers of TSR2. Lord Louis Mountbatten, then Chief of the Defence Staff and firmly loyal to the Navy, thought the RAF was wasting money on the TSR2. He felt they should be buying Buccaneers, at a considerable saving, and did everything he could to undermine the project, warning the Australians that the plane might never be completed. Dazzled by the offer provided by the Americans, and heavily influenced by the views of a man as highly respected as Mountbatten, the Australian Government tilted towards General Dynamics' TFX.

Under pressure from BAC, who desperately wanted the sale, the Ministry of Aviation was persuaded to cut another ten per cent off the price of TSR2. By that time the final decision on the project had reached the highest level, and in October 1963 Britain was without a Prime Minister. Macmillan had resigned, and in the absence of an occupant of Number Ten, no senior minister was prepared to take the decision instead. By the time Sir Alec Douglas-Home, the new Prime Minister, finally gave his consent it was too late – the Australians had already announced that they were buying American. The Australian Prime Minister Sir Robert Menzies called the American offer one 'no government could have refused'. TSR2 had been outbid by the financial might of the Americans and frustrated by the rivalries within the British military. Its days were now numbered.

In 1964 the first Wilson Government was looking for ways to trim the defence budget. The pressure on TSR2 was increased by the new Government's failure to cancel the joint Anglo-French project to develop the supersonic Concorde – then in its development stages and proving to be highly expensive. Within days of the election, the Labour administration published a white paper, signalling their intention to pull out of the Concorde project. But they then discovered a clause in the original agreement (inserted, ironically, to guard against a French decision to withdraw) which provided for penalty payments of almost £150 million to the other party if one pulled out. It had suddenly become too expensive to contemplate pulling out of the project.

That left TSR2 at the top of the list of projects to be cut. The plane was expensive, had failed to secure any foreign orders, and there was the F-111, an aircraft that could be bought for the RAF to replace it. Although the TSR2 had proved highly successful in early tests, by spring 1965 the decision had been taken – the project was to be scrapped. Also cut were two other major aerospace projects, a large transporter for the RAF, and a supersonic vertical take-off fighter being developed by Hawker, who later developed the less-complex Harrier from the same technology.

To replace the TSR2, Defence Secretary Denis Healey told Parliament that Britain would take an option on fifty of the F-111s. He said that it had been 'a difficult decision to take', but that the prospect of continuing escalation in the cost of developing what was already a very expensive plane was, the Government believed, more than was sensible. He defended the option on the F-111s by adding that it would have been irresponsible not to have provided the RAF with an alternative to carry out the tasks which TSR2 would have done. The cost of TSR2, he said, had been 'out of all proportion to its military value'. The F-111 was available at 'a cost the nation can afford'.[8]

There was fury both from within the aerospace industry and from the Conservative opposition. Christopher Soames, later Lord Soames, accused the Government of seriously damaging the aerospace industry, committing Britain to a huge dollar expenditure on the F-111s and ending up spending a combined total for the cancellation fees and the new plane which wouldn't have been much less than the cost of keeping the TSR2. 'It is natural that their American competitors are saying that the British industry is on its way out,' he said, '. . . and that anyone who buys British aircraft needs their heads examined. It is like . . . buying a car from a firm that is going out of business. No wonder they are cock-a-hoop in Washington.'[9]

Whatever the merits of the respective arguments, the Pentagon greeted Labour's decision with ill-concealed glee, and a firm resolve to turn the option into a firm order. Along with orders for Phantom fighters and Hercules transport planes, it was an amazing triple coup for the Americans. Henry Kuss visited London towards the end of the year to begin discussions about the terms of the sale, and British journalists were flown to the United States to be shown the merits of the American plane.

The key stumbling-block was payment. Britain would have to find an extra £280 million to buy the F-111s, most of that in dollars. Together with the Phantom and Hercules purchases, the sum was far beyond the means of the British economy. From the start a deal depended on the Americans providing some kind of offset agreement giving Britain sufficient dollar earnings to pay for the F-111s.

By the end of 1965 the balance of payments situation in London was beginning to give serious cause for concern. High-level diplomatic discussions took place between London and Washington in order to find a way to ensure significant dollar sales for Britain. The first such sale came within weeks, and almost entirely through the influence of McNamara, Kuss and the Pentagon. At that time Britain, France and the American corporations were fighting hard for a contract to boost the air defences of Saudi Arabia, which was becoming increasingly concerned about Nasser's activities in Egypt. Although the American corporations wanted the deal, the Pentagon considered a British sale to the Saudis an obvious way to help offset the huge cost of Britain's own purchases. It would also provide a useful fillip to the industry of an important ally, without really affecting the dominance of American companies. A joint package of British-made Lightning fighters and American-made Hawk missiles was put together for the Saudis.

It was a delicate situation; had the American corporations realized that the Pentagon was working behind the scenes to secure a sale for the British and defeat them, all hell would have broken loose. Quiet, diplomatic overtures were made to the Saudi leadership and the Saudis agreed to take the Lightnings. Britain had secured her biggest-ever export order. When all was in the open, Healey admitted to Parliament that the order would never have been won without the Americans. Such was the power of the formidable American arms sales machine.[10]

The Saudi agreement was one of the lynchpins of the deal to buy fifty F-111s which was announced a few weeks later, in February 1966. Almost the whole cost of the planes was to be covered by offset agreements. The Americans agreed to buy more British defence equipment, and to help the Ministry of Defence increase British exports by putting together more joint packages than the Saudi one.

But the deal was hardly satisfying for the British defence industry, which had to fulfil a quota to help the Government pay for a huge order from the Americans – for a plane that had taken the place of the flagship project of the domestic industry. Even more ironic was the fate of the F-111. The devaluation of sterling in 1967 led Britain to reduce its commitments in the Middle East and to decide it could no longer afford the F-111s. The order was cancelled. The Australian order also faltered – the F-111 ran into so many difficulties in its development that it wasn't delivered until the early 1970s – years late – and never lived up to expectations.

The decision to cancel TSR2 and to buy the F-111s brought home to Britain the strength of the American marketing machine. During the offset negotiations Henry Kuss became something of a bogeyman to British politicians and media alike. His low profile led one newspaper to nickname him the new Pimpernel. Twelve Conservative Members of Parliament signed a motion warning Harold Wilson to 'beware the slick salesmen of the American aircraft industry' and an opposition MP called a visit by Kuss to London 'very sinister'.[11] And as events would reveal, when the Lockheed bribes scandal broke a decade later, there *had* been a sinister side to the determination of some American salesmen. But that was not at the root of the British problem, though it showed how far some Americans were prepared to go to win major overseas orders.

But by failing to rationalize early enough, by failing to produce one British plane in each category, and by failing to divert all the best of British design into single projects, the chance was lost. Britain could have had a series of military and civil aircraft capable of winning vital export markets and providing the core of a successful defence industry.

By the time the Labour Government cancelled TSR2 the damage had already been done, though an opportunity still existed to salvage something from the wreckage. The P1127, also cancelled that year, eventually evolved into the highly successful Harrier, and now, ironically, more than twenty years later, there are plans to develop a supersonic version – in other words, a plane that could have been ready in the 1970s.

Although Britain's defence industry would never have been able to prevent the spread of American equipment after the arrival of Henry Kuss, it could have evolved on similar lines to the French defence industry, with greater prospects of success. There, the close links beween Marcel Dassault, the effective founder of the French aerospace industry, and Charles de Gaulle, gave France the support Britain lacked. France's Mirage jets proved highly successful and were exported around the world largely because they had French Government backing, had no rivalries in the domestic market and were guaranteed sales. Dassault turned the French defence industry into a significant force on the world markets, even though immediately after the war the French industry had been virtually non-existent. Britain, on the other hand, had a huge head start, yet ended up with little to show for it.

However, there was a solution to the rise of the American military-industrial complex, and Denis Healey realized it when he cancelled TSR2. He told Parliament:

> 'No country of our size can any longer afford to produce the more sophisticated modern weapons. That makes nonsense of all this talk by the Opposition that by co-operating with our allies we are somehow giving up our independence. They know perfectly well that independence in defence has been impossible for many years. Interdependence is the only possible basis for a defence policy in the second half of the twentieth century.'

That same day he announced that Britain was pressing ahead with plans to see whether it could begin joint collaborative programmes within Europe.

9

☆☆★☆☆

TOWARDS A EUROPEAN
ALTERNATIVE

*Within Western Europe collaboration is not infrequently treated as a
dose of somewhat unpleasant medicine, taken primarily to prevent the
ill of buying American.*

Colin Green, United Technologies Corporation.

IT HAS taken a quarter of a century for Western Europe to make real
moves towards widespread international co-operation in the production of defence equipment and to an increasing extent in civil industry as
well. Today there is collaboration on specific projects; there are shared
research facilities, and European products are beginning to have an
impact on international markets. But the European alternative is
scarcely much more than an industrial convenience to enable countries
to compete with the United States. There has yet to be a major defence
project involving all the major European companies; European countries
still tend to develop systems in parallel with each other, with all the
duplication and waste of resources that entails.

By the mid-sixties Britain had lost its place in the world defence sales
league and the decline has continued ever since. In 1965 British
industry still held almost 20 per cent of the world market. But by the
1980s that market had fallen by 75 per cent, and today Britain's share in
the total world defence export market is less than 5 per cent, despite
the huge proportion of its scientific and technical research resources
devolved to defence.

Britain's share is now roughly the same as the West Germans' – and
twenty years ago the German industry was still small and inexperi-
enced. Competition from the other side of the Atlantic has furthered the
move towards European rather than national industries and has led to
collaboration in both the civil and military aerospace industries. In the
defence field there have been three key projects: the Anglo-French
Jaguar aircraft, the Tornado, and now the European Fighter Aircraft,
which is due in service in the 1990s. The civil side of the aerospace

industry was already moving towards collaboration as Britain re-evaluated its own defence projects – the British and the French had been working together on Concorde since the late 1950s. Although Concorde proved a white elephant on the world markets, it set a precedent for collaboration; it was followed in the late 1960s by the European Airbus project, which has succeeded for the first time since the 1950s in breaking the American stranglehold on the passenger aircraft market.

But establishing a European alternative to the American industry has been fraught with difficulty. Although the planes produced over the course of twenty years have ultimately proved relatively successful, and have managed to win a reasonable share of the market and valuable export orders, progress towards developing the European alternative has been slow and complex. None of the major defence projects has attracted participation from all the major Western European industries together, and on more than one occasion joint projects have even faced competition from within Europe.

The problem has been primarily that each of the major projects has emerged, not from a general consensus throughout the continent but from the needs of one particular group of countries. So when the British and the French decided to go ahead and build Jaguar as a light battlefield and reconnaissance plane and as a trainer, the Germans refused to join them because they saw their priorities elsewhere.

If the Germans had participated, development costs would have been spread between the three countries and the guaranteed extra orders from Germany would have substantially reduced the costs per plane. Instead Jaguar had severe problems of cost throughout its development period, and lost some valuable export orders because it simply couldn't compete with American planes on cost.

And the collaboration between Britain and France in the Jaguar project broke down in the mid-seventies when Dassault launched an aggressive campaign to sell a new version of one of their other planes to the Dutch and the Belgians in direct competition to Jaguar. Dassault's fierce nationalism has proved a major obstacle to the success of collaboration. Marcel Dassault and de Gaulle were close friends and the Gaullist view of France was the prime motivation behind the French determination to produce their own planes and the aggressive market-ing of the Mirage series of jets. Indeed, with the exception of Jaguar, the French have steered well clear of collaborative projects in develop-ing military aircraft.

The largest of the military collaborative projects began in the late 1960s, with the establishment of an Anglo–German–Italian consortium to build the Tornado – a plane with a long-range strike capability and yet adaptable to other defence roles, particularly in combat. It was needed by Britain to fill the gap left by the cancellation of TSR2 and the decision not to buy the F111s. Tornado has not been an unqualified success, though it has won some lucrative export orders and is now in front-line service with NATO. Again it lacked one of the major players. The French refused to join the consortium. Instead Dassault pressed ahead with a new generation of Mirage jets in direct competition to Tornado – to the fury of the other European nations.

The Tornado project highlighted perfectly the difficulties of international collaboration. The Germans and Italians had already begun feasibility studies when Britain joined the consortium, and although Britain had by far the most modern and capable industry, the project was established in Germany. It was also run on an equal basis – with all three countries having equal weight in deciding what was done.

British aerospace executives involved in the project defend this arrangement, claiming that it did no harm to British interests even though project leadership was handed to a less experienced industry. But the arrangement certainly did have its disadvantages. The Germans were acutely aware of the huge amount of money the Americans were spending on defence in West Germany; American firms were positively encouraged to set up enterprises there, and given huge tax incentives if they did so. That meant that American companies were able to find their way into the European collaborative programmes by collaborating with German firms. On this occasion, too, the Germans pressed their partners to permit an American involvement in the project – allowing American firms to tender for the contract to supply engines for the new plane, even though, in Rolls-Royce, the consortium countries already had one of the world's foremost aero-engine manufacturers. Only after much debate and evaluation was the engine contract given to the British company. Further problems arose from the stipulation that the work load should be shared out proportionately. The German industry on its own could not hope to meet such targets, which gave the Americans a way into the project.

Despite this Britain still needed the Tornado programme – unlike the French, it had no will to go it alone. And British industry did not get the deals it wanted; even in all-European projects the American sales machine could not be avoided. One American firm was so keen to involve itself in the project it hired a top European aviation analyst to advise it on winning contracts – at a salary of $300,000 a year. In 1972 the British Electronic Engineering Association said that Britain had, as a result, lost out in areas of electronics where it had previously been a world leader, and so had lost ground in export markets for related technologies.[1] To the Labour Government of the late sixties, collaboration had seemed essential, but it also came at a price.

In addition, collaborative projects which involve an outlay of money on the scale required by the development of a new aircraft, seem to be constantly dogged by indecision. Before Jaguar ever left the drawing board it was the victim of constant rumours about a possible French withdrawal. And when Tornado was in the research stages there was talk of an Italian withdrawal (because they were in favour of a one-seater plane while the British and the Germans insisted on a two-seater). Although both projects reached the production stage without losing participants, such publicly aired doubts inevitably damaged export potential, as customers, fearing cancellation, looked for an alternative, safer source of the aircraft they needed. In practice that usually meant buying American.

In terms of exports both Jaguar and Tornado have ultimately done relatively well, with Tornado winning Britain's biggest overseas order, in 1986, in a deal with Saudi Arabia. The total value to Britain was some £5 billion. More recently the Kuwaitis have also bought Tornado.

Despite these successes the French have refused to join the most recent of the major collaborative projects – the European Fighter Aircraft, which is currently being developed by Britain, Germany, Italy and Spain for introduction in the 1990s. The French refusal to participate in the Eurofighter is understandable – since the 1960s they have been the only producers of standard fighter aircraft in the world outside the United States. Projects like Tornado have been on a larger scale, producing more versatile aircraft but at greater cost. For the French to have entered the Eurofighter project would have been to abandon a part of a lucrative market.

But it has been the civil aviation industry which provides the best example of successful European collaboration. The European Airbus, established in the late 1960s, has proved so attractive to airlines that it is now regularly at the centre of trade rows with the Americans who claim that it is being unfairly subsidized by Europe so that it can increase its share of the commercial airliner market. The degree of concern emanating from the American manufacturers about their rival is quite unprecedented. Yet the history of the European Airbus hasn't been wholly free from the problems that have dogged military projects. The idea of Airbus first emerged in 1967 after discussions between ministers from Britain, France and Germany, which concluded that only a European industry could compete with the United States.

The original Airbus was to fly over short-range flights, with a passenger capacity of 200 or 300 people. It was thought by many to be a lucrative market – in the United States Lockheed and McDonnell Douglas were both working on similar planes. But the European competitor had an inauspicious start. Indeed, for a long time, the British Government was reluctant to participate in the project. It was dogged by disputes within the consortium over its specification. It suffered cost overruns in the initial development stages which led to some of the more ambitious parts of the programme being abandoned.

Furthermore, the BAC was itself developing a plane aimed at the airbus market – the three-eleven. Inevitably it lobbied hard in Whitehall to get Britain out of the European Airbus project and to back a British alternative. The arguments in favour of this were highly attractive. Britain was the only country of the European consortium with a sizeable civil aerospace industry, and BAC argued strongly that the French were trying to use Airbus as a vehicle to climb on to the back of the British firms and establish themselves as the leaders of a European industry. In 1969 the Government pulled out of partnership with France and Germany, and BAC immediately asked for funding to develop the three-eleven, but were thwarted by the defeat of Harold Wilson's Labour Government in the 1970 General Election. The new Conservative Government spent some time re-evaluating both projects before announcing that it would not support either. But although Britain had pulled out of Airbus, Hawker Siddeley, the other main British aerospace manufacturer, remained involved in the project as a sub-contractor building the wings. Eventually, that link would prove the door by which Britain would rejoin the project.

After its troubled start – and an initial shortage of orders – the Airbus Industries consortium, based in southern France, emerged as a force in world aviation. By 1978 it had won firm orders of 95 planes from 12 leading airlines, and had options on 44 more. It began work on a new series of jets, and in the same year made its first real breakthrough into the American market with a $778 million sale of 22 jets to Eastern Airlines.

The development of new planes inevitably required extra finance, and the French and the Germans then threatened to build the wings themselves if Britain did not return as a full member of the project. The loss of the contract would have been a major blow to the newly amalgamated British Aerospace (BAe), which had taken over Hawker Siddeley's sub-contract, and would have cost thousands of jobs. There was little option – Britain put £600 million into the new research projects in exchange for a 20 per cent stake in the project and a seat on the board of Airbus Industrie.

Yet though the Airbus project now involved the major Western European aerospace industries, it has traditionally bought American and not British engines, as it has done so far since the first A300 airliners rolled off the production line at the consortium's assembly plant at Toulouse. Indeed, Airbus recently provided General Electric with its biggest ever order for aero engines, worth around $2 billion. Although American engines were only used in airbuses after Britain first pulled out of the project, it still makes little sense for an increasingly integrated European industry not to rely on indigenous manufacturers for key components. Since Britain re-entered the Airbus scheme, the consortium has continued to gain ground in the lucrative American market, with sales of 28 planes to Pan-American, 100 to Northwest Airlines and 25 to American Airlines. Yet the British commitment to the project has remained uncertain. When British Aerospace approached the Government in London in 1986 requesting help to finance a project to build a range of new long-haul jets, it received scant co-operation, and eventually received an offer of far less than the amount BAe claimed was the minimum needed.

Furthermore the British Government has been pressing Airbus to link up with the American firm McDonnell Douglas to build a long-range jet as a means of spreading development costs. The American firm is developing its own long-range plane, the MD11, in direct competition with Airbus's jet the A340. The Department of Trade and Industry in London has always doubted whether there is room for three planes in competition for the high capacity, long-range market. More recently the French have voiced interest in some kind of collaboration with McDonnell Douglas. It would be indeed ironic if Airbus was forced into partnership wtih one of its less successful American rivals.

Even so, the Airbus Consortium is still having a remarkable impact on world markets, and continues to cause disquiet in the United States. In 1976 some 90 per cent of planes used by Western airlines were American built. As early as 1981 a Congressional committee in

Washington was warned that the United States' domination of the civil
airliner market was under threat. By July 1987 a senior executive from
McDonnell Douglas, Louis Harrington, warned that the American
corporations, so long able to crush their rivals because of their size,
were now themselves being dwarfed by the four nations in the Airbus
project. 'If we, as a country,' he said, 'are going to allow the Europeans
to distort the competitive environment by heavily subsidizing Airbus,
over the long haul one could see the commercial manufacturing industry
shifting from the United States to Europe. Under those conditions,
whether it's us or Boeing, neither is big enough to compete . . . .'[2]
Today Airbus has moved into second place in the industry, ahead of
McDonnell Douglas, and is beginning to make inroads into the dominant
position held by Boeing. Despite the transatlantic arguments over
subsidies, Airbus has, more than anything else, shown the Europeans
that collaboration can and does work.

The success of large-scale co-operation in the aerospace industry has
set a precedent now being followed in other defence and civil sectors.
As part of its attempt to develop a single integrated market in Europe
and to reduce European dependency on high technology imports from
abroad, particularly from the United States and Japan, the EC has
backed a series of international development projects in the field of high
technology. Around fifty pan-European projects have now been
approved in computers, semi-conductors, telecommunications and
allied fields.

The European Space Agency (ESA) is one of the most established
collaborative programmes and enjoys almost as high a profile as the
major aerospace projects. But in recent months it has provided a clear
example of the problems of promoting collaboration. The Agency was
set up in the early seventies, largely after pressure from a British
minister whose passionate Europeanism would later project him into the
headlines – Michael Heseltine. The initiative came when Heseltine was
approached by British industry to provide funding to keep British space
research ahead of the French and Germans. 'It was,' he says, 'a
ludicrous idea.' It was hardly relevant, when the United States and the
Soviet Union were spending millions on their massive space programmes, for Western European countries to be spending trivial amounts
trying to compete with each other. But he did discover that the
combined budgets of the European nations on space research, while not
nearly as great as the amounts being spent by the superpowers, were
nonetheless significant. Out of that realization, and following much

persuasion of both British and European colleagues, the European Space Agency was born.

The role of the ESA has been to co-ordinate space research across Europe to avoid duplication of resources. It has backed existing projects, and worked to ensure that each member develops its own specializations. France, for example, had been involved in the development of the Ariane rocket well before the Agency was formed and has continued to lead European rocket research. Even before the American space shuttle Challenger blew up in 1986, the Ariane project had built itself a market share of around 50 per cent. Britain, on the other hand, has led the way in developing European satellites, and British Aerospace is now the third biggest satellite-maker in the world. In January 1987 the company won a £100 million order for a new communications satellite for NATO – the first time such an order has gone to a European firm. The Agency has also given smaller countries such as Belgium and Denmark, without the resources but with the technical expertise to develop space programmes of their own, the chance to participate in major space projects. The results have been generally successful, as the examples of Ariane and British Aerospace show.

But the future of British participation in the ESA is now increasingly in doubt. The Agency's plans for the future included the development of a manned space programme using a new generation of Ariane rockets and a European space shuttle. Two plans exist within Europe: for a British-designed craft – the Hotol (which stands for Horizontal take-off and landing, and would be powered by a revolutionary new form of air-breathing engine) and the French Hermes craft, based on a much more traditional design, and costing around a third of the amount needed to develop the British space plane. The other members of the ESA are planning to press ahead with the Hermes project and see it as a key to future research. But it is a decision which the British refuse to back. The reason owes less to national interest than to the principle of spending vastly increased amounts on space research. When he announced the Government's decision not to join the programme in November 1987, the Trade and Industry Minister Kenneth Clarke said he couldn't justify vast expenditure on manned space travel when that was something achieved twenty years earlier by the United States. 'The Government,' he said could see no 'sufficient scientific, industrial or commercial benefits to justify such a huge increase.'[3] Britain will continue as part of some other European space projects, notably the Columbus space station, but its contribution and influence in the projects remains much smaller than countries like France and West Germany.

There has been strong opposition in Britain to the Government's lack of commitment to the European space alternative. Many members of Mr Clarke's own party expressed their dismay about the decision in Parliament – going so far as to say that the Government had got it totally wrong. One, Robert Rhodes James, MP for Cambridge, said he and his constituents would not 'accept a situation that this nation is going to become a division three country, and research and development is going to be relegated'.[4] And another MP Richard Page told the Minister: 'Columbus discovered America on state aid – should we not do the same?'[5]

Well before the announcement became official Roy Gibson, the Director of Britain's National Space Centre, resigned over the fact that he thought the Government no longer willing to countenance substantial spending on the European effort. British Aerospace's Chief Executive Sir Raymond Lygo says the withdrawal 'is bound to have an adverse impact' on its space operations, and on those of many other British companies working in the field. But BAe say that it is too early to be certain how serious that effect will be. What is certain, though, is that the decision will damage the prospects for growing co-operation and collaboration in technological development across Europe. The progress towards a European alternative to American and Japanese industry remains vulnerable to national politics.

The other main forum for European collaboration to emerge in the past decade is the Independent European Programme Group (IEPG) It was set up in 1976, with thirteen member-countries, to co-ordinate European defence research and development, but has only really played a significant role in the 1980s. The chief aim of the IEPG is to bring countries together at the start of each project, and to combine their efforts on all aspects of research and development. Trying to pull together projects between countries that had begun their own research was one of the key weaknesses in the big aerospace programmes. There was certainly far less incentive for the French to join Tornado or the Eurofighter, for example – given that they already had ongoing development programmes, unlike the Germans, who had none. By bringing countries together at the start the IEPG has been able to harmonize what the defence establishments refer to as staff targets – that is, encouraging countries to work out their future requirements together and then introducing joint specifications. In the two-and-a-half years leading up to the 1987 British Defence White Paper, thirteen European staff targets had been agreed, all of which were intended to evolve into fully-fledged collaborative projects.

Britain is now working on a wide range of joint projects, but on a much smaller scale than ventures such as Tornado and Eurofighter. For example, the United Kingdom has linked up with Germany and Italy to develop a 70mm howitzer for use on the battlefield, and is working with the Germans and the Norwegians on developing a short range air-to-air missile.

Despite the fact that the Europeans have sometimes been unenthusiastic about working together in defence and civil projects, the experience in the last twenty years suggests that Europe is likely to be more successful working as a unit than as fragments.

But the biggest problem lies in finding a balance between working within Europe and working with the rest of NATO – the United States, in particular, is showing increasing enthusiasm for joint production of defence equipment. Britain must decide whether to be fully European or to make individual project decisions. That there are problems ahead was only too clearly shown by what was probably Britain's most serious domestic political crisis of recent years, which burst unexpectedly into the limelight in the autumn of 1985.

10

☆☆★☆☆

WESTLAND AND THE FUTURE OF THE DEFENCE INDUSTRY

We, all of us, simply are being priced out of the ability to have an effective and efficient defence.

Sam Nunn, Chairman of the
Senate Armed Services Committee.

IN EARLY 1986 the Thatcher Government came close to being brought down by an internal dispute over a private company with a turnover of only £300 million. Two senior ministers resigned, and the Prime Minister herself had to defend herself in Parliament against charges of lying. It was, by any standards an extraordinary affair that managed to get totally out of hand.

Although the issues at stake were lost amid a welter of personality clashes within the Government, the conflict brought into question the whole future of the British defence industry and its relationship with Europe and the United States.

The crisis was caused by the financial troubles of the Westland company, based in the small town of Yeovil in the West of England. The company had been in financial difficulties for nearly two years when it announced in autumn 1985 that it needed a large injection of capital from another company to keep it afloat. The most likely candidate was the United States firm United Technologies, which already had close links with Westland.

Westland's problems were largely caused by its size. Alone among the major producers of helicopters – both in Europe and the United States – it is a specialist company without the backing of a larger parent or of other divisions with sufficiently varied operations to cushion one part if it ran into trouble. Westland was therefore particularly vulnerable to serious recession in the helicopter market. In fact the final crisis in the company's finances was brought on by a recession in civil rather than military aircraft, particularly the failure to secure adequate orders

for the company's W30 civilian helicopter. Although Westland was near
bankruptcy, the possibility of the relationship between Westland and
United Technologies developing into more than just a working one
caused uproar among British politicians committed to the European
collaboration. The most vocal opponent of such a link was the Secretary
of State for Defence, Michael Heseltine.

Although with a much lower profile than the large-scale collaborative
projects like Tornado and the Eurofighter, the European helicopter
industry had probably the most successful collaborative record of all.
From 1967 onwards the British and the French, through the Aerospa-
tiale Corporation rather than Dassault, had been working together on a
long series of projects, producing in all some 2,500 Lynx, Gazelle and
Puma helicopters. In 1975 there was a move to expand that collaboration to include the Italians and the Germans as well.

In 1978 the four Governments signed an agreement to develop a new
series of European helicopters for the 1980s and 1990s. One of the
objects of the agreement was to try to maintain a strong European
helicopter industry in the face of American competition. The strength of
the American corporations in helicopter development is enormous. Bell,
the dominant company in the field with a market share of around 50 per
cent, has more than 4,000 of its Iroquois series helicopters in service
with the United States Army alone – almost double the total number
produced by the Anglo-French collaborative programme.

The surge in United States military spending after Reagan's election
further strengthened the domination of the American firms, providing
huge new resources for development and making them still more
powerful exporters. By the end of 1984 competition from America was
becoming almost too strong for Westland and the other European
companies. The then Westland Chairman Lord Aldington told Michael
Heseltine that 'neither Westland, nor any European helicopter manufacturer has the financial resources required to design and develop a major
new advanced, state of the art helicopter . . . No European government
is likely to be willing to match the enormous sums which the United
States has available.'[1] He said the company believed that the only way
for it to survive in the future was to link up with a leading American
manufacturer. A year later financial necessity had turned that belief into
company policy.

Westland's first choice for such a link up was with the Sikorsky
Division of the United Technologies Corporation, with which it had a
long working relationship. Westland had entered the helicopter market

in 1947 with a licence agreement to build the Sikorsky S-51 in Britain and has now built three further Sikorsky-designed aircraft, including the highly successful Sea King. In fact Westland has sold more Sea Kings overseas – to nine countries in all – than Sikorsky itself has done. By 1986 the British firm had built more than 1,200 Sikorsky planes under licence – a significant proportion of which was for export markets.

But to such a confirmed supporter of greater European collaboration as Heseltine, the idea of Westland becoming financially dependent on – if not actually a subsidiary of – United Technologies, was an anathema. It was also potentially damaging to British credibility in other fields of collaboration. Westland and Sikorsky's plan for a link up centred on a new licence agreement for Westland to build another American helicopter, the Black Hawk. But the Black Hawk was a direct competitor to one of the European projects under development, the NH90.

In autumn 1985 Heseltine tried to find an alternative rescue package for Westland. He was instrumental in bringing together a consortium of European companies willing to provide the necessary investment, made up of Westland's partners in the European industry, British Aerospace and GEC. He also arranged a meeting of the National Armaments Directors of the four European countries involved, and which not only came out strongly in favour of the European alternative for Westland, but recommended that in future European armed forces should buy all their middle-range helicopters from European companies.

This attempt by the five European companies to mount a last-minute rescue bid for Westland was, no doubt, motivated by the fear that Sikorsky would use Westland as a Trojan Horse to gain access to the European market. The British Aerospace Chairman Sir Austin Pearce admitted at the time to a fear in Europe that American competition within Europe as well as in export markets would make it hard for the other helicopter manufacturers to survive.[2] The American firm would have access to what had been a restricted market, in which European governments bought all their helicopters from their own firms. And it would also give the Americans access to details of the latest European technology, greatly strengthening their ability to compete in other export markets. But although the Ministry of Defence in London and the European companies worked hard to come up with a proposal to satisfy the Westland Board, there was never any real doubt that the final decision would be for a link with the Americans. Westland itself stressed the company's responsibilities to its shareholders, and the response to the initial discussions with United Technologies was rapid, professional and reassuring. Despite fierce pressure from the Ministry of Defence and a wave of public hysteria over what was presented as an American takeover, the Sikorsky option was eventually recommended to the shareholders and accepted.

The breach in the Government over the issue showed clearly just how uncertain Britain is over the way it sees defence collaboration heading in the future. Michael Heseltine's fervent search for a European alternative was born out of a long-standing commitment to the continuation of European programmes. He had been involved in the establishment of the European Space Agency, and later in the negotiations that set up the Eurofighter project, and turned the IEPG into a more potent force in European industrial development. But he was a minority voice. Throughout the Westland crisis the official Government view was that it was a company matter and not one for ministers to interfere in directly. Heseltine's direct and active intervention brought him into direct confrontation with colleagues and with Margaret Thatcher, and forced his resignation.

During the Westland crisis critics of Heseltine's campaign made it clear that their opposition was not to the principle of European collaboration, but rather to that of following the European route in every case. But this argument is not accepted by the European lobby. 'The only way', says Michael Heseltine, 'to ensure real industrial and economic progress within Europe is to be seen to be making every effort to achieve it.' He remains fiercely critical of what he calls the 'minimalists' within the British establishment who want Britain to look after its own interests rather than taking a broader view, but stresses that this is not intended to be anti-American. He argues that 'co-operation with the Americans should be on the basis of European strengths rather than weaknesses' and points to the strong American interest in playing some part in the Eurofighter project. That form of co-operation, he believes, is to be encouraged.

But there are also fears that Britain's relationship with the United States could be damaged if Britain goes too far down the European road. During the Westland crisis much of the fury against Michael Heseltine – which emerged from other members of the Government – was provoked by the anti-American feeling that Heseltine's pro-European campaign was generating. The then Trade and Industry Secretary Leon Brittan, who also lost his job because of the crisis and became the most outspoken critic of the Defence Secretary's actions, told a parliamentary committee afterwards that he had felt that the pro-European campaign could badly damage other British economic interests – particularly Airbus – in the American markets. Indeed British Aerospace was warned by an American subsidiary during the crisis that there was a real danger of that happening.[3]

The links between the British and American defence industries, and bilateral interest in working together in defence procurement, had been building up steadily since the mid-1970s. There were two reasons for this. The first was impatience in Britain and the rest of Europe with the United States' policy of giving its own contractors a huge price advantage when it came to handing out new contracts. The second was the increasing lack of co-ordination between the armed services in NATO countries and particularly of the weapons they used. In 1974 it became clear just how serious this lack of co-ordination had become when, during a mock battle over the North Atlantic, the forces representing NATO in the exercise shot down half their own planes because the communications systems in each country's aircraft weren't inter-operable.

In 1975 Britain and the United States signed a memorandum of understanding aimed at making it easier for their respective defence industries to compete in each other's markets. Two years later at a summit of NATO leaders in London, President Carter said he wanted to see the opening up of what he called the 'two-way street'[4] in arms procurement within NATO. The summit went on to adopt the idea as official alliance policy.

Initially there was a marked reluctance, particularly in the Pentagon, to open up American markets to foreign competition. Robin Beard, who recently finished a term as Assistant Secretary General of NATO, and served as a Congressman in the seventies and early eighties, says that on many occasions the Pentagon 'misled Congress' on precisely what was available abroad. 'When I voted for one particular programme, it was the only real option presented to me. No one told me that there was a German system, on the shelf, already in use, that we could have fielded almost immediately at so little cost compared to the $2 billion we put into our new system – which never even saw the light of day after fourteen years . . . . We were not even aware that there were European options – there might be American options but never European options.'

But the two-way street, as it is known, has now made a real impact on NATO procurement. The biggest beneficiaries have been smaller component manufacturers in Britain and Europe, winning what are, in

American terms relatively small orders but which are vitally important and highly profitable to them. The British company Fairey Marine, for example, recently won an order to supply support boats for pontoon bridges to the United States Army. It was worth around £30 million – a sizeable order for a medium-sized British firm. Other companies such as Lucas Aerospace and Doughty have won contracts to supply components for the new American B2 bomber, again a potentially highly profitable area. British defence officials say that this is the real benefit of the two-way street, though there have been some sales of major systems as well – most notably the Harrier and Hawk aircraft, and Royal Ordnance's 81mm Howitzer.

In the 1970s American firms enjoyed a four-to-one trade surplus over their British rivals. By the mid-1980s that figure had halved, and senior British officials and politicians would like to see the trend go further still. In practice it is unlikely that Britain will ever be able to sell as much to the United States as it buys, if only because of the vast amount the United States spends on research and development – at the most conservative estimates, around twice as much as Europe. That means the United States is likely to continue buying most of its equipment from domestic suppliers to defray research costs. Some British firms have also benefited from the development of offset agreements. These are agreements used in cases where the United States has been competing to make a major sale of equipment to one of its allies, and that ally has demanded a quid pro quo in terms of orders for its own industry. In Britain the best known example of this was the Nimrod. In late 1986 the Government decided to scrap the Nimrod early-warning aircraft, which had suffered from a long series of design difficulties, and buy the AWACS plane from Boeing. It was a painful political decision, which entailed writing off around £2 billion of investment and ten years of design effort.

One of the key factors that persuaded the Thatcher Government to abandon the Nimrod project, despite the strong political pressure not to do so and the lobbying campaign by the manufacturers, GEC, was the deal offered by Boeing. The American firm offered Britain a 130 per cent offset agreement; in other words, it said it would spend 130 dollars on contracts with British companies for every 100 dollars the British spent on AWACS. That meant that when the offer came under consideration, companies like Plessey who stood to benefit heavily from the Boeing offer, were heavily on the side of the Americans.

Like Westland, the Nimrod affair revived concern about the Anglo-

American relationship. Its opponents said the Government was repeat-
ing the mistakes of the sixties, abandoning the best of British research
and handing the rewards over to the Americans.

There has also been concern about the effectiveness of the deal. The
weakness of the dollar in 1987 and early 1988 has made it increasingly
difficult for British companies to win contracts, and for Boeing to comply
with the agreement without paying an excessively high price for its
purchases. In April 1988 Boeing strenuously denied allegations in the
British media that it wasn't living up to its side of the bargain, saying it
had done its utmost to give British firms the right to tender, but pointing
out that contracts still had to be won on price, quality and delivery time.

Ironically, the deal was also debated in Washington where there is a
lobby vociferously opposed to offset agreements. They argue that such
arrangements, which have become increasingly common among NATO
defence industries, are wasteful because contracts are won through the
best offset deal rather than because a product is the best. That view is
not shared by the British Government. The Defence Secretary George
Younger told a meeting of American and British businessmen in 1987
that offset arrangements motivate major American contractors to look
for British suppliers. He argued that 'work should be placed with our
companies on a competitive basis. If British firms cannot be, they
should not win the business.'[5]

Robin Beard says that many British firms have only recently come to
terms with the American market, and learned to sell their products
effectively. 'There was', he says, 'a real European industrial naivety as
to how to market in this country. Their idea of marketing in this country
was to get a public relations agency, and take out a four-page ad in the
Armed Forces Journal with colour pictures of their system, and just
know that in good conscience the services would come to them and say
"please let us buy your system". They just had no idea of how to work
the system. So now you see more of them setting up offices here,
establishing licensing arrangements or whatever to try to work the
system better.' And he says that the same thing is happening with
American companies in Europe.

The third major development in defence procurement over the last
ten years has been the growth of collaborative projects with the United
States as well as with the rest of Europe. Throughout the sixties and
early seventies there was very little defence collaboration between
Britain and the United States. There were a few exceptions – such as
the Harrier vertical take-off aircraft, one of the most notable successes

of the Falklands War – but they were few and far between. The Harrier was originally developed by Hawker Siddeley during the latter part of the 1960s after the more complex supersonic P1127 project was scrapped. It entered service at the end of the decade, and attracted immediate interest from the United States. The American marines ordered 114 planes, and Hawker Siddeley agreed a licensing arrangement with McDonnell Douglas whereby the British company would provide the first sixty planes, and the remainder would be built in the United States.

The first generation Harriers proved enormously successful, and the American marines expressed a strong interest in second generation, more technically advanced planes. Early development studies were begun jointly by McDonnell Douglas and Hawker Siddeley in the mid-seventies, but without any development finance from the British Government – the Pentagon wanted planes for delivery by 1981, but there was little enthusiasm for such early development within the Ministry of Defence. The RAF, for example, said there was no obvious need for it in Britain until at least four years after the Americans wanted it.

In the 1980s Harrier became a joint programme but with the Americans heading the project. Most of the design work was carried out in the United States, and although British Aerospace (which absorbed Hawker Siddeley when the industry was nationalized) assembles the plane for the British market and provides a significant proportion of the airframe components, the Harrier is now essentially an American plane with British participation.

A second area where there has been a high degree of transatlantic co-operation has been in the development of aero-engines. As the cost of developing new engines over the years has escalated, so it has become more and more difficult for individual companies to produce their own range of products. Indeed, in the case of Rolls-Royce the problems were apparent as long ago as 1971 when the company was bankrupted by the rocketing cost of developing its RB211 engine, and had to be rescued by the Government. Today Britain's only major aero-engine manufacturer is still a force on the world market although it can barely meet the huge costs of the industry. That has led it to seek joint projects elsewhere – which, in the aero-engine industry, means the United States.

Rolls-Royce has worked on a series of engine developments with the American firm Pratt and Whitney – also a part of United Technologies.

The two companies are currently collaborating on a five-nation project to develop the V2500 engine – a highly advanced turbofan engine – and have been working together with the French company Turbomeca on the RTM 322 helicopter engine, which, ironically, is being used to power the Sikorsky Black Hawk – a fact that was played on heavily by the Americans during the Westland crisis.

Until 1986 the scope for collaboration with United States firms in defence research and development was limited by American regulations in the form of the Arms Control Export Act. That meant that even if a company had invested money in a project in the United States, if it wanted to buy that product for its own forces it had to go through the channels set aside for arms sales to foreign countries. In other words, Britain had to buy products it had developed as if it was an entirely separate third party – clearly a disincentive to collaboration. The British Embassy in Washington and the companies concerned had to use considerable ingenuity to launch collaborative projects. In the case of the Harrier, that was done by setting up what was essentially a dual production programme, with British Aerospace and McDonnell Douglas working together, but also in parallel to each other. There was no joint management system as there had been with the European collaborative projects, nor was there any sharing of production to create efficiency. The British built their plane in Britain and the Americans built theirs in the United States.

American laws on the transfer of technology, which are discussed at greater length in a later chapter, have made it more difficult for British and other European firms to link up with American companies in developing defence systems. The restrictions can mean that equipment built in Europe using some American or largely American components may not be able to be exported from Europe to third countries. This is a prime concern for any company looking for a United States link-up.

In addition many British defence executives feel that joint ventures with American firms have been less attractive than those with other European firms because of the strident American business approach. Whereas in European projects each participant has always had an equal voice in management – even if the workload was apportioned – any company with a minority share of a project with an American firm was considered a minority voice.

But since the early 1980s interest has been growing in the United States for collaboration in NATO in developing defence systems and co-ordinating defence procurement. That interest is emerging both within political circles in the United States and within the United States' defence industry itself. British officials in the field of defence procurement do not believe that this increased interest has any one specific cause – although they recognize that as the problems of the American budget deficit have mounted during the second Reagan term, so the possibility of saving money by spreading NATO resources has become more attractive. They believe that the greater American willingness to work with its NATO allies arises from the efforts of a few people in the Pentagon and of European NATO officials who have supported greater harmonization of defence procurement by NATO countries. American industrialists also recognize the need for international collaboration. In June 1987 a senior executive from United Technologies, Colin Green, told a conference in Paris that his company wanted to see real moves in that direction, and highlighted what he called the 'crippling, wasteful duplication in NATO's defence research efforts'.

Politicians, officials and the defence contractors also now accept that collaboration will have to begin at the start of research. One of the biggest obstacles to defence collaboration was that voiced by European firms during the Westland crisis – namely, that by working with Americans they would be handing over their trade secrets to a rival. If companies are only brought together after a research project has begun, the fear that original work is being lost will always be present. This problem has hampered some of the early European collaborative projects, and stands in the way of NATO-wide collaboration.

Sam Nunn, the scourge of the European members of NATO over defence spending, has also been the prime force in the United States behind the move towards greater harmonization of arms development and the economies that go with it. As far back as 1977 he was responsible for giving the United States Defence Secretary the power to by-pass the Buy American Act if he felt it would promote the concept of a two-way street in defence procurement within NATO. In 1983 Nunn, along with two other prominent senators John Glenn and William Roth, went on to promote the concept of 'memoranda of understanding' between the United States and its NATO allies aimed at harmonizing weapons development. More recently, he launched the so-called Nunn initiative, which began as an amendment to the annual National Defence Authorization Act in 1985. It led to the provision of $100 million of new funding for NATO procurement projects, and another $25 million for testing equipment produced by other members of NATO, with a view to developing the two-way street.

The amendment received widespread support in Congress, and was passed overwhelmingly. That was at least partly due to the emphasis on co-operation from the very start of a project. Senator Nunn himself believes that collaboration in any other form would immediately run into difficulties because of both the 'Buy American' mentality and because American corporations would have to make sacrifices if development was already underway. Both these factors would have provoked opposition in Congress.

The Nunn amendment money has been used in a wide range of projects, including a NATO frigate replacement for the 1990s, 155mm guided shells, an advanced sea mine and continued development of the vertical take-off and landing technology in the Harrier. The scale of the projects has varied. The NATO frigate replacement involves nine countries: The United States, Canada, Britain, France, West Germany, Belgium, Holland, Spain and Italy. Other projects simply involve two nations – such as the vertical take-off technology project between Britain and the United States.

Projects are chosen for Nunn amendment finance after being nominated by any one of the allies, by NATO or by the Independent European Programme Group. Not all are accepted – in 1986 the IEPG suggested six likely candidates, of which only four were eventually given funding. Ultimately the decision lies with America, though the merits of each one are discussed within NATO. Various conditions are attached; the most important that the military service backing each project must be willing to take over the development funding once the Nunn amendment money has run out, and that they must provide clear provision for this in their long-term financial plans.

By autumn 1987 a total of fifteen projects had reached the stage where either memoranda of understanding had been signed or statements of intent issued. Eighteen more projects are under consideration and a total of $2.9 billion has been assigned over the next four years.

The Nunn amendment was followed by a second – and perhaps even more important – legislative change, introduced by Senator Dan Quayle of Indiana. While the Nunn amendment motivated the American armed services to become involved in international collaboration, the Quayle amendment removed many of the legal obstacles which had hampered such ventures. It gave the Secretary of State the power to override those aspects of United States defence legislation which had made it difficult or impossible for American firms to join international development projects. For example, contracts in European collaborative ventures had been divided according to the country's investment. But American law demanded that all contracts should be put out to competitive tender. The Quayle amendment provided the means to bypass such legislative handicaps. Quayle himself believes that an increase in collaborative projects can only benefit NATO by improving standardization and efficiency. And, he says: 'It is a recommitment to the alliance, to the principles of NATO, that we're here to stay; we've got to have this as a joint effort. I think that people are beginning to see that this is an efficient way to do business with our allies.'

There was, though, an important disadvantage to the Quayle amendment, which in the event of a collaborative project breaking down at an early stage, gave the partners in the project the right to stop the use of those early technological developments elsewhere. In other words, if the United States pulled out of a joint development project with Britain, Britain could only turn to other potential partners if the United States Government gave its blessing. That restriction has yet to be tested in practice, but could jeopardize future collaboration if the United States really did pursue those provisions.

The Nunn amendment system also has its drawbacks. Money provided for these NATO-wide projects has to be spent within the United States, which inevitably means that most of it goes to American firms. Furthermore, the Nunn Amendment system represents only a tiny proportion of the total American defence research budget: currently the United States spends around £1 billion on collaborative projects – less than 3 per cent of the total. By contrast, the major European collaborative programmes have taken up well over 10 per cent of European research budgets.

There are other uncertainties. Britain and its European allies don't yet know to what extent the Americans will provide their most advanced technology to projects involving other countries. Nor can they be certain about the long-term commitment of the United States to projects like those established with the Nunn money. But although Britain recognizes these problems, the onus is very much on the Americans to show their hand, rather than vice versa. It will be American pressure, more than anything, which pushes NATO-wide collaboration in the future.

The Nunn amendment projects have provided a means of improving NATO-wide collaboration but they have also – like the Westland affair – served to highlight the dilemma that faces Europe. The American armed forces are by far the biggest single market for defence systems, but despite the moves towards the two-way street in arms supply that Sam Nunn has so enthusiastically endorsed, there is little prospect of the Americans buying a complete, major defence system, such as the Eurofighter, from its allies. In projects of that scale it will always buy American, if only because of the political pressures to do so. Equally, there is as yet no sign that the Americans are going to pass project leadership on key NATO developments to its allies.

Furthermore, in projects where the Americans have been willing to share research and development effort, the Europeans have found that their share has failed to live up to expectations. The classic example of that was over the American decision to let some of its allies develop part of the technology for the Strategic Defence Initiative – President Reagan's 'Star Wars' project. In June 1987 the British House of Commons Select Committee on defence revealed that British industry had only been given SDI contracts worth around £20 million, with expectations that the figure would reach £100 million by the end of 1987. The Government had declared it expected to get a total of £1.5 billion. That report led to criticism of the United States from the British Defence Secretary George Younger, who accused the Pentagon of not giving British companies similar opportunities to those open to American contractors in Europe.

In addition, the two-way street, whether in collaboration or sales, depends on political will in the United States. The size of the American trade deficit is certain to renew protectionist tendencies in Congress and in the United States administration. Protectionist pressure was already strong in Congress before the Stock Market crash in October 1987 highlighted the severe deficit problem the United States faces, and the scale of the trade deficit is certain to increase this. Senators and Congressmen are never likely to be particularly enthusiastic about plans to give a contract that might have gone to a corporation in their own state to a foreign supplier. The British Government was already worried about the threat to the two-way street well before the crash – in his speech to the American Chamber of Commerce in London four months earlier George Younger said he was worried by 'the failure of many important and influential individuals in Congress . . . to realize the true nature of the two-way street'. He argued that with a healthy trade surplus over the rest of NATO in defence equipment American industry had more to lose than its European competitors from a cut-back in trade.[6]

The Westland issue showed that the British have several options. It is now widely acknowledged that international collaboration between defence industries will become more and more common. Sam Nunn and his supporters have created a framework for that collaboration to develop on a NATO-wide basis, but almost certainly with the United States as the key partner. Michael Heseltine and his supporters want Britain to play a key role in a European defence industry that both competes with and sometimes works together with its American counterpart. Though the two-way street has increased British defence sales in the United States, events like the Nimrod affair demonstrate that the American industry retains much of the financial power it enjoyed twenty-five years ago. Britain could not pay for a contract-winning offset arrangement like that offered by Boeing to British industry.

Like Britain at the time of the TSR2 cancellation, the United States is beginning to discover that it is expensive to do everything itself. But although the United States may be keen to participate in international projects, it has yet to demonstrate that it is prepared to become involved in projects such as Tornado, and to buy the end product. As long as that situation exists, Britain will have to continue its involvement in European projects competing with the United States. The two-way street has not removed the basic inequalities between the industries of Britain and the United States.

If the British Government allows its commitment to Europe to be compromised by incidents such as the Westland crisis it runs the risk of losing the benefits of twenty years of collaboration. And until the United States can prove that its view of international defence collaboration goes considerably further than the Nunn amendment system, Britain cannot afford to lose those benefits. Otherwise the future of the British defence industry will be as no more than a component supplier dependent on favourable offset arrangements. That would be the ultimate come-down for an industry that forty years ago had few equals.

11

☆☆★☆☆

INDUSTRIES ABROAD

*There are about 20,000 companies on our computer involved in
Anglo-American trade. You'd be amazed by the things that are sold –
starting with candles at one end of the scale, there's a lot in fashion
wear, in furniture, and in foods and wines – and much the same
thing applies in reverse into the United States – one firm that's
expanded over there in the past two years makes door furniture.
Really you can hardly find areas where they're not.*

Harry Cressman, Director General of the
American Chamber of Commerce in London.

AMERICAN products and businesses are to be found throughout
British life. On a typical day the average Briton will breakfast on
American cereal, like shredded wheat or cornflakes, made by Nabisco
or Kellogg, perhaps washed down with a mug of Maxwell House coffee
(part of General Foods) or a glass of American-produced Florida orange
juice. The British may be wearing blue jeans made by Wrangler or Levi
Strauss. The family car is likely to be American – a Vauxhall or a Ford –
and even the petrol could come from one of the three big American
firms: Esso, Mobil and Texaco. The evening's entertainment is also
heavily dependent on America: you may go to one of the big American
fast-food chains, such as McDonald's or Pizza Hut, for a cheap meal out,
or watch an American-made television series such as *Dallas*, or perhaps
a Hollywood-made film. Even if you go to a pub, you could well be
drinking a few glasses of one of the increasingly popular American
beers, like Miller Lite and Budweiser. The British public shop in
department stores like Selfridges (which originated in North America)
or in huge indoor shopping centres (such as Brent Cross) of the kind
found all over the United States.

American industry in Britain, although vital to the British economy,
has been highly controversial at times – the plan to sell British Leyland
trucks and Land Rover to the Americans in 1986, for example, caused
almost as much debate as the Westland affair had done. The aggressive
marketing by American companies with factories in the United Kingdom
and by American-based firms looking for opportunities in the British

market is often seen as the reason for the 'Americanization of the British way of life'. Although that is too simplistic a view, it is nonetheless indicative of just how successful American companies have been in Britain. The American industrial presence in Britain – and the growing number of British firms with divisions in the United States – is another example of the way nations have become increasingly inter-dependent since the war. Although American companies have operated in the United Kingdom throughout this century, American subsidiaries in the United Kingdom are now part of an international production system, making components for factories in other countries and products for sale overseas. A strike by the British-based work-force at Ford in early 1988 brought production to a halt at Ford plants in other Western European countries. The spread of American business around the world and increased high costs in the United States have led many American companies to shift production overseas, often to developing countries as well as to Europe, with the result that while there are vast numbers of American firms operating in Britain, many of the largest can no longer be properly called American. They are multi-national in the true sense of the word.

The industrial interchange over the years has been so great that few people realize that many companies and products regarded as inherently British – Esso, Mars, Vauxhall – are in fact American. That phenomenon is seldom experienced by British firms operating in the United States, although one of Britain's biggest companies, Hanson Trust, recently ran an advertising campaign highlighting the fact that many Americans did think it was American.

But although there are British companies in the United States, and American companies in Britain, their relative impact on the two economies is vastly different. Few British firms operating in the United States are major employers or play a significant role in the market, in contrast to the situation in Britain, where the American multi-nationals play a very important part. Major industries such as the motor and computing industry are dominated by American firms, and millions of people depend on American companies for their livelihoods.

Britain began the exchange of investment between the two countries in the mid-nineteenth century. Many of the early British investors were textile companies, firms like J. and J. Clark which set up a cotton thread factory in New Jersey in 1864 and J. and P. Coats which opened a plant five years later. They were followed by the Northern Irish firm William Barbour and Sons, and then by Courtaulds, which developed a flourishing rayon business in the United States. Other industries invested in the United States as well, British firms bought American breweries in the 1880s, and other companies investing there included part of what would eventually become ICI. But by the turn of the century many American firms had started to invest in Britain. Samuel Colt's gun company was one of the first arrivals, to be followed by companies like Kodak, which arrived in 1891, and Ford, which started producing cars in Manchester in 1911 and within two years had captured a quarter of the market.[1]

The flow of American investment into Britain and Europe was dramatically increased by the First World War. Not only did the war increase demand for American products, it also destroyed Britain's position as the world's foremost foreign investor. In 1914 Britain still provided nearly 50 per cent of the world's foreign investment while the United States provided less than 20 per cent. By the start of the Second World War the United States had overtaken Britain and by 1950 it was investing three times as much abroad as Britain. And much of that was in Britain itself.

That flow of investment was not visible with the arrival in Britain of many of the biggest American firms, many of which have since become household names in Britain. General Motors bought Vauxhall in 1925, and has been here ever since. The tyre companies Goodyear and Firestone opened factories, as did the food conglomerates Nabisco, Mars and General Foods. Hoover, which was already selling its appliances in Britain, opened a factory there in 1932.

American investment and the impact of American products in Britain was most prominent in the 1950s. The United States economy was buoyant in the years after the Second World War and a vast new consumer product industry grew up to supply a richer America. But the same consumer sector took much longer to develop in Britain because its economy remained depressed until the early 1950s, with rationing and relatively little expenditure on household equipment (such as washing machines and refrigerators for example). As the British economy picked up in the 1950s, so the demand for consumer products started to build up. At the same time the meteoric growth that American firms had experienced in the United States in the late forties was slowing down, and they began to focus instead on the potential in Europe, investing in new factories and opening or re-opening local networks of dealers.

A typical example of the type of firm that developed its business in

Britain in the mid-fifties in response to the resurgent market was the California Packing Corporation – better known for its Del Monte trademark. It had had factories in the United Kingdom since the late nineteenth century, and had exported produce to Britain in the inter-war years. But for some fifteen years between the start of the war and the mid-fifties the business dried up because of rationing and wartime austerity, and the company ran down its British operations. In the early fifties Del Monte found its ability to expand in the United States was limited; the steady growth in sales through the years of post-war prosperity in the United States was beginning to tail off. Around that time a senior executive from the corporation was visiting Europe, and was surprised by the relative prosperity of the cities he visited. It was clearly a market to be exploited. And so Del Monte revived its British operations, and established a new sales structure and an advertising campaign to boost its products. The corporation, which is now part of Nabisco, has been a brand leader with its food products ever since.[2] In the post-war years, successive American Governments actively encouraged their companies to invest overseas as a means of cutting the huge balance of payments problem that built up during the 1950s because of America's enormous military commitments. Generous tax incentives were provided to companies planning to go multi-national. But there was little reverse flow of investment. Manacled by exchange controls, few British companies were able to establish themselves in the United States.

The flow of American investment in Britain reached a high point around 1960, when it amounted to almost 60 per cent of total American investment in Europe. Since then the proportion has fallen to less than 40 per cent in 1971, and then to 32 per cent in 1981 – although it has now grown back to around 40 per cent. The total investment is enormous. By 1977 American firms had invested nearly \$55 billion in the United Kingdom out of around \$155 billion in the EC as a whole. A significant part of the relative decline in the 1960s came with the formation of the European Economic Community, and its plans to form a tariff and duty-free zone in Western Europe. The possibility that this might be achieved induced many American firms to invest in continental Europe. The opportunities provided by such a huge, harmonized market were enormous, but there was also the risk that if American firms didn't move fast, they would lose out to a resurgent European manufacturing industry. After Britain joined the EC, American invest-ment returned to Britain. Today, this country is the most popular

European centre for American firms, securing, for example, more than twice as much American money as the West Germans.

By the end of the 1960s some 10 per cent of British industry was owned by the Americans. That figure has remained constant ever since, and today around a tenth of the private sector work-force is working for subsidiaries of, or directly for, American companies. American firms also pay round 13 per cent of the total wage bill of that work-force.

Many American firms have become the dominant employer in their area, leaving communities dependent on them. Typical examples are General Motors, whose Vauxhall subsidiary is the key employer in Luton, and IBM, which dominates Greenock in Scotland. American companies have also been heavily involved in the growth of many of Britain's new towns. There are now, for example, more than seventy American firms operating in Warrington/Runcorn, near Manchester, and a similar number in Britain's best known new town, Milton Keynes. American firms have played an important role in the development of Scotland's so-called Silicon Glen, in and around the town of Livingstone, and near Edinburgh, and in the high technology corridor that has grown up along the M4 motorway west of London.

One typical example of a town that has benefited enormously from American investment is Swindon at the western end of the M4 corridor. The town grew up as an engineering centre for Brunel's Great Western Railway, but in recent years has seen heavy job losses and the closure of its railway workshops. Today it has become a centre for high tech companies, many of them American. More than 5 per cent of the town's work-force, or around 6,500 people, is now employed by American-owned companies, including well-known names like Union Carbide, Monsanto, Doubleday and Semi-Conductors.

Britain is uniquely placed to attract American investment is its geographical position, which is ideal for an American company looking to establish manufacturing bases in Europe. The lack of a language barrier, and the similar culture, has made it easier for American managers to deal with local bureaucracy and regulations. It has also made it easier to recruit and train local work-forces and managers. Companies are also attracted by the similarities between the British and American legal systems, and in accounting practices. Because of these advantages Britain is likely to remain the prime European recipient of American finance in the foreseeable future.

In addition, the severe problems caused by high unemployment in Britain led central government to pursue a policy of special development in the worst-hit areas. In practice, that has meant particularly attractive financial deals for American companies looking to invest in Europe – and prepared to establish themselves in badly-affected parts of Britain. In areas like Livingstone, for example, the Scottish Office has given grants of 15 per cent of capital investment to companies moving into the area. In a few particularly badly hit parts of the country even higher grants have been on offer, up to a theoretical – though seldom reached – 40 per cent of the total investment in a new venture. And manufacturing companies have also enjoyed a substantial reduction in business rates if they locate in badly hit areas. Those financial benefits have undoubtedly contributed to the large number of new American ventures in the United Kingdom in the past few years.

United States firms have played a particularly important role in sustaining employment in Northern Ireland, which has suffered more than any other part of the United Kingdom from unemployment. While some ventures – notably the abortive De Lorean sports car and the Lear Fan jet airliner – have proved fiascos (millions of pounds of taxpayers' money remains unaccounted for after the De Lorean collapse, for example), there are several flourishing American ventures in the region. In late 1987 a total of twenty-five American firms operated in Northern Ireland, employing more than 11,000 people and producing a variety of products ranging from motor parts to chemicals and tobacco. Some of those firms have had problems in recent years, though not because of events in the province. The tobacco-maker Gallahers, for example, owned by the firm American Brands, has been forced to run down its long-established Belfast factory, although it is switching some production to another plant in the Province. But others have also been arriving, including the engineering giant McDonnell Douglas which has a growing computer software division on the edge of Belfast.

The Americans play an important and influencial role in the British economy, particularly since the widespread closures in the British manufacturing sector in the early 1980s. The most influential companies are the big multi-nationals, particularly the two big motor manufacturers Ford and General Motors; the major oil companies Esso, Mobil and Texaco; and the giant computer manufacturer IBM. The third largest major American car maker, Chrysler, no longer has a British operation. Its United Kingdom subsidiary ran into serious financial difficulties in the 1970s, and was eventually sold to the French firm Peugeot.

Although the Japanese have also entered the world market, the two

American motor giants dominate the British car market, and until the recent slump in demand for freight vehicles, held a sizeable share of British truck production as well. Ford's car division has consistently held a market share of around 30 per cent in the 1980s, and during the severe recession in the United States' industry after the 1979 oil crisis, Ford's European operations were said to be propping up the American parent. General Motors' Vauxhall subsidiary has, by revamping its model range, built its share up from less than 10 per cent in the 1970s to something over 15 per cent. It is now in second place in the manufacturers' league table, ahead of the all-British Rover Group which a decade ago rivalled Ford as the market leader. However, both firms import many of the cars and components they sell in Britain from their other Western European operations, leaving their plants in Britain to concentrate on specific parts of the model range. But although the motor industry is dominated by American-owned firms, they do not attract the suspicion that the Japanese face in Britain. The British think of Ford UK and Vauxhall as British in a way that they certainly don't – yet – think of the Nissan operation that recently began production in North-East England.

One significant exception to this view of American companies was the Government's plan in early 1986 to sell the Austin-Rover car group to Ford, and to sell other parts of the state-owned British Leyland group – including its Land Rover and Range Rover divisions and the largest British-owned truck producer Leyland Trucks – to General Motors. The proposals provoked anger in Britain, from politicians and industrialists to graffiti writers! The idea was eventually shelved because of this outcry, particularly over the plan to include Land Rover in the sale. No doubt some of the indignation hung over from the Westland affair a few weeks earlier, but nonetheless it was a good indicator of how nationalistic the British can be.

A second area of British industry where American firms play an important role is in computing. Computer hardware production in Britain is dominated, as it has been in other countries, by IBM. The IBM range of personal computers aimed at the business leader has been the industry standard since it was first released – taking around 40 per cent of the market – and the company has also dominated sales of main-frame computers, well ahead of its only British rival ICL, which narrowly escaped going into liquidation in 1983. A similar situation exists in computer software.

But perhaps the most important contribution made by American industry to the British economy in recent years was in developing Britain's most precious asset in the 1980s – North Sea Oil. Although successive British governments have tried to ensure that as many North Sea development contracts as possible went to British firms, in the early days Britain did not have sufficient technical knowledge to develop its energy resources alone. And there simply weren't enough British operators to fund the massive investment needed to develop the resources.

By contrast, American firms had already spent years working in the Gulf of Mexico and off the shore of California and had both the necessary equipment and the technical expertise. Around half the oilfields in the North Sea have been developed with an American company as the operator – the company that actually runs the rigs and the developments – and many other fields have American firms as partners but not operators.

Furthermore the percentage of fields operated by American firms does not take into account the huge role played by the world's biggest oil company Exxon/Esso. In 1965 it went into partnership in North Sea oil development with its part-British rival Shell, an arrangement which has been highly successful. Essentially the arrangement meant that the two pooled their expertise in offshore oil development from the start, and divided all oil recovered from the North Sea as soon as it was shipped ashore. But Shell remains the operating company. The decision to establish this working relationship between the two multi-nationals was taken for two reasons. Firstly, Esso believed it would benefit from the British infrastructure that Shell already had in place, because Shell is a part-British operation. And it already had expertise in offshore development in areas like the Gulf of Mexico. Esso admits that it benefited from the link with one of Britain's best known companies which helped when the two companies applied for licences to develop new parts of an important British asset. Although the huge resources of Esso and its American parent might suggest that the company could have made its own way in the North Sea, it has been a remarkably successful example of transatlantic industrial co-operation. The joint venture has been the single largest producer of oil and gas in the North Sea over more than twenty years.

But though the multi-nationals are mostly of American origin, in the 1980s it is becoming increasingly difficult to view them as American. More than anything, they typify the way business transcends geographical and political boundaries, drawing countries like Britain and the

United States into a wider economic network. Most of the multinationals now operate on a regional basis, co-ordinating production from a
single headquarters that covers an entire continent, allowing individual
countries and plants to specialize in a small part of the product or
component range. The 1988 dispute between Ford UK and its work-
force provided a perfect example of this. Even before the strike began,
the veteran Engineering Union official Jimmy Airlie had predicted that
'Ford's European operation will collapse'.[3] When the action began it
closed plants in Belgium and West Germany, because of shortages of
British-made components. The diesel version of the Ford Fiesta, for
example, is made in Germany, but its engine is built in Britain. Likewise
some Ford Transit vans are made in Belgium, but their engines are built
on the other side of the English Channel.

Traditionally, most British subsidiaries of American firms are encouraged to be autonomous, with their American parents retaining a
watchful eye – rather than direct control – over what they do. Today
General Motors, Ford and IBM all have corporate headquarters for
their European operations – Ford in the United Kingdom, IBM in Paris
and General Motors in Zurich – as do the big household product groups
such as Proctor and Gamble, and General Foods, both of which have
European offices in the United Kingdom.

General Motors is one of the most recent to make the transition, ten
years after their main rival Ford. General Motors' main British
subsidiary is the Vauxhall motor company and, until its sale in 1987, its
Bedford trucks division, although the company does have several
smaller subsidiaries, including the newly acquired Lotus Cars. At its
peak Vauxhall was one of Britain's major employers, with a total
work-force of around 37,000, and able to develop products out of its
own resources, giving it a high degree of independence from the
American parent in Detroit. Because of the stark variations in demand
for cars which involved producing huge gas guzzlers for the Americans
as well as smaller cars for British families, subsidiaries like Vauxhall
were left relatively free to design and develop their own vehicles.

But changes in the motor industry have changed Vauxhall's position
dramatically. Although the oil crises of the 1970s, and regular labour
difficulties and strikes, made it harder for subsidiaries like Vauxhall to
make money, the real cause of the decline has been the escalating cost
of new technology. The result has been to draw what was once an
American-owned British company into a worldwide corporation.
Rationalization within General Motors has altered the position of its

British operations. General Motors Europe was formed in 1986 to structure the company's European operations so that they catered for the whole European market rather than having individual subsidiaries catering for particular countries. Because of those changes, Vauxhall, for example, has now lost its role as a car designer to its counterpart in Germany, Opel, while all General Motors' European truck design has been concentrated in Britain. And Opel now designs those cars for the European market. Opel cars in Germany are almost identical to Vauxhall cars on the road in Britain, but with different names.

In the computer industry IBM has also incorporated its British subsidiary into a wider structure although on a different basis to that of General Motors. All the company's research and development effort is controlled by the corporate headquarters in the United States, although the work is done globally. For example, IBM's research laboratory at Hurstley in Hampshire did much of the graphic design for the second generation of the company's personal computer, while the hardware was designed in Florida. But the British laboratory is controlled from the United States and has no direct link with IBM UK. That arrangement means that all product investment and development decisions are taken in the United States.

The company's manufacturing effort is organized regionally. The two IBM plants in Britain, at Greenock and Havant, near Portsmouth, are under the direction of the headquarters in Paris. Each plant usually produces one part of the product range for its own particular region – the Greenock factory, for example, produces the IBM personal computer for the European market while another in North America produces the same product for that market. There are occasional exceptions, such as where a product is aimed at such a small market that it isn't worth producing it in more than one place. But, in general, companies like IBM try to regionalize their production to cut costs.

Within IBM, the subsiduary, such as IBM UK, is responsible for marketing the product, and as such acts as an independent entity, although there is some co-ordination of pricing policy to make sure it isn't cheaper to buy the company's products in another country.

There are a few companies that have abandoned the concept of European headquarters. Esso, with its American parent Exxon, is an example of this, taking the globalization of business still further. For around twenty years there was an Esso Europe, based in London, which supervised the work of the various subsidiaries throughout Western Europe. But that office was closed in 1986 as part of a world-wide restructuring of the company. Esso claims that the improvement in communications available to companies was responsible for the changes. It argues that an efficient internal computer system, linked by modern networks, reduces the need for American parent companies to keep a close watch on the operations of their subsidiaries, by actually being geographically close at hand. Esso executives can now send messages directly to each other's desk top computer terminals right across the globe. 'It doesn't even matter if he's out,' one said. 'He'll get the message when he gets back from lunch' – or if it's a different time zone, 'when he's woken up and come to work.'

Although there are no immediate signs that many other companies will follow suit, the continuing advance of communications technology is likely to make that option increasingly attractive. One advantage of such a move is that the cost compares favourably to that of keeping American executives stationed in Europe. The Anglo-American Chamber of Commerce in London estimates that it costs an American firm around two-and-a-half times as much to keep an American executive in Europe as it does to employ a local man or woman. Whilst the majority of American companies employ a mostly British work-force and management in their United Kingdom subsidiaries, increasingly top management is becoming international. Where the large corporations have European corporate headquarters a significant proportion of the staff will tend to be from the American parent. Both IBM Europe and General Motors Europe, for example, have American presidents. General Motors, however, is more conservative in its appointment of managers to its subsidiaries. In Britain the top General Motors executives are always recruited from the corporate headquarters in the United States. There are now fewer American board members in British operations than there have been in the past, though the two most powerful positions, Managing Director and Finance Director, are still held by Americans.

In fact most of the large corporations operate on international management career patterns. American executives will work for two- or three-year assignments in Europe while British executives will spend time working in the main headquarters in the United States. Exxon, for example, tends to give executives marked out as directors of its European subsidiaries work experience in the United States and a short period shadowing one of the directors of the corporation's main board. That process has also worked in some British firms operating through subsidiaries in the United States. Shell, for example, regularly posts its high-flying manager to the United States. In a company like IBM, where the local subsidiary plays a lesser role in the global corporation, the flow of managers across the Atlantic is smaller. There are no American managers currently working for IBM UK, though there are two or three British managers on assignments in the United States. There, most management exchanges are through IBM Europe.

Interestingly, while the interchange of employees in the large corporations is limited to senior levels, in smaller companies the reverse is true. There, staff lower down the ladder go to the United States, whether for technical training or to get experience of operating methods in other parts of the company. This is because in the smaller subsidiaries the management team is small, and members cannot easily be spared.

The globalization of business can have detrimental effects as well as benefits. The fact that a subsidiary in Britain is doing well does not shield it from problems elsewhere. The most obvious example in recent years was the closure of the Caterpillar tractor plant near Glasgow in 1987 with the loss of more than 1,200 jobs. Only four months before, the company had announced a massive investment programme in the plant. Caterpillar in America admitted at the time that its Scottish operation was highly efficient and that it had an excellent record of labour relations. But the company had been forced to review its operations after deciding that it had too much capacity world-wide.

Despite the scale of American investment in Britain, Britain invests as much money in the United States as the United States does in Britain – although the relative impact of the two flows of investment is vastly different. The United States employs 10 per cent of workers in British industry, whereas the British role is tiny in an economy on the scale of the United States.

Even so, the flow of British money into the United States since the lifting of exchange controls in 1979 has been startling. British firms have been frenetic in their takeover operations in America in recent years. Indeed there was one ironic incident at the time of the Westland and Land Rover disputes. The two crises coincided with detailed negotiations by a British consortium looking to buy two major American airports, including Washington National on the outskirts of the capital. It needs little imagination to predict the political row if it were announced that an American company wanted to buy London's Gatwick Airport. Yet American officials in Washington say that moves by British companies into the American market would never create anything like the furore seen over Westland and Land Rover. As one put it: 'The American public tends to be far too provincial. They just don't worry about individual companies that are in a different part of the country.' That said, even the Americans have begun to take notice of the way Britain and other countries have been buying their industries. An issue of *Time* magazine in autumn 1987 had the following front page caption: 'The Selling of America – Foreign Investors Buy Buy Buy'.[4] The range of American operations that have been bought up by foreign investors taking advantage of the decline in the United States dollar – which fell by 40 per cent between 1985 and 1987 – has been staggering.

British investors now own around $1 billion-worth of property in Washington DC, including part of the now infamous Watergate complex, along with considerable parts of Manhattan and other American cities. Britain owns such famous American brands as Smith and Wesson handguns, Smith Corona typewriters, Baskin Robbins and Dayvilles ice cream, Jaccuzi whirlpool baths; it owns California vineyards, chains of American petrol stations, shoe-makers, and America's biggest employment agency – even the famous department store Saks Fifth Avenue. Between 1980 and 1986 British investment in the United States rose from $14.1 billion to $51.4 billion, more than twice as much as Japan and almost three times as much as West Germany. Only the Dutch, traditionally heavy investors in the United States, come anywhere near the British total with around $43 billion. Some British takeovers of American firms have been astonishingly audacious. In June 1987 the little-known London advertising agency WPP launched a successful $566 million takeover of the world's most famous agency J. Walter Thompson – a company many times its size. Two months later the relatively small London employment agency Blue Arrow spent $1.3 billion on acquiring the huge American employment agency Manpower, again a much bigger company.

The best known predators for American companies in recent years have been two of Britain's most colourful industrialists, Sir James Goldsmith and Lord Hanson. The Hanson Corporation now employs nearly 40,000 Americans in nine companies acquired in recent years. It also added a touch of irony with its most recent purchase, the consumer product group Kidde, bought in November 1987. It was Kidde's British subsidiary that fell foul of President Reagan's attempt to stop strategic exports at the time of the Siberian gas pipeline affair in 1982.

But there are now signs of some American resistance to British takeovers. The British firms Beazer, and BAT, both faced strong political and legal resistance to their attempts to win control of the American companies Koppers and Farmers respectively, and the resistance may increase when future British takeovers are launched in the USA.

Despite the flow of British finance into the United States, there is little likelihood that British industrial firms will establish themselves in the American market in the way the Japanese have done, or on the scale that American firms have in the United Kingdom. American products, sold with highly effective marketing techniques, have had a great impact on all parts of British society over the course of forty years. The Americanization of Britain has become something of a cliché in recent years, and there is no doubt that American concepts and products have been highly influential in the United Kingdom since the 1950s.

American marketing executives argue that it is too easy to put down the so-called Americanization of the British way of life to the aggressive actions of large American multi-nationals. They say that the American firms were doing no more than respond to a growing consumer demand in the United Kingdom. The American corporations did well because their experience of the American market gave them a head start in both marketing techniques and in finding the right products to offer. Fast-food chains, for example, have done well because the changing needs of the public have meant that people want to be able to eat swiftly and inexpensively. For example, as more British women entered full- or part-time employment so the need for convenience food has developed. In fact, though McDonalds has established itself as one of the most successful restaurant chains in Britain since opening its first branch in London in 1974, there were Wimpy bars in Britain long before that. What companies like McDonalds have done is to market their product more effectively and provide a better service over the years.

A considerable part of that success lies in the strength of the American advertising industry. When American corporations invested heavily in Britain in the 1950s, their advertising agencies also came here. During the Second World War there had only been four American advertising agencies with offices in London, but by 1960 that figure had risen to thirty-six, with a total, between them, of 281 offices in Britain. Some started from scratch, but the majority bought out British firms and used those firms as vehicles to move into the British market. That trend continued for more than twenty years, with only four of the top twenty firms in the early 1980s being British. However, WPP's takeover of J. Walter Thompson, and the rapid expansion of agencies like Saatchi and Saatchi, are clear signs that the trend looks to be in reverse.

The mid-fifties was the perfect time for the American promotional machine to set to work on the British public. Wartime restrictions on food and other products remained well into the fifties, and restrictions on hire purchase, which had kept down the sales of household appliances, were only lifted in 1954. The British had been deprived of things that their American counterparts had enjoyed throughout the years of hardship, and demand was buoyant. The appearance of commercial television for the first time in 1955 provided an important visual outlet for the advertising agencies. In real terms the amount spent in Britain on advertising has more than doubled every decade since the end of the war. But for much of that time British agencies were behind their American rivals in terms of marketing techniques and market research. The United States' agencies developed high-profile brand marketing, and many of the brands that benefited from their efforts were those the American corporations were trying to sell abroad.

By contrast, British firms wasted many opportunities. The British Motor Corporation – the predecessor of today's Rover Group – should have made substantial profits from its highly successful Mini, launched in 1957. Instead the company failed to use modern methods of market research, and priced the car lower than its customers would have been willing to pay, making it an instant success but not a great money spinner. When the company tried to break into the American market after the Second World War, it sent a shipload of cars to New York with no plans for what to do with them once they got there. On arrival there was no berth waiting to store the cars, which had to be unloaded elsewhere. And there were no dealers lined up to sell the cars once they were unloaded. The cars sat in port for weeks until outlets could be found to sell them. There were a few British achievements in that era – Beachams successfully launched several products, including Macleans toothpaste and Brylcreem in the United States, and both Schweppes and EMI enjoyed some success in American markets – but they were not the norm. Although the majority of British firms did eventually adapt to new marketing techniques and the realities of global competition in Britain, they did so only after the American firms had built up a sizeable market share, and after many export opportunities had been lost.

That head start American firms enjoyed over their British counterparts in the fifties and sixties is the real reason for the apparent Americanization of British society. Although the way Britain has developed over the years since the war appears to match very closely many aspects of life in the United States, that has been due to the fact that the needs of the modern consumer have been very similar from country to country. Where the Americans succeeded was to take advantage of those to win a healthy share of highly lucrative European markets. Even in particularly high-profile areas, for example the marketing of American television programmes, such as *Dallas, The Muppets*, and *Starksy and Hutch*, with all the hype and glamour attached to them, is at root no more than a question of companies selling their product overseas successfully. No American concept or product has been forced upon the British – they have done well because the consumer wanted them, or because advertising succeeded in creating a demand for them.

Interestingly, advertising executives in New York say the wheel has now come full circle. While in the past it has been the United States that was widely acknowledged to be the best at marketing its own products and at developing new advertising techniques, it is now Britain that is the most highly regarded. The growth of British ownership of American companies, and the revival of such high-profile products as the Jaguar luxury motor car have reversed a trend of thirty years. It is, of course, wholly unreasonable to expect Britain in the future to play anything like the role in the American economy that the United States has played in British industry. But equally it is clear that in the years ahead business will continue to break down borders, and more and more British entrepreneurs are going to be looking to the other side of the Atlantic as the place to expand.

12

☆☆★☆☆

EXTRATERRITORIALITY AND INTERNATIONAL TRADE

This invasion of our sovereignty is wholly unacceptable to all sections of political opinion in Britain.

Spencer Batiste MP, on the use of American laws
against companies operating in Britain.

IN THE past thirty years there have been regular trade disputes between Europe and the United States, often acrimonious and potentially highly damaging. One issue stands above all others as controversial and divisive. That is the degree to which the United States attempts to impose its laws beyond its boundaries in cases that it believes are crucial to its national interest. This is known as extraterritoriality, and has caused a long series of confrontations between the British and American Governments over what is seen as unwarranted and unjustified intrusion by the United States into British sovereignty.

Although it has been the cause of a wide range of disputes between the British and the Americans, the area where extraterritoriality is most contentious is in the application of strategic export controls – the transfer of the West's most advanced technology to another country.

The United States and the West as a whole have regulations to maintain a close supervision over the application of that technology. The United States has been widely criticized for the way it puts those restrictions into practice, and there is deep hostility in Europe and in industry on both sides of the Atlantic to many of its actions. One of the greatest complaints from Europe is that the framework for controlling the transfer of such technology is another relic of the transatlantic post-war relationship, and hasn't adapted to meet the changing economic realities of the 1980s.

Yet the motivations behind the controls are entirely logical. It is United States Government policy to do all it can to prevent the Soviet Union and its allies from getting hold of crucial technology that could enable them to deploy far more effective weapons systems against

NATO than would otherwise have been the case. Official United States Government figures suggest – in so far as it is possible to quantify such things – that the Soviet Union is roughly ten years behind the West in its technological ability, particularly in the field of computers.

However, the system established to monitor and control the transfer of American technology around the world is now highly divisive. It is resented throughout Europe and has cost the United States billions of dollars-worth of business, both with other Western countries and with the rest of the world. Indeed, some of the features of the current system are absurd in the extreme. The British-based subsidiary of an American firm wanting to ship a piece of high technology to another Western European country, say France or Belgium, has to apply to the United States Government for a licence enabling it to export the product. That process can take up to three months. The same company wanting to ship the same piece of equipment to the People's Republic of China does not need a licence. It is an area that has provoked fury in Britain, where Members of Parliament from all sides of the spectrum have attacked the United States for excessive interference in other countries' affairs. In the United States a strong body of opinion believes that the allies simply aren't pulling their weight in what is regarded as a crucial area of Western security.

There are two mechanisms for monitoring and controlling high technology exports. The first is through Cocom, the Co-ordinating Committee on Multilateral Export Controls, an international organization based in Paris. The United States also unilaterally restricts the flow of some products, blacklisting any firm that doesn't apply to it for permission to sell the American-originated technologies concerned abroad.

Cocom was formed in 1949 by all the NATO countries with the exception of Iceland, but including Japan. It emerged from a general consensus established in the aftermath of the war that some of the West's future strategic plans should be based on the fact that the United States totally dominated much of the world's research, development, and manufacturing capacity – because it alone had escaped the war unscathed. The NATO allies recognized that they could economize numerically in their military strength if the quality of their defence systems remained ahead of the opposition. So while the Soviet Union maintained a massive conventional force, NATO hoped to match them through their huge technology lead. The concept was called the 'force multiplier strategy', and it is still the *raison d'être* behind American concern about high technology imports.

Cocom has three major functions. It draws up the lists of proscribed and restricted goods, of which there are three. The first two have seldom been matters of contention, as they are concerned with nuclear technology and munitions, which are highly unlikely to form part of legitimate sales to the Soviet Union from the West. It is the third list, the industrial list, that has proved so controversial in recent years. That is because of the difficulty of defining civil, and commercial products, and what can be used for strategic purposes. The list is subject to regular review, with 25 per cent of it revised each year. Many industrialists argue that this is far too infrequent, as each individual item only comes up for discussion every four years. Ironically, though Cocom has always been dominated by the Americans, the original lists were based on a British munitions list. In addition, Cocom acts as the forum for requests from member-countries to ship goods on the Cocom lists to third parties, particularly in restricted countries in the Soviet Bloc. And it serves as a co-ordinating body for member-countries' administration and enforcement of the regulations.

However, despite its influence, Cocom has no concrete powers. Individual member-governments have the ultimate right of sovereignty over technology transfer, although there have been no cases in its thirty-eight year history of any of the sixteen members enforcing that right. Ever since it was formed Cocom has been secret – for many years none of its member would acknowledge officially that it existed – and some European government departments, particularly in West Germany, still refuse to admit it exists.

Although there were disputes between members in the early years of Cocom, the real difficulties posed by the system only emerged in the 1970s. Throughout the 1950s and 1960s much of the West's scientific research began in the military field in the design of new weapons technologies which were later adapted for civil use. That left much of the emphasis within Cocom on the munitions and nuclear lists, which have never posed many difficulties to the NATO allies.

But during the 1970s that situation changed, and now, considerable amounts of the West's technological development come from companies operating in the civil field, whether building main-frame computers for business use, or high-technology cash registers to use in supermarkets. The spread of what has become known as 'dual-use technologies' has posed enormous problems for governments. While the cash register in the supermarket is in itself a perfectly harmless piece of equipment, it may well contain a microelectronic component that could be taken out of it and put to use in a weapons system. In the hands of the Soviet Union, so the argument goes, that harmless cash register component could turn a second-rate weapon into one capable of matching the systems deployed by the West.

The United States has deployed considerable evidence demonstrating that the Soviet Union has already used legitimate means to acquire technology that has vastly improved its military capability. A CIA document drawn up in 1985 claimed Moscow had been receiving thousands of pieces of Western equipment and many tens of thousands of classified and unclassified documents a year, with benefit to almost every Soviet military research project. It argued that the assimilation of Western technology has been so broad that the United States and its allies have effectively been subsidizing the Soviet military build-up.

That view has been the driving force behind the United States determination to control the movements of its high technology. The determination has gone even beyond the provisions of the Cocom lists – there are now twenty-seven specific categories of technology unilaterally controlled by the United States. That means that any company – inside the United States or abroad – has to apply for an export licence if it wants to re-export American products that fall into the restricted categories. The same is true if its own products contain parts manufactured in the United States, or with American technology, that fall into the same categories. If it seems complex – it is. The regulations themselves have confused and hindered businesses throughout the Western world. And United States restrictions go further. The Chairman of ICL has confirmed that American engineers need an export licence to work for his company in the United Kingdom, because of technical knowledge they acquired in the United States. And if an American engineer working for ICL writes a piece of software, that software is also subject to American export control restrictions. In 1985 British engineers were told they could only attend a scientific conference in the United States if they were vetted, and signed American export control agreements.[1] Furthermore, the restrictions also cover spare parts. So a supplier asked to provide a replacement for a broken component would need an export licence for that as well.

Hardly surprisingly, the whole question of technology transfer dominates the trade relationship between Britain and the United States, and accounts for most of the duties of Department of Trade officials in London and at the Washington Embassy. Under America's unilateral restrictions, and the provisions of Cocom – which the United States Government enforces rigidly – any company using technology in any way connected to the United States is operating in a legal minefield. And any business found by the Americans to have contravened the strict regulations is liable to be placed on a Government denials list, which makes it illegal for any other company to sell it American technology. There have been several instances of firms going out of business as a result – something that has enraged politicians in the United Kingdom. And there have been allegations that the CIA has monitored and on occasions raided British firms to check on movements of technology.

One company which went out of buisness after becoming embroiled with American restrictions was a Leeds-based firm called Systime. It re-exported equipment produced by the American firm DEC and managed to undercut DEC's own United Kingdom subsidiary by obtaining its supplies through American dealers rather than direct from DEC. But American restrictions put the British firm at a disadvantage. To re-export the United States equipment to, say, France, it needed a licence from the British and from the Americans – a process taking up to a year, making it harder to compete against the American firm. So Systime broke American regulations – though not British law – and sold the equipment with only a British licence. The company was fined $400,000 dollars by the United States Government – with the threat that it would be placed on the United States' denials list if it didn't pay. Allegations from DEC that it had also been trading with the Soviet Bloc followed, leading to Systime being cut off from all American supplies. The combination of this, the prospect of an investigation into the DEC allegations, and the heavy fine caused the company's collapse.[2]

It is this power over British firms that has provoked such anger among British MPs. Even Government ministers have condemned the policy. In July 1985 the Attorney General Sir Michael Havers said in a parliamentary reply to the Liberal Member of Parliament Paddy Ashdown that the policy of extraterritoriality was an 'unwarranted encroachment on UK jurisdiction . . . and contrary to international law'.[3]

The most serious dispute between the two countries over the high technology trade wasn't, in fact, directly linked to strategic considerations. In the late 1970s the Soviet Union negotiated an agreement with several Western European countries to build a pipeline linking those countries to vast reserves of natural gas in a remote part of Siberia. The agreement meant vast amounts of work for Western companies – in

West Germany alone the initial estimates were for equipment makers to be given orders worth nearly £5 billion. The project was always strongly opposed by the United States, which argued forcefully that it would make countries such as West Germany over-dependent on Soviet gas for its energy. The final intention was for the Germans to get about 30 per cent of their needs through the pipeline.

But in 1982 the Reagan administration turned the pipeline project into a weapon against the declaration of martial law in Poland and the crushing of the independent Solidarity trade union. Hard-liners in the administration, particularly the then Defence Secretary Caspar Weinberger, argued forcefully for a direct response against Moscow. The target was to be the Siberian pipeline, with a ban on the use of American technology in building it. Within weeks the White House stepped up the embargo, ruling that it would apply to equipment produced by American manufacturers operating abroad, or by foreign firms operating under licence agreements with American firms.

The European countries affected by the ban – Britain, France, West Germany and Italy – were furious, accusing the United States of infringing their sovereignty. After an abortive attempt to persuade the Americans to back down the British Government ordered the British-based companies involved to fulfil their contracts and to ignore the American instructions. In all, six British companies were affected, including the Glasgow-based John Brown Engineering. They had been contracted to supply six turbines for the pipelines, which had been built with parts from the giant American manufacturing corporation General Electric, and as such were directly affected by the embargo. When John Brown went ahead with its contract and shipped the finished turbines to the Soviet Union at the end of August 1982 it was blacklisted by the United States Government, as were two French firms that did likewise.

Strategically the equipment involved in the pipeline embargo was useless. One of the European-based companies affected was the British-based subsidiary of the United States Kidde Corporation, which had a contract to supply fire prevention equipment for the pipeline. The ban went way beyond any of the norms established within Cocom, and it was this presumption by the United States that they could direct the use of all technology linked to them that provoked such a strong and unified reaction from the four European Governments involved. The British went so far as to invoke trade legislation that would have left the companies involved liable to unlimited fines had they not fulfilled their contracts. Faced with such strong defiance of their action the Amer-

icans were forced to back down. After a month of talks between the two
sides the White House agreed to drop the sanctions.

Despite the lessons of the Siberian pipeline affair – that the United
States' allies are not prepared to tolerate blatant extraterritoriality of
the kind seen during the crisis – the problem of American legislation and
its impact beyond the American borders has not gone away. Perhaps
the most blatant example of the extent of the American regulations
came the year after the pipeline affair when a routine letter from IBM to
thirty of its biggest leasing company customers provoked massive
outcry in Parliament. The letter was intended by IBM as no more than a
clarification for those customers of American law as it affected them,
but the implications were astonishing. The letter told the customers
concerned that under American regulations they would have to get
licences from the United States Commerce Department if they wanted
to reassign any of around a thousand main frame computers installed in
the United Kingdom, to sell them to someone else or to change their
use. In other words, if a company wanted to move a computer from
Manchester to London it had to ask the permission of the United States
Government first.[4]

But what may prove to be the most divisive of all United States
extraterritorial involvement is still to be enacted, buried in a massive
piece of trade legislation for the 1988 session of Congress. It follows
what is widely regarded to have been the most serious breach of
strategic export restrictions in recent years, by the Japanese company
Toshiba and the Norwegian firm Kongsberg. In 1987 it was revealed
that the two companies had sold equipment to the Soviet Union that has
enabled the Russian Navy to make its submarines far harder to detect
than they have been in the past. The two companies were both dealt
with severely by their respective Governments – in Japan Toshiba were
fined, senior executives forced to resign and the junior managers
responsible were arrested and prosecuted. In both countries the
revelations have led to a tightening of restrictions on high technology
exports.

But the reaction in Washington has been stronger still. The United
States is particularly sensitive when the Soviet Bloc succeeds in getting
hold of important Western technology, since it funds much of NATO's
research and development efforts. After the revelations, the feeling in
the United States was that it would cost a substantial amount of money
to fund research to restore the United States Navy's ability to track
Soviet submarines to what it was before the Toshiba sale. The result

has been a furious reaction on Capitol Hill, with an amendment to the 1988 trade legislation that, if enacted, would mean a lengthy ban on the sale of Toshiba products to American firms and their affiliates.

It is there that the scope for a major new confrontation between the United Kingdom and the other EEC countries and the United States exists. By including American affiliate companies – the subsidiaries operating in Britain – in the Toshiba legislation, Congress is threatening to blacklist any European-based subsidiary that buys Toshiba products. The Reagan administration is doing its utmost to have the legislation modified so that it would be discretionary rather than mandatory, but if the amendment goes ahead in the form it was tabled, it seems almost certain to provoke a trade war between the EEC and the United States. Britain in particular, after years of hostility towards American extra-territoriality, could hardly stomach such a blatant infringement of its sovereignty.

The United States faces a second problem with its plan for the rigid enforcement of strategic export controls in the years ahead. In 1992 the EEC is due to introduce the single market in Europe, removing trade and customs barriers between members, with the object of making it as easy to ship goods from one part of the Community to another as it is to ship from one state to another in the United States. But at present American restrictions make it compulsory for firms dealing in American high technology to get a licence to move goods within the EEC. Unless the American restrictions are modified before the EEC changes come into effect, a British high technology company using components falling within the United States' parameters will be unable to take advantage of the benefits of the new freedom of movement within the community. Firms will be unable to spread their production processes around Europe, with part of a product built in one place, and the rest in another, even though non-sensitive industries will have that ability. The legislation will also throw open the whole question of the legality of the United States restrictions. If a contract is not fulfilled because of delays caused by American laws operated within Europe, there is a real possibility that a suit for breach of contract would succeed, and hence invalidate those American laws.

British companies are particularly angry about the way the American restrictions may hinder the creation of a single market in the European Community. ICL is one example. It has an American subsidiary, and markets products made by that subsidiary, and is at the same time an enthusiastic supporter of what has been dubbed 'the single market' or

'Europe sans frontières'. Yet it is not yet certain whether it will be able to reap the benefits of the new situation after 1992. In the years ahead a company like ICL will have no products that do not feature on the Cocom lists or in America's own unilaterally restricted categories. So a leading European high-technology manufacturer will be unable to operate in its own market without regular licencing applications to the United States. That, says ICL, is a situation that simply can't be tolerated and must be changed before 1992.

Companies like ICL face a second threat to their business as a result of the Cocom restrictions. There is now a growing second-hand market in computers around the world, with the result that many third parties are now equipping themselves with mix-and-match computer systems, using personal computers from Third-World producers and parts of larger Western produced systems obtained on the second-hand market. Although such systems are less efficient, they do get round the West's restrictions, and as such are attractive to would-be purchasers in other parts of the world.

The regulations governing British companies using American-made technology components in their products state that components making up more than 25 per cent of the finished item must have an export licence. The figure is reduced to 10 per cent if the sale is to a country classifed by the United States as a 'bad' country. This has created a disincentive for British and other firms to use American components at all. A recent study by the National Academy of Sciences and Engineering in the United States estimated that American industry had lost out heavily in the past few years as overseas customers bought components elsewhere. During the pipeline crisis, for example, when John Brown was cut off by American restrictions from its supply of American parts for its turbines, it was able to get equivalent equipment from a French company. The United States' study revealed that more than 50 per cent of American companies involved in exporting high technology products had lost out because of the restrictions, seeing their business go to rivals not affected by strategic export controls. Its authors found no evidence of United States firms themselves trying to get round the restrictions by getting their British and European subsidiaries to use non-American components instead – though they say that route is available to companies, and certainly could become more common in future.

Many MPs believe that American strategic export controls have been manipulated to benefit American companies at the expense of their competitors here. But the United States has caused itself enormous harm by persisting with such a stringent approach to the control of trade in high technology. In 1985 around 40 per cent of American exports needed a licence, and the National Academy of Sciences' study estimated that the total cost of the restrictions to the American economy was running at the rate of $9 billion a year, and at the expense of around 200,000 jobs. The United States is increasingly dependent on exporting manufactured goods. In an era where it has been running a huge trade deficit, it is hard to see how it can continue to run such a restrictive licencing system in the future – particularly when not only other Western countries, but also the developing nations, such as South Korea and Taiwan, are increasingly able to provide companies with an alternative supply of the parts they need.

The senior State Department official concerned with strategic exports Allan Wendt says the United States accepts the need for reform, but that it cannot be done without parallel reforms throughout all the Cocom countries to ensure that restrictions are absolutely firm. At the moment, he says, some of the Cocom members are making very little effort to enforce the controls on strategic exports that they themselves have gone along with.

In early 1987 there was a strong movement in Congress for a significant reform of the Cocom system. It was felt that the time had come for wholesale reductions of the numbers of goods on the restricted list, which would free many American and foreign companies from the need to get licences. Their minds had been concentrated by letters from two European firms – British Aerospace and the Dutch firm Philips – to the American computer manufacturer Hewlett Packard, advising them that they would be reluctant to buy from them in future unless there was some kind of assurance that the items concerned were not subject to export restrictions. The letters were circulated widely in Congress, and did much to convince its members that something had to be done.

But the revelations of the Toshiba affair a few weeks later has done enormous damage to the case for relaxing American export controls. At a stroke they removed any likelihood that Congress would agree to a major programme of reform – instead the best that can now be hoped for is a small reduction in the number of goods that come under the restrictions.

Ironically, there is little difference in the objectives of all sides involved in the Cocom debate. Everyone, in both government and industry, wants to see the creation of a licensing-free zone within the Cocom countries, whereby high technology goods can be shipped between member-states without any form of restriction whatsoever. The problem lies in the United States where there are concerns about how far the individual members are prepared to go to enforce restrictions on shipping goods outside that area. But if this goal was achieved it would remove the whole question of extraterritoriality at a stroke, as well as the danger of future confrontations between Britain and the United States. There is also no doubt that the way individual products and categories of products are categorized will have to change. ICL say the four-year review system simply doesn't work in an area where products are changing every two years.

There is also a broader reason why change to the Cocom structure has acquired such importance. Disputes over the transfer of technology have serious implications for the unity of the West and particularly of the NATO alliance. For example, as long as the restrictions exist, it will prove difficult to develop a wide-ranging programme of transatlantic defence collaboration, since British companies participating in joint programmes can still find the end product subject to American restrictions. There is also a question about whether the United States will even consider allowing its allies to work on projects and use its most significant technological breakthroughs. At present those technologies are often classified as 'no foreign' – no matter who the foreign country may be. That degree of suspicion can only weaken trust in the NATO alliance.

Furthermore, as long as there is the feeling in Washington – whether in the State Department or Congress – that many allies simply can't be trusted, NATO is also likely to suffer. That is particularly true at a time when the whole question of the United States' commitment to the defence of Europe is under scrutiny. If members of Congress don't think Europe can be trusted with key technology, it is inevitable that they will ask whether the United States should continue to defend it. According to the authors of the study issued by the National Academy of Sciences, there is reason to believe that has already started to happen.

The key problem with Cocom is that it simply hasn't evolved over the years. It was created in the early days of the Cold War, when the United States provided the backbone of Western defence, and when its strategies had the paramount influence in NATO. Cocom simply doesn't take into account either the gradual shift in the balance of power in the Western world, or the way that companies and economies have become globalized. In the 1980s Cocom, as structured at present, has become inappropriate. There is now a move towards reform, but what remains to be seen is whether that reform will come in time to prevent further divisions across the Atlantic.

There have been other areas where the principle of extraterritoriality has been contentious – and the two Governments have taken steps to lessen the potential divisiveness of the United States' regulations. In the late seventies and early eighties, disputes over attempts to apply American anti-trust laws to other fields led to serious confrontation between the two Governments. The two most highly publicized centred on court cases brought in the United States against British-based companies.

The first of these was in 1977, when the American firm Westinghouse took legal action against the British mining conglomerate Rio Tinto Zinc (RTZ) under the anti-trust laws. The case centred on allegations that RTZ had been part of an international cartel that had collaborated to fix the price of uranium, and led to strong diplomatic protests from Britain over the presumption that the American legal system had judicial rights over companies and activities wholly outside the United States. In 1979 Britain responded by passing the Protection of Trading Interests Act, used during the Siberian pipelines crisis to force John Brown to deliver the turbines it had contracted to supply. Then after the collapse of his airline Skytrain in 1982, the businessman Freddie Laker forced a judicial investigation of a number of airlines, including British Airways, under the anti-trust laws alleging price fixing to drive him out of business. Again the case focused on activities outside the United States, and the British Government, using the Protection of Trading Interests Act, had to order British Airways not to comply with United States orders to hand over documents relevant to the case. Margaret Thatcher put pressure on President Reagan, and eventually the investigation was dropped.

In the autumn of 1983 a junior minister in the British Government Malcolm Rifkind visited the State Department in Washington and proposed a series of bilateral talks aimed at healing the differences over extraterritoriality. Both sides agreed to differ over the actual principle, but accepted that there was a need to lessen the impact on bilateral relations of disputes over extraterritorial action. Those talks began the following year, and have resulted in a series of agreements on ways to reduce tension. They include the agreement on providing information for criminal inquiries which led to the United States supplying the

evidence that exposed the Guinness scandal. But though those agreements have gone some way to reducing the potential for disputes in
many areas, they have not removed the risk of confrontation of a kind
that might emerge from the Toshiba affair, nor have they eased British
resentment over extraterritoriality.

Despite their significance, the disputes over strategic export controls
and extraterritoriality are only part of a long series of difficulties in the
transatlantic trading relationship. There have been a succession of
disputes between the United States and the EC over their respective
trade policies. In Europe all major trading decisions are now taken by
the EC in Brussels, with only such questions as anti-trust cases and
strategic export controls being left to the individual governments to
handle. The British Department of Trade and Industry has a staff of
around a hundred people in Brussels dealing with questions such as
tariffs, quotas and disputes over trade in items like foodstuffs and steel,
which have caused particular problems to the transatlantic relationship
in recent years.

In fact the degree of acrimony that surfaces with regularity over trade
issues is remarkable, considering that the combatants are political and
military allies. In September 1987 the EC warned the United States of
'very grave consequences' for its economic relations with Western
Europe if the 1988 trade legislation was put onto the statute book. In a
major dispute over agricultural sales in 1986 the Europeans said
Washington had adopted a 'confrontational approach'. Washington accused the Europeans of 'unjustified escalation' of what was a relatively
minor trade dispute. And a senior official added: 'We will not allow our
rights to be infringed upon.'[5] In May 1986 Washington imposed quotas
on various EC products. A White House spokesman said: 'When they
put a hit on us, we'll come back and do a likewise hit on them.' Those
involved in the debate over strategic export controls have said that it is
often necessary to remind people in Washington that the targets of
vitriol or irritation are in fact friends and allies. The same point certainly
applies to other trade matters.

That disputes over trade do arise is both disturbing and predictable.
The United States and the EC are the second biggest trading partners
in the world today, after Canada and the United States. Between them
they account for more than half the world's gross national product, and
the trade between them amounts to around $120 billion a year. The two
main points of difference in recent years have been steel production and
trade in agricultural products.

The most recent outbreak of the dispute over steel came in the early eighties when American steelmakers launched a lobby in Washington against the growing quantities of steel imports from the EC that were reaching the American markets. Those fears were partially alleviated in 1982 by an agreement between the Reagan administration and the EC to impose modest limits on the amount of steel sent across the Atlantic. But the 1982 agreement only covered specific parts of the industry. The following year urgent appeals from the parts of American industry not covered by the earlier deal led to the administration imposing temporary tariffs and import quotas on their European competitors. That provoked a furious response from the Europeans. The worst breach over agricultural trade in recent years came in early 1986 when Spain and Portugal joined the European Community. The Americans lodged a strong protest against changes to their trade regulations planned by the two countries to bring them into line with practice elsewhere in the EC. The changes were extraordinarily complex, but essentially meant that the United States was likely to lose around $400 million-worth of sales of feed grain to Spain. It argued that the changes would directly benefit British farmers and their counterparts elsewhere in the EC, at the expense of American producers. Ronald Reagan wrote in strong terms to Senate leaders, and threatened sanctions in retaliation: 'We cannot allow the American farmer, once again, to pay the price for the European Community's enlargement.'[6]

The Reagan administration's reponse was to announce a plan to impose 200 per cent duties on £400 million-worth of European business in the United States. The package of measures was carefully spread around the members of the EC – it affected Dutch cheese, British gin and French wine among others. The administration admitted that the aim was also to produce what was called 'same dollar impact' – all business lost to the Americans would be matched by United States action against Europe.

Although the dispute over the Spanish and Portugese markets has now been solved – a final deal was put together in January 1987, a year after the row broke out – it served to highlight just how serious the divide between the two sides has become. As has been the case over the Airbus project, the Americans have strongly resented the way European unity and co-operation has hit their agricultural exports. Although the EC remains the biggest purchaser of American agricultural produce, the farms of the Mid-West have been steadily losing ground to their European competitors since the 1960s. Grain and other foodstuffs have long been a vital component of United States trade – in 1981 they provided a surplus of more than $25 billion for the balance of payments. That surplus has now fallen by nearly 75 per cent – and at one point in 1986 the agricultural trade actually went into deficit for a few months for the first time in twenty years. The United States has also seen a dramatic turn round in its agricultural trade with Britain and other EC countries. Until 1984 it had a constant balance of payments surplus with the European Community – reaching a peak of $18 billion in 1980. That situation has now been completely reversed: in 1986 America had a trade deficit in agricultural produce of nearly $30 billion.

It is hardly surprising, therefore, that Britain and the other EC countries have received such a strong American backlash against the changes within the EC; although in the row over Spain and Portugal the EC argued strongly that American producers would benefit overall – that there would be more who increased sales to the EC as a result than lost out. But the United States has had some grounds for concern. A recent study into the effects on American interests of Greece entering the EC in 1981 revealed that American exporters lost both industrial and agricultural sales to European competitors as a result. Nor is there any likely end to competition in the agricultural markets in the near future, since both the United States and the Europeans are over-producing vast quantities of food. That will inevitably mean that the two will come into conflict as they try to dispose of the surplus.

Furthermore, the United States remains deeply hostile to many aspects of the European Community's Common Agricultural Policy (CAP). The CAP is essentially seen as a subsidy for European producers, and its policy of selling off excess produce to the Eastern Bloc at greatly discounted rates to reduce surpluses, is seen as giving the EC substantial advantages over American farmers. That has prompted the United States to provide substantial subsidies to its own producers to enable them to compete in what has become a very expensive international subsidy war. In 1986 the United States and the EC spent almost $60 billion between them on agricultural support programmes. In October 1986 a senior State Department official warned that the continuing confontations over trade and the battle for the agricultural produce market could ultimately have an adverse effect on the transatlantic relationship as a whole.[7]

It is particularly interesting to see the balance of power in the negotiations over trade issues in recent years. Leaving aside the question of strategic export controls, the United States and the EC have essentially faced each other as equals, giving way only after considerable brinksmanship over particular issues. For example it was the EC who finally yielded over the Spain/Portugal dispute. After several weeks of complex negotiations over the problem, with an American deadline of 1 July for the imposition of its sanctions against European products waiting only hours away, the EC negotiators agreed to a temporary truce which delayed the effects of the new Spanish and Portugese trade system on American farmers for six months. When the six-month deadline expired without a further agreement, the American administration went ahead with its measures against European produce. That produced both the threat of retaliatory action against other American produce and some concessions from the EC. After lengthy negotiations and genuine alarm about the possibility of a trade war, the two sides agreed on a settlement which allowed the United States to sell some grain in the EC at reduced prices to compensate American farmers. But interestingly farmers from both sides of the Atlantic condemned that deal as a sell-out, each saying it went too far towards giving the other side what it wanted. That, as much as anything, suggests that trade disputes are now really between equals, that American and European negotiators both talk with the knowledge that each has the power to do serious harm to the other's economy.

13

☆☆★☆☆

CONCLUSION

*Decision-makers in Washington must face the awkward and
enduring fact that the sum total of the United States' global interests
and obligations is nowadays far larger than the country's power to
defend them all simultaneously.*

Paul Kennedy, *The Rise and Fall of the Great Powers.*[1]

THE publication of Professor Paul Kennedy's book *The Rise and Fall
of the Great Powers* has highlighted the increasing reassessment in
the United States about the role of the United States. Kennedy's
analysis of the decline of a series of powerful nations since the sixteenth
century carries important lessons for the United States in the years
before the twenty-first century. He argues that the decline of great
powers begins when their international commitments become too big
for their economies to sustain; although the United States' decline is
relative, and should be seen within the context of the rise of the Asian
economies and of Europe, that is precisely what is happening to the
United States.

As Professor Kennedy is the first to admit, this analysis is not new.
In 1970, while America was embroiled in South-East Asia, David Calleo
was writing on exactly the same theme, saying that 'by the late sixties,
a sizeable proportion of the American political elite as well as the
general public appears to have decided that the country's international
role was demanding a dangerously excessive proportion of its
resources.'[2] And it is easy to find similar warnings from other professors over the years.

When Senator Mike Mansfield first began putting pressure on Europe
in the 1960s, the United States was still enormously strong economically, despite the burden of the Vietnam War. The scale of Japanese and
German economic recoveries was only just becoming fully apparent.
But today the United States is the world's biggest debtor nation and
although the White House and Congress have begun to tackle the
budget deficit, it is likely to face economic difficulties for some years to
come. That means that the United States is simply not going to be able

to afford to sustain its present commitments – more than 300,000 troops in Europe and even more in other bases around the world, an expanding Navy – and to develop the new generations of missiles, ships, tanks and aircraft, and the Strategic Defence Initiative.

The budget deficit will lead to further pressure on Western Europe to contribute more to its own defences. This is likely to take two forms. Firstly, it seems unlikely that the United States will continue to maintain such a huge military presence in Europe, which would mean a reduction in the number of troops. Ronald Reagan's successor will have to make major cuts in the defence plans just to fulfil the terms of the deficit-cutting Gramm–Rudman Act. And anyone who wants to make serious inroads into the deficit – whether Republican or Democrat – will have to go even further than Gramm–Rudman. Secondly, the United States is certain to pursue further collaboration with its allies in the development of new weapons systems in order to reduce its own research and development costs.

As Henry Kissinger and Cyrus Vance have put it: 'the weaknesses of the United States economy may be among the most serious and urgent foreign policy challenges to the next President.'[3] What is remarkable about the current debate in the United States is how it is mirrored within the Soviet Union by the debate about reasonable sufficiency of defensive power. Behind the debates is the gradual acceptance by both superpowers that the obsession with military superiority leads to a reduction in political power if it results in economic weakness. This is at the heart of the current rapprochement between the two superpowers.

Mikhail Gorbachev's determination to reduce the Soviet Union's defence burden by a series of initiatives to attempt to tempt the West into arms control agreements, transformed the rhetoric of East–West relations, just at the time that the scale of American defence spending was coming under serious question. But the warmth in the rhetoric of superpower relations has not made a major impact on the substance so far, and it remains to be seen how far the rhetoric will transform the perception of the mutual threat which has been the justification for arms spending for forty years.

The implication of the reduced military power of the superpowers is the concept of what Soviet spokesmen call 'a multi-polar world'. In other words, the superpowers accept that the world is not simply divided into two blocs. It also implies more instability as the old certainties of the Cold War are removed. The relationship between the two Germanies, and the position of the countries in Eastern Europe will be increasingly important. Their political and economic crises will be an unpredictable factor in East–West relations. The shift to a multi-polar world can only be gradual, since the two superpowers will remain the most powerful nations and because the economic power of Japan or West Germany has yet to be transformed into major political power, partly as a result of their self-restraint which stems from their immediate histories.

But the effect will be as dramatic on West–West relations. Since the Second World War, the United States has played the role of 'leader of the free world', and has used the protection that they gave their allies as the justification for that position. And if the United States is to persuade Europe to contribute more to its own defence, which there is no doubt that Europe must do, then the United States will have to accept a greater European input into American decision-making. In practice, it would mean giving Western Europe a say over certain American foreign-policy decisions, something which the United States shows no sign of being willing to consider. The alternative is likely to be a further drawing apart of the two sides of the alliance.

The economic relationship underlies the military and political relationship. The changing international economic system has created a situation where governments are no longer in a position to pursue key policies without taking into account market forces. This applies not just to economic policies, but also to other issues such as defence, where a government's determination to carry through its manifesto commitments could be undermined by a run on its currency.

The sheer fragility of the international stock-markets and the interdependency was of course highlighted by the stock-market crash in October 1987. The role of multinational companies is another aspect of internationalization of the world economy. As this trend continues in the future – with the integration of economies, particularly within Europe – so more and more power will pass from governments to the world of business and finance – and particularly to transnational corporations. After 1992, in the single European market, the European Commission will have considerable powers, but it will not be a government. Since political integration is lagging behind economic co-operation, the result will be to give multinationals, many of whom will be of American origin, a much freer hand, even with national laws applying.

This highlights the need for greater European co-operation to strengthen the power of the European countries and to reduce the loss of autonomy of the members of the European Community as a group. This involves a ceding of autonomy by each individual government within the European Community. In an increasingly interdependent world, niceties of national autonomy have to be given second place to avoid a real loss of power.

The reality is that Britain now functions as part of Europe, and although its ties with the United States will continue, in today's inter-related international systems the focus of future British policy must be within Europe. If NATO does develop an effective European pillar, and if the European Community continues on its path towards greater economic unity and collaboration, Britain cannot afford to remain doubtful about its links with Europe.

FOOTNOTES

INTRODUCTION (page ix)

1 Peter Jenkins: 'One Woman out in the European Triangle'. *The Independent*, 27 January 1988.

2 Alan Bullock: *Ernest Bevin, Foreign Secretary* p.395 (Heinemann, 1983).

3 Ibid., p.602.

4 John Baylis: *Anglo–American Defence Relations 1939-1984*, p.209 (Macmillan, 1984).

1 THE ERA OF UNITED STATES SUPREMACY (Pages 1–11)

1 Quoted in *On Every Front – the making of the Cold War*, by Thomas G. Paterson, p.23 (Norton, 1979).

2 Ibid., p.31.

3 Alan Bullock: *Ernest Bevin, Foreign Secretary*, p.370 (Heinemann, 1983).

4 Roy Jenkins: *Truman*, p.101 (Collins, 1986).

5 Ibid., p.408.

6 Ritchie Ovendale: *The English-Speaking Alliance*, p.64 (George Allen and Unwin, 1985).

7 Bullock: op.cit., p.529.

8 Ovendale: op.cit., p.76.

9 Ibid., p.78.

10 Treasury Papers, November 1956 (Public Record Office, Kew).

11 Ibid.

2 POLITICAL TIES (Pages 12–25)

1 Harold Macmillan: *Riding the Storm*, p.195 (Macmillan, 1971).

2 Macdonald Daly and Alexander George: *Margaret Thatcher in Her Own Words*, p.41 (Penguin 1987).

3 BBC, *Panorama*, 4 January 1988. (Mrs Thatcher is not, of course, Head of State).

4 *The Economist*, June 11 1988.

5 Duncan Campbell: *The Unsinkable Aircraft Carrier*, p.318 (Paladin, 1986).

6 Simon Duke: *US Bases in the United Kingdom, A Matter for Joint Decision?*, p.165-6 (Macmillan, 1987).

7 *The Economist*, 10 March 1984.

8 Ibid.

9 Tip O'Neill: *Man of the House*, p.366 (Bodley Head, 1987).

10 Interview on BBC World Service, 20 October 1985.

11 Duke: op.cit., p.165. Henry Kissinger: *Years of Upheaval*, p.713 (Weidenfeld and Nicolson, 1982).

12 *The Economist*, 10 March 1984.

13 From a lecture by Henry Kissinger to the Royal Institute of International Affairs, London, May 1982.

14 Ibid.

15 L.B. Johnson: *The Vantage Point*, p.255 (Weidenfeld and Nicolson, 1969).

16 Louis Heren: *No Hail No Farewell*, p.231 (Harper and Row, 1970).

17 Duncan Campbell: op. cit., p.142.

18 Alexander Haig: *Caveat*, p.269 (Weidenfeld and Nicolson, 1984).

19 *The Economist*, 3 March 1984.

20 David Dimbleby and David Reynolds: *An Ocean Apart*, p.315 (BBC/ Hodder and Stoughton, 1988).

21 *The Economist*, 3 March 1984. *An Ocean Apart*, op. cit., p.314.

22 *The Channel Four Enquiry*, 24 September 1986.

23 *International Herald Tribune*, 4 June 1987.

24 Chris Mullin: *A Very British Coup* (Hodder and Stoughton, 1982). Televised in June 1988.

25 *Sunday Telegraph*, 4 November 1979.

3 ECONOMIC LINKS (Pages 26–41)

1 Quoted in Jeffrey A. Frieden, *Banking on the World*, p.115 (Harper and Row, 1987).

2 Ibid., p.85.

3 *Sunday Times*, 1 November 1987.

4 Frieden: op.cit., p.175.

4 US & BRITISH NUCLEAR DETERRENT (Pages 42–64)

1 John Simpson: *The Independent Nuclear State*, p.22 (Macmillan 1986).

2　Andrew J. Pierre, *Nuclear Politics, British, Experience with an Independent Strategic Force 1939–1970*, p.31 (OUP, 1972).

3　Pierre: op.cit., p.38.

4　Ibid., p.60.

5　Simpson: op cit., p.45.

6　William Snyder: *Politics of British Defence Policy 1945-1962*, p.231 (Ohio State University, Columbus, 1964).

7　BBC Radio 4: 'A Bloody Union Jack on Top of it', 5 May 1988.

8　Margaret Gowing: *Independence & Deterrence*, Vol.1, 1945–1972, p.243 (Macmillan, 1972).

9　Dean Acheson: *Present at the Creation*, p.321 (Norton, New York, 1969).

10　*The Times*, 1 January 1988.

11　AJR Groom: *British Thinking About Nuclear Weapons*, p.190 (Francis Pinter, 1974). (Eden said later the threat wasn't taken literally.)

12　Andrew J. Pierre: op.cit., p.103.

13　Ibid., p.93.

14　Ibid., p.263.

15　BBC Radio 4: 'A Bloody Union Jack', 12 May 1988.

16　Victor Macklen interview: *Our Bomb*, London Weekend Television, 6 April 1986.

17　John Baylis: *Anglo-American Defence Relations, 1939–1984*, p.158 (Macmillan, 1984).

18　Public Accounts Committee, House of Commons, 1981-82, Ministry of Defence Chevaline Improvements to the Polaris Missile System. Dr Jones AWRE evidence p.20, 17 March 1982.

19　Defence Committee, House of Commons, 1980-1, Strategic Nuclear Weapons Policy. BAeD Memorandum, p.183.

20　*Our Bomb*, 6 April 1986.

21　Ian Bellany: *Naval Forces*, Vol.VII, No.V, 1987, pp.80–89.

22　*Financial Times*, 30 October 1987. *The Independent*, 29 October 1987.

23　*The Independent*, 26 January 1988. Tim Sainsbury MP: Written Answer, House of Commons, 10 February 1988, column 241.

24　Shaun Gregory: *The Command and Control of Nuclear Weapons* (Bradford University, 1986).

25　*Our Bomb*, 6 April 1986. House of Lords, 18 December 1979, column 1628.

26　John Simpson: Appendix to Minutes of Evidence before the House of

Commons Expenditure Committee (Defence and External Affairs Sub-Committee), p.244 (1979).

27 A.W. Sullivan: *National Defense*, January 1988.

5 THE INTELLIGENCE CONNECTION (Pages 65–88)

1 David Dimbleby and David Reynolds: *An Ocean Apart*, p.25 (BBC/Hodder and Stoughton, 1988). Ray Cline: *The CIA Under Reagan, Bush and Casey*, 1981, p.44 (Acropolis Books, Washington DC, 1981).

2 John Ranalegh: *The Agency: The Rise and Decline of the CIA*, p.27 (Simon and Schuster, 1986).

3 Interview with Ray Cline: 25 January 1988, Washington DC.

4 William Stevenson: *A Man Called Intrepid*, p.84 (Macmillan, 1976). A junior Embassy official, Tyler Kent, was arrested 20 May 1940.

5 Stevenson: op.cit., p.148.

6 Op.cit., p.148.

7 Ibid., p.151.

8 Jeffrey Richelson and Desmond Ball: *The Ties That Bind*, p.137 (Allen & Unwin 1985). Stevenson: op.cit., p.105.

9 Nigel West: *GCHQ*, pp.283–5 (Coronet, 1986). Jeffrey Richelson: *The US Intelligence Community*, p.196 (Ballinger Publishing, Cambridge, Massachusetts, 1985).

10 Ranalegh: op.cit., pp.42–3.

11 Stevenson: op.cit., p.274.

12 Phillip Knightley: *The Second Oldest Profession* (André Deutsch, 1986), p.218.

13 Cline: op.cit., p.51.

14 Knightley: op.cit., p.218.

15 Thomas Powers: *The Man who kept the Secrets: Richard Helms and the CIA*, p.28 (Weidenfeld and Nicolson 1979). John Prados: *The Soviet Estimates: US Intelligence and Russian Military Strength*, p.57 (Dial Press New York 1982). Jonathan Bloch and Patrick Fitzgerald: *British Intelligence and Covert Action*, p.65 (Junction Books 1983).

16 Nigel West:*The Friends*, p.61 (Weidenfeld and Nicolson, 1988).

17 Christopher Andrew: *Secret Service*, p.493 (Heinemann, 1985).

18 Nicholas Bethell: *The Great Betrayal*, pp.205–6 (Coronet, 1984).

19 Robert Lamphere: *The FBI–KGB War*, p.133 (W.H. Allen, 1986). Chapman Pincher: *Too Secret Too Long*, p.140 (Sidgwick and Jackson, 1984).

20 Bruce Page, David Leitch, Phillip Knightley: *Philby*, p.271 (Sphere, 1969).

21 Thomas Powers: op.cit., p.32 and p.68.

22 Page et al: op.cit., p.211.

23 Bethell: op.cit., fully documents the case against Philby. West (1988) argues the operations would have failed anyway.

24 Ranalegh: op.cit., p.157.

25 Ibid., p.236.

26 Chapman Pincher: *Too Secret Too Long*, pp.197–8. (Sidgwick and Jackson, 1984).

27 Ibid., p.197–8.

28 Ibid., p.157. Trevor Barnes: 'The Secret Cold War in Europe 1946–1956', *Historical Journal*, Vol.24 1981, pp.339–415, and Vol.25 1982, pp.649–670.

29 Ranalegh: op.cit., p.254.

30 Kim Philby: *My Secret War*, p.182 (Panther, 1969).

31 Nigel West: *Molehunt*, p.26 (Coronet, 1986).

32 Duncan Campbell: *The Unsinkable Aircraft Carrier*, p.125 (Paladin, 1986).

33 Ranalegh: op.cit., p.254.

34 Interview with Ray Cline, 25 January 1988. Ranalegh: op.cit., p.254.

35 Cline: op.cit., p.147.

36 Ibid., p.146.

37 Brian Lapping: *End of Empire*, pp.217–8 (Granada Publishing, 1985).

38 Ibid., p.218.

39 Andrew: op.cit., p.495.

40 National Archives, Washington DC. Draft memorandum from Chief of Staff by Joint Strategic Plans Group, 18 December 1951.

41 Ranalegh: op.cit., p.139.

42 Pincher: op.cit., p.314.

43 Christopher Dobson and Ronald Payne: *A Dictionary of Espionage*, pp.165-6 (Harrap, 1984).

44 Richard Deacon: *'C': A Biography of Sir Maurice Oldfield*, p.118 (MacDonald and Co. 1984).

45 Op.cit., p.138.

46 *The Observer*, 22 July 1984.

47 Andrew: op.cit.

48 Pincher: op.cit., p.473-4.

49 Ibid., p.511.

50 Powers: op.cit., p.101.

51 Ray Cline interview, 25 January 1988.

52 Ray Cline interview: BBC Radio 4, 23 August 1981: *The Profession of Intelligence.*

53 Christopher Dobson and Ronald Payne: Op.cit., pp.182–4 (Grafton Books, 1986). John Simpson: *Behind Iranian Lines*, p.99 (Robson Books, 1988). *Washington Post*, 12 November 1985. *Daily Telegraph*, 20 November 1985.

54 *Washington Post*, 8 August 1986. Jeffrey Richelson: *Foreign Intelligence Organizations*, pp.27–28 (Ballinger, Cambridge, Massachusetts, 1988). West: *The Friends*; op.cit., p.163.

55 BBC TV *Panorama*, 11 November 1985. Cord Meyer interviewed.

56 BBC TV *News*, 12 December 1986. Cord Meyer interviewed. It is still unclear if Gordievsky's evidence sheds any light on earlier penetrations and whether Sir Roger Hollis, the former MI5 Director-General, was a Soviet agent. Cord Meyer believes that Gordievsky would be able to provide conclusive proof as he would have reviewed the history of the London station. (BBC *News*, 12 December 1986). However the writer Chapman Pincher said on television in March 1988 that he had been told by a British Government minister that Gordievsky could provide no information about Hollis. Challenged on this, Ray Cline said Gordievsky's state of knowledge on Hollis is of 'almost no consequence' in proving his innocence or guilt. London Weekend Television: *The Trial of Sir Roger Hollis*, 3 April 1988.

57 *New York Times*, 9 August 1986.

58 Interview with Ray Cline, 25 January 1988.

59 *Washington Post*, 8 August 1986.

60 *New York Times*, 9 August 1986. Jeffrey Richelson: *Foreign Intelligence Organizations*, pp.27–8.

61 *The Economist*, 3 March 1984, pp.23–4.

62 William Burrows: *Deep Black*, p.250 (Random House, New York, 1986).

63 Bob Woodward: *Veil*, p.212 (Simon and Schuster, 1987).

64 Ibid., p.212.

65 Arthur Gavshon and Desmond Rice: *The Sinking of The Belgrano*, p.82 and p.225, note 5 (New English Library, 1984).

66 Ranalegh: op.cit., p.649.

67 Lamphere: op.cit., p.127.

68 BBC Radio 4, 30 August 1981: *The Profession of Intelligence*. Frank Snepp interviewed. David Atlee Phillips quoted in *The Guardian* 20 December 1987. Ray Cline interview 25 January 1988.

69 Woodward: op.cit., p.78.

70 Jeffrey Richelson and Desmond Ball: *The Ties That Bind*, p.152.

71 Cline: op.cit., p.146. Richelson and Ball: op.cit., p.152.

72 Campbell: op.cit., pp.146–7.

73 Ibid., pp.143–4.

74 Cord Meyer: *Facing Reality*, p.223 (Harper and Row New York, 1980).

75 Cord Meyer: interview 20 January 1988.

76 Meyer: op.cit., p.166.

77 Barnes: op.cit., *Historical Journal*, Vol.24 1981, pp.412–13.

78 Jeffrey Richelson: interview, 26 January 1988, Washington DC.

79 Ranalegh: op.cit., p.246. Cline: op.cit., p.151.

80 Philip Agee and Louis Wolf: *Dirty Work: the CIA in Western Europe*, p.168 (Zed Books, 1981).

81 Campbell: op.cit., p.147.

82 Ranalegh: op.cit., p.246.

83 Campbell: op.cit., p.147.

84 *The Guardian*, 31 December 1976.

85 Cord Meyer: interview, 20 January 1988.

86 Meyer: op.cit., p.170.

87 Campbell: op.cit.

88 Barnes: op.cit., *Historical Journal*, p.667, Vol.25, 1982. Memo to Director of NSA, 1 June 1954, declassified 21 February 1978. US National Archives, Washington DC.

89 James Bamford: *Puzzle Palace*, p.336 (Sidgwick and Jackson, 1982).

90 Campbell: op.cit., p.152.

91 Bamford: op.cit., pp.XIV–XV.

92 House of Representatives Appropriations Committee, Military Construction Hearings 1984, Part 5, p.320. Campbell: op.cit., p.158.

93 Jeffrey Richelson: *The US Intelligence Community*, p.211 (Ballinger Publishing, Cambridge, Massachusetts, 1985). Ian Stewart MP: Written Answer, House of Commons, 27 April 1988.

94 *The Independent*, 21 September 1987. Ian Stewart MP: Written Answer, House of Commons, 9 June 1988, column 661.

95 Duncan Campbell: *New Statesman*, 27 April 1984.

96 Bamford: op.cit., p.210–211.

97 Ibid., p.210–211.

98 Duncan Campbell and Linda Melvern: *New Statesman*, 18 July 1980.

99 Bamford: op.cit., p.332. Bamford: Telephone interview, 20 May 1988.

100 Jeffrey Richelson: interview 26 January 1988.

101 Campbell: op.cit., p.164–5.

102 Nigel West: *GCHQ*, p.343 (Coronet, 1986).

103 Bamford: op.cit., pp.333–4.

104 Ibid., p.333.

105 Ibid., p.331. West: op.cit., p.343.

106 Ibid., p.331. *Sunday Times*, 14 March 1982.

107 *New York Times*, 30 September 1982; and Richelson and Ball: op.cit., p.262.

108 Duncan Campbell: op.cit., p.158.

109 Bamford: op.cit., p. XV.

110 Pincher: op.cit., p.558 and p.621.

111 Bamford: op.cit., p.xxxxiii.

112 *Sunday Times*, 8 February 1987.

113 *The Times*, 6 August 1987.

114 Jeffrey Richelson: *Foreign Intelligence Organizations*, p.61, footnote 55.

115 'Europe's Future in Space' (Royal Institute for International Affairs), 1988. *Le Monde*, 10 April 1987.

116 Chapman Pincher: *Inside Story*, p.38 (Sidgwick and Jackson, 1979).

6 WHO PRESSES THE BUTTON? (Pages 89–106)

1 William Arkin and Richard Fieldhouse: *Nuclear Battlefields – Global Links in the Arms Race*, p.234 (Ballinger Publishing, Cambridge, Massachusetts, 1975).

2 Ibid., pp.234–5. William Arkin estimates the US stockpile in Britain as 1,268 warheads. Greenpeace: 'UK's Involvement in the Naval Nuclear Arsenal' estimates the US arsenal at 1,726 warheads. As well as the 6 locations where nuclear warheads are stored, a contingency store at RAF Bentwaters is under development, according to *The Observer*, 13 July 1986.

3 Simon Duke: *US Defence Bases in the United Kingdom. A Matter for Joint Decision?*, p.31 (Macmillan Press, 1987).

4 Notes of the Month, *The World Today*, August, p.320 (Royal Institute of International Affairs, 1960).

5 David Dimbleby and David Reynolds: Op.cit., p.188. Duke: op.cit., p.58.

6 *The Washington Post*, 1 December 1950.

7 Ibid., 1 December 1950.

8 Roy Jenkins: *Truman*, p.178 (Collins, 1986).

9 *Washington Post*, 6 December 1950. Acheson: *Present at the Creation*, p.478 (Norton Books, New York, 1969).

10 Duke: op.cit., p.66. Acheson: op.cit., p.484.

11 Simon Duke: 'US Bases: A Matter for Joint Decision?' (*ADIU Report*, Vol.9, No.1, January 1987, citing *Foreign Relations of the United States*, Vol.VII, 7 December 1950, p.1462. US Government publication).

12 Campbell: op.cit., p.307. Dean Acheson interview. *The Listener*, 8 April 1971.

13 Acheson: op.cit., p.478.

14 Ibid., p.484.

15 Acheson: op.cit., p.484. Harry S. Truman: *Years of Trial and Hope 1946–1953*, p.435 (Hodder and Stoughton, 1956). Truman says he asked 'what the Prime Minister's constituents and his Government would do if they could see a picture of the British Ambassador on his knees to the President of the United States'.

16 *Foreign Relations of the United States*, 1950, Vol.III, p.1781.

17 Duke: op.cit., p.68.

18 *Washington Post*, 8 December 1950.

19 BBC TV *Brass Tacks*, 30 May 1983. Interview with Lucius Battle.

20 *Arms and Disarmament Information Unit (ADIU) Report* 9:1. January–February 1987, p.3. (University of Sussex).

21 John Bayliss: *The World Today*, p.156. August–September 1986, Royal Institute of International Affairs.

22 BBC TV *Brass Tacks* interviews with Robert McNamara and Paul Warnke, 30 May 1985.

23 Duke: op.cit., pp.133–4.

24 Ibid., p.145.

25 Campbell: op.cit., p.146.

26 Ibid., p.311.

27 *New York Times*, 14 April 1983.

28 *The Guardian*, 18 April 1983.

29 BBC TV *News*, 27 May 1983.

30 BBC TV *Brass Tacks*, 30 May 1983.

31 David Steel: speech, House of Commons, 16 April 1986. *Hansard*, Column 889.

32 Campbell: op.cit., p.52. Shaun Gregory: 'Nuclear Accidents involving Britain', p.2 (Nuclear Age Peace Foundation, Santa Barbara, California 1987).

33 Campbell: op.cit., p.219. Shaun Gregory: op.cit., p.3. Gregory claims there have been five 'acknowledged' incidents involving US nuclear weapons, and 9 'suspected' accidents in Britain or within approximately 200 miles.

34 *The Independent*, 15 July 1987.

35 Ian Stewart MP: Written Answer, House of Commons, 25 February 1988, column 134, *Hansard*.

36 Headquarters US European Command: USINCEUR CONPLAN 4367–87 'Response to Nuclear Accidents/Incidents within the theatre', pp.4–5, p.9 [obtained by Peter Wills, University of Auckland, New Zealand, under US Freedom of Information Act].

37 Press Release, Peter Wills (1987).

38 Ian Stewart MP: Written Answer, House of Commons, 2 November 1987, column 6070. *The Independent*, 2 April 1988.

39 Joint Nuclear Accident Co-ordinating Centre: Field Command Defence Nuclear Agency '1987 Nuclear Accident Response Capability Listing' (NARCL).

40 *The Times*, 20 January 1987.

41 Andrew Burrows: 'Preparing for a Nuclear Weapons Accident. UK and US Accident Response Teams and their Joint Training' (Natural Resources Defence Council, Washington DC, October 1987). US Department of Defence 'Nuclear Weapons Surety'. Annual Report to the President, 1984 (Section D and E). Obtained by William Arkin.

42 *The Independent*, 15 July 1987. Roger Freeman MP: House of Commons, 15 July 1987, column 1129 et seq.

43 US DOD 'Nuclear Weapons Surety', op.cit., section E.5. Andrew Burrows: op.cit., p.3.

44 Ian Stewart MP: Written Answer, House of Commons, 26 April 1988, column 1878.

45 Information supplied by Richard Guthrie: June 1988.

46 Ian Stewart MP: Written Answer, House of Commons, 26 April 1988, column 1878.

47   John Stanley MP: Written Answers, House of Commons 1 May 1987, column 298–9; and 22 April 1987, column 594. Norman Lamont MP: Written Answer, House of Commons, 7 February 1986, column 305.

48   Figures from 'The Military Balance 1987–1988', p.25. International Institute for Strategic Studies. There are reports Britain has agreed to the stationing of another 50 F-111 aircraft in Britain.

49   Ian Stewart MP: Written Answer, House of Commons, 24 March 1988, column 180.

50   Campbell: op.cit., p.255.

51   Campbell: op.cit., pp.175–177.

52   Duke: op.cit., p.179. Duncan Campbell: op.cit., p.267.

53   Ian Stewart MP: Written Answer, House of Commons, 20 April 1988, column 502.

54   Ian Stewart MP: Written Answer, House of Commons, 29 April 1988; and *Sunday Times*, 17 April 1988.

55   Campbell: op.cit., pp.176–7.

56   *The Observer*, 9 November 1984, Press Release: US Information Service, 27 May 1988.

57   *Washington Post*, 27 September 1984, p.1.

58   Duke: op.cit., p.194. *The Times*, 13 June 1986. *Milav News* (undated), in files of Arms and Disarmament Unit, Sussex University.

59   *Aviation Week and Space Technology*, 2 May 1988. Information from British–American Security Information Council, June 1988. *Omaha World-Herald*, 12 June 1988.

60   *A Guide to the Third Air Force* (Third Air Force Public Affairs Office, March 1988). Desmond Ball and Jeffrey Richelson: *The Ties That Bind*, p.183 (Allen and Unwin 1985). Jeffrey Richelson: *American Espionage and the Soviet Threat*, p.214. Ballinger, Cambridge, Massachusetts, 1987). Duncan Campbell: op.cit., p.132.

61   *Janes Defence Weekly*, 17 November 1984.

62   John Ranalegh: *The Agency: the Rise and Decline of the CIA*, p.318 (Simon and Schuster, 1986). Desmond Ball and Jeffrey Richelson: op.cit., p.233.

63   Duke: op.cit., p.233.

64   Desmond Ball and Jeffrey Richelson: op.cit., p.233. Duke: op.cit., p.134.

65   *Washington Post*, 31 December 1984. Duncan Campbell: op.cit., pp.260–6. Duke: op.cit., p.204. *The Observer*, 13 July 1986. Ian Stewart MP: Written Answer, House of Commons, 20 June 1988, columns 431–2.

66   There are reports that submarines of the classes capable of carrying sea-launched Cruise missiles have used Holy Loch in Autumn 1987. The

presence of nuclear weapons is never confirmed. There is speculation that SLCMS may be assigned to NATO. Greenpeace: *The UK's involvement in the Naval Nuclear Arms Race*, 1988.

67 William Arkin and Richard Fieldhouse: op.cit., p.234. *A Guide to the Third Air Force*, op.cit., p.52.

68 Campbell: op.cit., p.171.

69 William Burrows: *Deep Black*, p.179 (Random House, New York, 1987).

70 Paul Bracken: *The Command and Control of Nuclear Forces*, p.38 (Yale University Press, 1983).

71 *Janes Defence Weekly*, 17 January 1987.

72 Malcolm Spaven: briefing paper on JOSIC, February 1988 (Arms & Disarmament Information Unit, Sussex University. Ian Stewart MP: Written Answers, House of Commons, 14 December 1987, column 411.

73 US Department of Defense Construction Appropriations for FY 1985, House Appropriations Committee 1984, p.185.

74 Campbell: op.cit., pp.179–84.

75 Tim Sainsbury MP: Written Answers, House of Commons, 7 December 1987, column 88; 11 January 1988, column 64; and 18 January 1988, column 484.

76 *The Independent*, 6 June 1988.

77 Greenpeace: The UK's involvement in the Naval Nuclear Arms Race (1988).

78 Sub-committee on Military Construction Appropriations for 1988. House of Representative Appropriations Committee 100th Congress, pp.584–5.

79 Duke: op.cit., p.194. Duncan Campbell: op.cit., p.186. *The Guardian*, 10 December 1982, 16 December 1982.

80 Campbell: op.cit., p.291.

81 Ibid., p.303.

82 Duncan Campbell: *New Statesman*, 13 December 1985.

83 Duncan Campbell: *New Statesman*, 8 March 1986.

84 Kenneth Clarke MP: Written Answer, House of Commons, 17 March 1986, column 82.

85 US Department of Defense. *Report on Allied Contribution to the Common Defence*, p.57, March 1983.

86 Headquarters United States European Command Wartime Host Nation Support Planning and Procedures in US European Commands. Appendix D, Appendix L.

87 Duncan Campbell: *New Statesman*, 13 December 1985.

88 *The Independent*, 4 March 1987, quoting an unclassified annual report of the US Air Force.

89 Tony Newton MP: Written Answer, House of Commons, 31 March 1987, column 492.

90 Baroness Trumpington: Written Answers, House of Lords, Vol.474, No.90, column 1026.

91 House of Representatives Sub-Committee on Military Construction, 99th Congress 1983, p.243.

92 Roger Freeman MP: Written Answer, House of Commons, 31 March 1987, column 454. Sub-Committee on Department of Defense Appropriations, House of Representatives, Part 3, 1988.

93 Duncan Campbell: op.cit., 303.

94 Lord Trefgarne: Written Answer, House of Lords, 7 May 1986, column 811.

95 Campbell: op.cit., 303.

7 THE EUROPEAN DIMENSION (Pages 107–133)

1 Representative Pat Schroeder, quoted in *Newsweek*, 7 March 1988.

2 Alan Bullock: *Ernest Bevin Foreign Secretary*, p.534 (Heinemann, 1983).

3 Ibid., pp.533–4.

4 *New York Times*, 28 April 1949.

5 Dean Acheson: *Present at the Creation*, p.285 (Norton Books, New York, 1969).

6 Stanley Sloan: *NATO's Future: Towards a New Transatlantic Bargain*, p.5 (National Defence University Press, Washington DC, 1985).

7 William Park: *Defending the West. A History of NATO*, p.16 (Wheatsheaf Books, 1986). Stanley Sloan: *Defence Burden Sharing: US Relations with NATO Allies and Japan*, p.5 (Congressional Research Service, Washington DC, April 10 1985).

8 Park: op.cit., p.17.

9 Ibid., p.18.

10 Sir Anthony Eden: quoted in *Questions of Defence*, 15 July 1986. BBC Television.

11 Sir Frank Roberts: interviewed in *Questions of Defence*, July 1986.

12 Stanley Sloan: *NATO's Future: Towards a New Transatlantic Bargain*, p.163.

13 Andrew Pierre: *Nuclear Politics: British Experience with an Independent Strategic Force, 1939–1970*, (Oxford, 1972).

14 Sir Frank Roberts: quoted in *Questions of Defence*, July 1986.

15 Park: op.cit., p.20.

16 General Andrew Goodpaster: interviewed in *Questions of Defence*, 22 July 1986.

17 Park: op.cit., p.89.

18 Stanley Sloan: *NATO's Future*, p.24.

19 Park: op.cit., p.41.

20 Ibid., p.45.

21 Ibid., p.47.

22 Ibid., p.57.

23 Ibid., p.89.

24 Ibid., p.91.

25 Barnet: op.cit., p.219.

26 Robert S McNamara: *Blundering into Disaster. Surviving the First Century of the Nuclear Age*, p.24 (Panthon Books, New York, 1986).

27 Robert McNamara: interviewed in *Questions of Defence*, 5 August 1986.

28 William Park: op.cit., p.92.

29 Sir Arthur Hockaday: interviewed in *Questions of Defence*, 5 August 1986.

30 Stanley Sloan: *NATO's Future*, p.42.

31 Sir Arthur Hockaday interview: *Questions of Defence*, 5 August 1986.

32 John Baylis: *Anglo-American Defence Relations 1981–84; The Special Relationship*, p.209 (Macmillan 1984).

33 Park: op.cit., p.80.

34 Phil Williams: *The Senate and US Troops in Europe*, p.133 (St Martins Press, New York, 1985).

35 Phil Williams: 'American Troops in Europe', p.126 *The World Today*, December 1987. Royal Institute for International Affairs.

36 Barnet: op.cit., pp.319–20.

37 Lawrence Freedman: 'Foreign Policy' 145, p.48–68

38 Kenneth A. Myers: *NATO the Next 30 years*, p.5 (Westview Press, Boulder, Colorado, 1980).

39 *Discriminate Deterrence*: Report of the Commission on Integrated Long-Term Strategy, p.30, January 1988.

40 William Pfaff: *Los Angeles Times Syndicate*, 15 January 1988.

41 *Time Magazine,* 14 March 1988.

42 Ibid.

43 Pat Schroeder: *New York Times,* 6 April 1988. Olivier Debouzy: *International Herald Tribune,* 13 May 1988.

44 Phillip Williams: 'American Troops in Europe'. Schroeder: op.cit.

45 *The Independent,* 16 February 1988.

46 Ibid.

47 Stanley Sloan: *Defence Burden Sharing,* p.15.

48 Ibid., p.17

49 *The Independent,* 16 February 1988.

50 *Christian Science Monitor,* World Edition, 2–8 May 1988.
    International Herald Tribune, 20 February 1988.

51 *New York Times,* 6 April 1988.

52 *International Herald Tribune,* 26 April 1988.

53 Phil Williams: 'American Troops in Europe', p.218.

54 *The Guardian,* 2 March 1988.
    Stephen Cain: 'Carlucci's budget avoids hard choices', p.44, *Bulletin of Atomic Scientists,* 1988.

55 Melvyn Krauss: *How NATO weakens the West,* pp.17–28 (Simon & Schuster, New York, 1986).

56 David P. Calleo: *Beyond American Hegemony,* p.217 (Basic Books, New York, 1987).
    David Calleo: 'NATO's Middle Course', pp.140–1. *Foreign Policy,* No.69, Winter 1987/8.

57 David P. Calleo: *Beyond American Hegemony,* p.217.

58 Paul Kennedy: *The Rise and Fall of the Great Powers,* p.515, (Random House, 1987).

59 *International Herald Tribune,* p.5, 4 May 1988.

60 Sir Geoffrey Howe's speech to Belgian Royal Institute for International Affairs, 16 March 1987. Olivier Debouzy: *International Herald Tribune,* 13 May 1988.

61 *NATO In the 1990s.* A Special Report by the North Atlantic Assembly Committee on NATO in the 1990s. 18 May 1988, p.16.

62 Stephen Shenfield: 'In Quest of Sufficient Defence'. *Détente,* No.11 p.29, 1988.

63 Ibid., p.27.

64 *Time Magazine,* 14 March 1988.

65   Ibid.

66   *The Independent*, 27 January 1988.

67   Stanley Sloan: *A New Transatlantic Bargain. An Essay on US Policy toward European Defence Co-operation*, pp.1–2, 1988.

68   Henry Kissinger: *The Troubled Partnership. A Reappraisal of the Atlantic Alliance*, p.40 (Doubleday, New York, 1966).

69   David Calleo: 'NATO's Middle Course', p.143.

70   Ronald Reagan speech to Centre for Strategic and International Studies, Washington DC, 14 December 1987, in *Europe*, January/February 1987/8, p.21.

71   Sloan: *A New Transatlantic Bargain*.

72   David Calleo: *The Atlantic Fantasy*, p.ix. (Johns Hopkins Press, Baltimore, Maryland, 1970).

8 THE BATTLE FOR THE DEFENCE MARKETS (Pages 134–145)

1   *Sunday Telegraph*, 25 September 1962.

2   Ibid.

3   *Daily Telegraph*, 16 December 1962.

4   *The Guardian*, 6 March 1965.

5   *Sunday Telegraph*, 25 September 1962.

6   *Sunday Telegraph*, 7 March 1965.

7   *Daily Telegraph*, 31 August 1960.

8   *Daily Telegraph*, 4 December 1965.

9   Ibid.

10   Anthony Sampson: *The Arms Bazaar*, p.162 (Hodder and Stoughton, 1977).

11   *Daily Telegraph*, 9 December 1965.

9 TOWARDS A EUROPEAN ALTERNATIVE (Pages 146–155)

1   *The Times*, 8 May 1972.

2   *Reuters*, 29 July 1987.

3   *Daily Telegraph*, 13 November 1987.

4   Ibid.

5   Ibid.

10 WESTLAND AND THE FUTURE OF THE DEFENCE INDUSTRY
(Pages 156–169)

1 House of Commons Defence Committee: 'The Defence Implications of the future of Westland Plc'. Senior 1985–6, HC.518.

2 Ibid.

3 Ibid.

4 *The Klepsch Report* (Brasseys, 1979).

5 Quoted in *Atlantic*, the Journal of the American Chamber of Commerce (UK), September 1987.

6 Ibid.

11 INDUSTRIES ABROAD (Pages 170–185)

1 John M. Stopford and Louis Turner: *Britain and the Multinationals*, chapter 3 (Wiley, 1985).

2 William Braznell: *California's Finest: The History of the Del Monte Corporation*, p.132 (Del Monte 1982).

3 *The Guardian*, 12 February 1987.

4 *Time Magazine*, 14 December 1987.

12 EXTRATERRITORIALITY AND INTERNATIONAL TRADE
(Pages 186–201)

1 Kevin Cahill: *Trade Wars*, p.179 (W.H.Allen, 1987).

2 Ibid., p.176–85.

3 Ibid., p.11.

4 *The Guardian*, 21 December 1987.

5 *Time Magazine*, 28 April 1986.

6 *Financial Times*, 11 April 1986.

CONCLUSION (Pages 202–205)

1 Paul Kennedy: *The Rise and Fall of the Great Powers*, p.515 (Random House, 1987).

2 David Calleo: *Atlantic Fantasy*, p.ix (Johns Hopkins Press, 1970).

3 Henry Kissinger and Cyrus Vance: *Foreign Affairs*, Summer 1988.

BIBLIOGRAPHY

Acheson, Dean: *Present at the Creation* (Norton Books, New York, 1969).
Agee, Philip: *Inside the Company – CIA Diary* (Penguin, 1975).
—— and Louis Wolf: *Dirty Work, CIA in Western Europe* (Zed books, 1981).
—— *On the Run* (Bloomsbury, 1987).
Alternative Defence Commission: *Without the Bomb* (Paladin, 1985).
—— *The Politics of Alternative Defence* (Paladin, 1987).
Andrew, Christopher: *Secret Service* (Heinemann, 1985).
Ashworth, William: *A Short History of the International Economy since 1850* (Longman, 1987).
Bamford, James: *Puzzle Palace* (Sidgwick & Jackson, 1982).
Barnet, Richard J.: *Allies: America, Europe and Japan Since the War* (Jonathan Cape, 1984).
Baylis, John: *Anglo-American Defence Relations, 1939–84* (Macmillan, 1984).
Bethell, Nicholas: *The Great Betrayal* (Coronet, 1984).
Bloch, Jonathan and Bledowska, Celina: *KGB-CIA* (Bison Books, 1987).
Bloch, Jonathan and Fitzgerald, Patrick: *British Intelligence and Covert Action* (Junction Books, 1983).
Blum, William: *CIA, A History:* (Zed Books, 1986).
Braznell, William: *California's Finest* (Del Monte Corporation, 1982).
Bullock, Alan: *Ernest Bevin, Foreign Secretary* (Heinemann, 1983).
Burridge, Trevor: *Clement Attlee* (Jonathan Cape, 1985).
Burrows, William: *Deep Black* (Random House, New York, 1986).
Cahill, Kevin: *Trade Wars* (W.H. Allen, 1987).
Calleo, David P.: *Beyond American Hegemony* (Basic Books, 1987).
—— *Atlantic Fantasy* (Johns Hopkins Press, 1970).
Cameron Watt, Donald: *Succeeding John Bull: America in Britain's Place* (CUP, 1984).
Campbell, Duncan: *The Unsinkable Aircraft Carrier* (Paladin, 1986, Revised Edition).
Cline, Ray: *The CIA under Reagan, Bush and Casey* (Aeropolis Books, Washington DC, 1981).
Cochran, Thomas, Arkin, William, and Hoenig, Milton: *Nuclear Weapons Databook, Vol.1 US Nuclear Forces and Capabilities* (Natural Resources Defence Council, Washington DC, 1984).
Coker, Christopher: *A Nation in Retreat, Britain's Defence Commitment* (Brasseys, 1986).
—— *British Defence Policy in the 1980s* (Brasseys, 1987).
Dean, Jonathan: *Watershed in Europe. Dismantling the East-West Confrontation* (Lexington Books, Lexington, Massachusetts, 1987).
Department of Trade and Industry: *Multinational Investment Strategies in the British Isles* (HMSO, 1983).
Dillon, G.M.: *Dependence and Deterrence* (Gower, 1983).

Dimbleby, David and Reynolds, David: *An Ocean Apart – The Relationship between Britain and America in the Twentieth Century* (BBC/Hodder & Stoughton, 1988).

Dobson, Christopher and Payne, Ronald: *Dictionary of Espionage* (Harrap, 1984).

Duke, Simon: *US Bases in the United Kingdom – A matter for Joint Decision?* (Macmillan, 1987).

Edmonds, Robin: *Setting the Mould: The United States and Britain, 1945-50* (OUP, 1986).

Freedman, Lawrence: *Britain and Nuclear Weapons* (Macmillan, 1980).

Freemantle, Brian: *CIA* (Futura, 1983).

Frieden, Jeffrey: *Banking on the World* (Harper and Row, 1987).

Galtung, Johan: *The European Community: A Superpower in the Making* (George Allen and Unwin, 1981).

Gilbert, Martin (Ed.): *A Century of Conflict, 1830–1950. Essays for A.J.P. Taylor* (Hamish Hamilton, 1966).

Gilpin, Robert: *US power and the multinational corporation* (Macmillan, 1976).

Gowing, Margaret: *Independence and Deterrence: Britain and Atomic Energy, 1945–52* (Macmillan, 1974).

Groom, A.J.R.: *British Thinking about Nuclear Weapons* (Frances Pinter, 1974).

Haig, Alexander: *Caveat* (Weidenfeld and Nicolson, 1984).

Harris, Kenneth: *Attlee* (Weidenfeld and Nicolson, 1982).

Heseltine, Michael: *Where there's a Will* (Hutchinson, 1987).

Jenkins, Roy: *Truman*, (Collins, 1986).

—— *Afternoon on the Potomac* (Yale, 1971).

Joffe, Joseph: *The Limited Partnership, Europe, the United States and the Burdens of Alliance* (Ballinger Press, Cambridge, Massachusetts, 1987).

Kennedy, Paul: *The Rise and Fall of the Great Powers* (Random House, 1987).

Kissinger, Henry: *Observations* (Michael Joseph/Weidenfeld and Nicolson, 1985).

—— *The White House Years* (Weidenfeld and Nicolson, 1979).

—— *The Years of Upheaval* (Michael Joseph, 1982).

Knightley, Phillip: *The Second Oldest Profession* (André Deutsch, 1986).

Krauss, Melvyn: *How NATO weakens the West* (Simon and Schuster, 1986).

Lamphere, Robert: *The FBI-KGB War* (W.H. Allen, 1986).

Lapping, Brian: *End of Empire* (Granada Publishing, 1985).

Leifer, Michael (Ed.): *Constraints and Adjustments in British Foreign Policy* (Allen and Unwin, 1972).

Lindsey, Robert: *The Falcon and the Snowman* (Penguin, 1979).

Lloyd, T.O.: *Empire to Welfare State, English History 1906–76* (Oxford, 1979).

Louis, W.M. and Bull, Hedley (Eds.): *The Special Relationship: Anglo-American Relations since 1945* (OUP, 1986).

Macmillan, Harold: *Riding the Storm, 1956–9* (Macmillan, 1971).

McNamara, Robert S.: *Blundering into Disaster: Surviving the First Century of the Nuclear Age* (Panther, 1986).

Malone, Peter: *The British Nuclear Deterrent* (Croom Helm, 1984).

McDonald, Ian: *Anglo-American Relations since the Second World War* (David and Charles, 1974).

McLean, Scilla (Ed.): *How Nuclear Weapons Decisions are Made* (Macmillan, 1986).

Meyer, Cord: *Facing Reality – From World Federalism to the CIA* (Harper and Row, New York, 1980).

Miall, Hugh: *Nuclear Weapons. Who's in Charge?* (Macmillan, 1987).

Nevins, Allan and Commager, Henry: *A Pocket History of the United States* (Pocket Books, 1981).

Odell, Peter: *Oil and World Power* (Penguin, 1981).

Ovendale, Ritchie: *The English-Speaking Alliance* (George Allen and Unwin, 1985).

Packard, Vance: *The Hidden Persuaders* (Penguin, 1981).

Page, Bruce, Leitch, David, and Knightley, Phillip: *Philby* (Sphere 1969).

Paterson, Thomas: *On Every Front – The making of the Cold War* (Norton, 1979).

Peninou, George, and others: *Who's Afraid of the Multinationals* (Saxon House, 1978).

Palmer, John: *Europe Without America* (Oxford, 1987).

Park, William: *Defending the West, A History of NATO* (Wheatsheaf Books, 1986).

Philby, Kim: *My Silent War* (Panther, 1969).

Pierre, Andrew: *Nuclear Politics – British Experience with an Independent Strategic Force* (OUP, 1972).

Pincher, Chapman: *Their Trade is Treachery* (Sidgwick & Jackson, 1981).

—— *Too Secret Too Long* (Sidgwick & Jackson, 1984).

—— *Inside Story, A documentary of the pursuit of power* (Sidgwick & Jackson, 1979).

—— *A Web of Deception* (Sidgwick & Jackson, 1987).

Plender, John and Wallace, Paul: *The Square Mile* (Century/LWT, 1985).

Powers, Thomas: *The Man who kept Secrets; Richard Helms and the CIA* (Weidenfeld and Nicolson, 1980).

Pringle, Peter and Arkin, William: *SIOP, Nuclear Warfare from the Inside* (Sphere, 1983).

Ranalegh, John: *The Agency. The Rise and Decline of the CIA* (Simon and Schuster, 1986).

Richelson, Jeffrey: *The US Intelligence Community* (Ballinger Press, Cambridge, Mass., 1985).

—— *American Espionage and the Soviet Target* (William, Morrow, New York, 1987).

—— *Foreign Intelligence Organizations* (Ballinger Press, Cambridge, Mass., 1988).

Richelson, Jeffrey and Ball, Desmond: *Ties that Bind* (George Allen and Unwin, 1985).

Roper, John (Ed.): *The Future of British Defence Policy* (Gower, 1985).

Sampson, Anthony: *The Arms Bazaar* (Hodder & Stoughton, 1977).

—— *The Money Lenders* (Hodder & Stoughton, 1981).

Schmidt, Helmut: *A Grand Strategy for the West* (Yale, 1985).

Simpson, John: *The Independent Nuclear State* (Macmillan, 1986).

Sloan, Stanley: *NATO's Future, Towards a New Transatlantic Bargain* (National Defence University, Washington DC, 1985).

Stephenson, William: *A Man Called Intrepid* (Macmillan, 1976).

Stopfor, John and Turner, Louis: *Britain and the Multinationals* (Wiley, 1985).

Treverton, Gregory F.: *Making the Alliance Work. The United States and Western Europe* (Cornell, New York 1985).

Truman, Harold: *Years of Trial and Hope, 1946–53* (Hodder & Stoughton, 1956).

Vernon, Raymond: *Sovereignty at Bay* (Longmans, 1971).

Verrier, Anthony: *Through the Looking Glass* (Jonathan Cape, 1983).

West, Nigel: *Molehunt* (Coronet, 1986).

—— *GCHQ* (Coronet, 1986).

—— *A Matter of Trust* (Weidenfeld and Nicolson, 1982).

—— *The Friends* (Weidenfeld and Nicolson, 1988).

Winks, Robert W: *Cloak and Gown* (Morrow, New York, 1987).

Wilson, Harold: *The Labour Government, 1964–70* (Penguin, 1971).

Williams, Phil: *The Senate and US Troops in Europe* (St Martin's Press, New York, 1985).

Wood, Derek: *Project Cancelled* (Janes, 1986).

Woodward, Bob: *Veil* (Simon and Schuster, 1987).

Wynne, Greville: *The Man from Odessa* (Hale, 1981).

INDEX